Teachers as Mediators in the Foreign Language Classroom

LANGUAGES FOR INTERCULTURAL COMMUNICATION AND EDUCATION

Series Editors: Michael Byram, *University of Durham, UK* and Alison Phipps, *University of Glasgow, UK*

The overall aim of this series is to publish books which will ultimately inform learning and teaching, but whose primary focus is on the analysis of intercultural relationships, whether in textual form or in people's experience. There will also be books which deal directly with pedagogy, with the relationships between language learning and cultural learning, between processes inside the classroom and beyond. They will all have in common a concern with the relationship between language and culture, and the development of intercultural communicative competence.

Full details of all the books in this series and of all our other publications can be found on http://www.multilingual-matters.com, or by writing to Multilingual Matters, St Nicholas House, 31-34 High Street, Bristol BS1 2AW, UK.

LANGUAGES FOR INTERCULTURAL COMMUNICATION
AND EDUCATION: 27

Teachers as Mediators in the Foreign Language Classroom

Michelle Kohler

MULTILINGUAL MATTERS
Bristol • Buffalo • Toronto

Library of Congress Cataloging in Publication Data
A catalog record for this book is available from the Library of Congress.
Kohler, Michelle - author.
Teachers as Mediators in the Foreign Language Classroom/Michelle Kohler.
Languages for Intercultural Communication and Education: 27
Includes bibliographical references and index.
1. Language and languages—Study and teachers. 2. Interlanguage (Language
learning) 3. Intercultural communication—Study and teaching. 4. Language teachers.
5. Mentoring. I. Title.
P53.K596 2015
407.1–dc23 2014033092

British Library Cataloguing in Publication Data
A catalogue entry for this book is available from the British Library.

ISBN-13: 978-1-78309-306-9 (hbk)
ISBN-13: 978-1-78309-305-2 (pbk)

Multilingual Matters
UK: St Nicholas House, 31-34 High Street, Bristol BS1 2AW, UK.
USA: UTP, 2250 Military Road, Tonawanda, NY 14150, USA.
Canada: UTP, 5201 Dufferin Street, North York, Ontario M3H 5T8, Canada.

Website: www.multilingual-matters.com
Twitter: Multi_Ling_Mat
Facebook: https://www.facebook.com/multilingualmatters
Blog: www.channelviewpublications.wordpress.com

The policy of Multilingual Matters/Channel View Publications is to use papers that
are natural, renewable and recyclable products, made from wood grown in sustainable
forests. In the manufacturing process of our books, and to further support our policy,
preference is given to printers that have FSC and PEFC Chain of Custody certification.
The FSC and/or PEFC logos will appear on those books where full certification has
been granted to the printer concerned.

Typeset by Deanta Global Publishing Services Limited.
Printed and bound in Great Britain by the CPI Group (UK Ltd), Croydon, CR0 4YY.

Contents

Introduction

For some decades there has been an increasing recognition and understanding of the place of culture in language education as a basis for more effective language learning and understanding of other world views. The global reality of superdiversity (Vertovec, 2010) and increasing multilingualism (Bloomaert *et al.*, 2012) has further focused attention on the importance of developing capabilities to engage with other languages and cultures in meaningful and mutually beneficial ways. The shift towards an intercultural orientation in language teaching and learning is viewed as a means of achieving these capabilities.

There is now a substantive body of work related to intercultural language teaching and learning which is largely theoretical in orientation, focusing on conceptual frameworks and considerations for practice. There is less work related to investigating practice and in particular how intercultural language teaching and learning occur in the foreign language classroom. There is little work in particular on mediation and the role of language teachers as mediators of intercultural language learning. This book focuses on precisely this area of practice. It examines in detail how teachers of languages mediate intercultural language learning with their students in the daily reality of school language programmes. It is an account of language teachers and their students who live the experience of intercultural language teaching and learning, and of the research process through which this account was reached. The main body of the book presents the findings of the research; however, the reader who is interested in the process will find in this introduction and in the detailed appendices an explanation of the 'participant action research' that was undertaken.

Context of the Study

This book presents a multiple case study of three foreign language teachers in Australian schools who participated in an investigation that I conducted into how teachers of languages mediate intercultural language learning in their teaching practice. The study evolved in response to my own interest and awareness of both an increasing critique in the field of applied linguistics and language education of communicative language teaching, and a shift towards intercultural language teaching and learning. This shift paralleled my own experience as a former secondary school language teacher with students who were not willing to undertake 'pseudo' communication tasks and who were demanding greater relevance, conceptually demanding and meaningful language learning experiences.

At the time, communicative language teaching heralded a new era of language teaching in which the social and purposeful nature of language was foregrounded. It did, however, become realised in ways that were not beneficial and one of the major criticisms has been that communicative language teaching has largely focused on an idealised monolingual, native speaker norm (Byrnes, 2006). It has assumed that both language learners and users have discrete languages and that the goal in teaching and learning is to acquire a further discrete language (the target language) in order to communicate fluently with native speakers of that language. Others' criticisms include that communication in this approach has become primarily 'transactional' in orientation, that it is biased towards listening and speaking, and often results in formulaic or rehearsed language that is detached from its real-world contexts and purposes of use (Eisenchlas, 2010; Legutke & Thomas, 1991; Leung, 2005; Scarino & Liddicoat, 2009).

The criticisms of communicative language teaching, together with emerging understandings of language and culture, have resulted in efforts over recent decades to generate new theoretical frames that recognise the significance of culture and context in language use (Byram, 1991; Damen, 1987; Kramsch, 1993, 1995). Sociocultural competence (Nostrand, 1991) and intercultural competence (Buttjes, 1991; Byram, 1988) were new models that attempted to do just that. Indeed, Byram and Alred (2002) suggested that the notion of an 'intercultural speaker' was a more appropriate goal for language teaching and learning, reflecting the difference between the processes of first language acquisition and one's primary socialisation, and that of additional language learning and tertiary socialisation. Others have proposed a goal that is oriented towards 'functional multilingualism' and the capability of language learners to navigate and move between multiple languages and cultures; being an intercultural meaning maker (Byrnes, 2006; Kramsch, 2006b; Risager, 2007).

Much of the initial work related to intercultural competence was theoretical in nature, attempting to conceptualise the area and identify considerations for research and practice (Buttjes, 1991; Byram, 1989, 1991; Byram et al., 1994; Byram & Zarate, 1994; Crozet & Liddicoat, 2000; Damen, 1987; Kramsch, 1993, 1995, 1998, 2008; Lo Bianco, 2003; Paige et al., 1999). Following this, work has become more practice oriented, addressing various dimensions. For example, studies have focused on evaluating textbooks in terms of their representations of language and culture in materials for language teaching (Kramsch, 1987; Sercu, 2000). In the area of curriculum, Byram *et al.* (2001) investigated teachers' planning and programming practices using learning objectives in a number of different countries and contexts. Liddicoat *et al.* (2003) developed a set of principles and outlined their related implications for curriculum, assessment, teaching and learning. Sercu (2005) has investigated language teachers' perceptions of the 'cultural' dimension of their work, finding that while they were willing to support cultural objectives in language teaching, they remained committed to a communicative orientation in practice. Sercu (2006) also found that despite expectations that language teachers were incorporating an intercultural orientation in their teaching, a significant number of them reported difficulties and remain focused on traditional pedagogies. More recently, Liddicoat and Scarino (2013) exemplify aspects of intercultural language teaching with vignettes of teachers' practice drawn from a number of research studies and professional learning programmes. In the higher education context, Diaz (2013) reports on curriculum design and implementation in Italian and Chinese programmes, highlighting various 'stumbling blocks' to implementing an intercultural orientation in practice, and proposing a framework to address what she regards as a theory and practice divide.

Hence, there is a growing body of work focused on practice, particularly in the areas of curriculum, programming, resourcing and, to a lesser degree, assessment. There remains little investigation, however, of the nature of intercultural language teaching and learning itself, and specifically the act of mediation. As Byram and Feng (2004: 164) argue, there is a gap in understanding 'how teachers and learners interact, how their discourse reveals their shared position as mediators, how their language reveals the acquisition of new concepts and rules whilst simultaneously revealing their ability to de-centre from their own and others' concepts to better understand both'. It is precisely this gap in understanding that this book aims to address.

Why Mediation Matters

Arguably the most common activity that language teachers and learners engage in every day is the process of mediation, and yet little is known about this dimension of language teaching and learning, particularly in relation to an intercultural orientation. Mediation is a term that is understood in various ways and is commonly associated with notions of conflict or resolution of difference. However, when applied to a learning context, and in particular intercultural language teaching and learning, such notions are found wanting. Hence, it is timely to reconsider the notion of mediation and investigate how it might be understood in the context of language teaching practice, drawing on understandings from both the fields of language teaching and sociocultural learning theory.

From the perspective of applied linguistics, and in particular language teaching, mediation has traditionally been associated with cross-cultural mediation (Dasli, 2011). A mediator is someone who acts as an 'intermediary' using his/her 'competence' to transfer meanings from one party to another, where these parties do not share the same language (Buttjes, 1991; Byram, 2003; Byram & Alred, 2002). Mediation, in this view, is a process of learning to 'read' a new linguistic and cultural system and transfer these meanings to another linguistic and cultural system. Understood in this way, mediation has largely been associated with the skill of translation and processes such as paraphrasing and summarising. Where mediation features in language curricula, and it seldom does, it has largely been framed as real-world problem-solving skills (Byram, 2013). In the area of 'cultural mediation', Zarate *et al.* (2004) argue that mediation is more than a skill and that greater attention is needed to the affective dimension of mediation including the role of attitudes and dispositions such as empathy, and the role of identity in engaging with otherness. Some recent work has begun to focus on areas such as identity (Tsai & Houghton, 2010), but it is not framed specifically in terms of mediation.

From a sociocultural learning theory perspective, mediation is the process whereby artefacts, both material and symbolic, are used to enable human mental activity (Lantolf, 1994; Lantolf & Thorne, 2006; Vygotsky, 1978; Wertsch, 1985). Understandings of mediation in education are greatly influenced by Vygotskian views that learning occurs on both interpsychological and intrapsychological planes (Vygotsky, 1978). That is, new ideas and experiences are presented to the learner through social interaction and are transformed by the learner through individual cognition into his/her own knowledge. Mediation occurs in the 'zone of proximal development' where the novice (learner) is presented with new information and ideas by an expert (teacher) who uses a range of 'tools' to enable the transformation of the 'new' into the 'known'. In a formal education context, the teacher is the primary mediator of learning. According to this theory, the ultimate mediation tool through which learning takes place is language, as it represents a symbolic artefact through which we carry out social interaction and private mental functions, and build our conceptual systems of mental activity (Cole, 1994; Lantolf, 1994; Lantolf & Thorne, 2006). In the foreign language classroom, language takes on even greater significance as it represents both a medium *for* learning (a symbolic artefact for social interaction and mental activity) as well as an object *of* learning (a symbolic artefact that represents alternative forms of knowledge and meaning).

This book brings together these perspectives on mediation as a basis for understanding how teachers mediate an intercultural orientation in language teaching. In doing so, the notion of mediation moves beyond a process of transferring meaning in communication or scaffolding knowledge for learning. Instead, it can be understood as the act of bringing (at least) two linguistic and cultural frameworks into a relationship, with an educative purpose. Mediation is thus an integral dimension of language teaching: a set of practices and ways of being that build connections between learners' existing and new language and culture frameworks, and in doing so, develop their own capability to act as intercultural mediators.

An Overview of the Study

The primary concern of the research study was to investigate teaching practice and address the specific question: How do teachers of languages mediate intercultural language learning in practice? This section provides an overview of the study in terms of its design and methodology, the participants, including myself, and the context(s) in which the study took place. Examples of materials used during the study are available in the appendices.

Design

The study was framed according to two key design features: case study and participatory action research (PAR). The study was based on case study methodology, adopting a collective case study in particular as it provides a basis for exploring both individual cases and the collective case overall, as Stake explains:

> ...a researcher may jointly study a number of cases in order to investigate a phenomenon, population, or general condition. ...collective case study... Individual cases in the collection may or may not be known in advance to manifest some common characteristic. They may be similar or dissimilar, redundancy and variety each important. They are chosen because it is believed that understanding them will lead to better understanding, perhaps better theorizing, about a still larger collection of cases. (Stake, 2005: 437)

The collective case study provided a number of benefits for the study. A collective case study does not require generalisability and instead takes as its starting point sensitivity to context. The study upon which this book is based was not intended to create generalisations about language teachers as a cohort but rather to investigate the lived reality of three teachers and their students, with sensitivity and nuance. The collective dimension is provided through consideration of the range of experiences and mediation practices across the teachers. That is, it is possible to understand the individual in her context and also develop some sense of how this relates to others' experiences:

> In a *collective case study* (or multiple case study), the one issue or concern is again selected, but the inquirer selects multiple case studies to illustrate the issue. (Creswell, 2007: 74)

The aim is not to describe a single, decontextualised instance, but to give a rich description of it and then some indication of how it may be connected or relevant beyond the individual instance. This kind of research aims to 'describe the cases in sufficient descriptive narrative so that readers can vicariously experience these happenings and draw conclusions' (Stake, 2005: 439).

A case study approach also provided the kind of flexibility and sensitivity needed to include a collaborative dimension that was crucial for the study. Drawing on the literature (Fantini, 1991; Papademetre & Scarino, 2000; Sercu, 2005) and my own teaching and research experiences, it was evident that it could not be assumed that the language teachers had already developed an intercultural language learning orientation in their teaching. Therefore, methods such as observation or interview would be insufficient and an approach was needed that could accommodate the teachers' development of this orientation. PAR (Denzin & Lincoln, 2000; Kemmis & Wilkinson, 1998; Reason & Bradbury, 2008) offered such an approach, providing support for the teachers to develop a considered understanding of intercultural language learning, while retaining the focus on mediation. As the teachers engaged in the research process, they explored understandings, experimented with their practice and reflected on the experiences and their views. The research process itself, with regular planning and debriefing discussions, enabled the participants to consider and adjust their views and practices over time. They were supported to reimagine and remake themselves through developing insights into their practice and underpinning theories and knowledge. This was a case of 'theory developing practice and practice developing theory' (Robertson, 2006: 309). This research method was also valuable in that it closely aligns with theories of intercultural language learning in which individuals encounter new ideas and ways of being, and are transformed through dialogue and critical self-reflection.

Case study and PAR were also chosen as they can accommodate a longitudinal research perspective. This was important in order to capture a range of mediation practices over time. Data were gathered over one full school year through an iterative process based on cycles of teaching and learning (see Appendix 1). The data show evidence of ways that the teachers build connections in learning over time such as referencing back and forth, and narrating their own experiences. While one school year was assumed to be sufficient, in the busy lives of teachers and their schools, the time proved to be quite limited and it was difficult to complete more than two full cycles of data collection. This longitudinal perspective on mediation is an area that is undertheorised and warrants further investigation in future research.

Participants and their context(s)

The participants in the study were three secondary teachers of Indonesian (as a foreign language) teaching in schools in South Australia. In addition, each teacher selected a class of students to participate; a Year 9, 10 and 12 class. The students in these classes were participants in the sense that they were involved in their regular role as students in the language programme. Furthermore, I was also a participant in the process both as researcher and as collaborator, as will be discussed in more detail later.

Teachers of Indonesian were chosen for two reasons. Firstly, Indonesian is my second language (in addition to English as my first language) and the language that I have taught and been associated with professionally for many years. Sharing the language used by teachers and students provided an important avenue for collaboration with the teachers and for analysis of the data. Secondly, Indonesian is the third most commonly taught language (almost exclusively as a foreign language) in Australian schools (Kohler & Mahnken, 2010; Slaughter, 2009), hence it is potentially a major site for advancing an intercultural orientation in language teaching. Despite being a widely taught language, Indonesian resides within a fragile language policy context. Language policy in Australia, particularly in recent decades, has been driven in the main by federal government strategies and targeted programmes, particularly for Asian languages (MCEETYA, 1994, 2005). States and territories have developed their own outcomes-based curriculum and assessment frameworks that are generic across all languages. Materials for teaching particular languages are not mandated, even at the senior secondary level, where Year 12 external examinations are conducted. Teachers are free to interpret curricula frameworks, and select and develop teaching materials and assessment as they choose. There is a strong culture of professional learning driven by teachers' own interests as well as encouragement to 'implement' local initiatives such as cross-curricula concepts and use of information and communication technologies. Intercultural language teaching and learning has emerged within this context. It is referred to in language planning documents but it is not mandated and instead is encouraged through professional learning programmes and materials (Scarino & Liddicoat, 2009; Scarino *et al.*, 2007, 2008).

In relation to the teaching of Indonesian specifically, there is a history of language programmes in schools being taught by teachers with limited formal training in the language or in languages pedagogy (Kohler & Mahnken, 2010; Worsley, 1994). Furthermore, in the tertiary sector, Indonesian is typically located in social sciences faculties, and is aligned with areas such as anthropology, political science and cultural studies (Worsley, 1994). The effect has been that many tertiary-trained language teachers have adopted a culture studies approach in their own teaching in schools. Combined with communicative language teaching, this has resulted in a somewhat positivist and 'exotic' treatment of culture as facts and information. In addition to the pedagogical orientation, Indonesian faces the challenge of how Indonesia and Indonesians are perceived in the Australian community. A number of traumatic events within Indonesia, such as the Bali bombings (2002), the Boxing Day tsunami (2004) and the arrest of a number of Australians on drug-trafficking charges (2004, 2005), have increased negative attitudes towards Indonesia in the community and exacerbated the decline in student participation in Indonesian language programmes in schools (Kohler & Mahnken, 2010; Slaughter, 2007, 2009). While these events had occurred several years prior to the research study, the attitudes among the Australian community continued to resonate (and still do) in schools, and were partly what the teachers in this study were attempting to counter in their teaching.

It is within this policy and social context that the three teachers agreed to participate in the study. The names of both the teachers and the students have been changed to pseudonyms in the interests of anonymity.

Collette

Collette has been teaching for over 15 years with experience in two large secondary schools, including her current school. She is of Anglo-Celtic background, with English as her first language, and she is married to an Indonesian, whom she met while studying in Indonesia, and with whom she has two children. She converted to Islam as part of her commitment to her husband's family.

Collette teaches Indonesian in a large, prestigious, non-denominational private school in the metropolitan area. She teaches Year 7 to Year 12 students who sit for the externally assessed Indonesian examination at the end of Year 12. The school prides itself on academic achievement and expectations of student achievement are high. School-based examinations begin in Year 8 and are conducted twice a year. The particular class that Collette chose for this study was her Year 9 Indonesian group. The class consisted of 12 students, 8 girls and 4 boys. Collette's reasons for selecting this group were that (a) they were highly motivated to learn, (b) the group was not too large or small with sufficient interaction without distracting the teacher and (c) the level was not 'high stakes' and therefore there was some degree of flexibility with the course content.

Kelly

Kelly learned Indonesian through her secondary school education and she spent time in Indonesia as part of her university study, completing a six-month intensive language course at an Indonesian university in central Java. Kelly is a first language speaker of English and grew up in a rural community in which she is now teaching; a community with German heritage and an area that is becoming increasingly culturally diverse.

At the time of the study, Kelly had five years' experience as a teacher of Indonesian. She had worked in one school and was the assistant head of house having responsibility for administrative matters. Kelly worked with one other teacher of Indonesian across Years 8–12 and she also taught physical education.

The school is a Catholic school located on the outskirts of a large country town, which is becoming an outer suburb of the metropolitan area. The school has approximately 800 students, male and female, most of whom live locally and are of predominantly Anglo-Celtic or European background. The school has a Catholic ethos, priding itself on community spirit as well as academic achievement. Indonesian is the only language offered at the school and it is compulsory in Year 8 for one semester.

The class chosen by Kelly for this study was Year 10 Indonesian. There were 15 girls and 6 boys in the group, with a couple having travelled overseas and the majority with some experience of having travelled within Australia, largely within South Australia. Kelly considered the group to be largely monocultural with rather limited experiences and narrow views of the world beyond their immediate environment.

Maria

Maria is multilingual, with Italian being her first language, and English, French and most recently Indonesian, as additional languages. After a period of 10 years living in Italy, Maria made a conscious choice to learn Indonesian because of the proximity of Indonesia to Australia and the perceived relevance of Indonesia to young Australians in the future. Being a recent student of

Indonesian (albeit at university), Maria feels particularly in touch with her students' needs and experiences as non-background learners of the language.

Maria is an experienced teacher of languages and is the coordinator of languages at an all-boys Catholic school that offers three languages, Indonesian, Italian and German. The school has a diverse linguistic and cultural cohort. Maria no longer teaches Italian as she prefers to teach Indonesian only. The class that Maria chose for the study was Year 12 Indonesian with three male students. The students were keen language students having begun their study in Year 7. One student was of Vietnamese background, one of Indian heritage and the other student was of Anglo-Celtic and German heritage.

The three participants in the study have distinctive linguistic and cultural biographies, teaching contexts and students. It is these distinctive people and their worlds that are at the heart of the account of mediation in this book.

Gathering the data

The data gathering process was based on an action research 'cycle' involving planning, teaching and reflection on language lessons. There were a number of cycles over a school year with each new stage being informed by the previous stage. The data gathering process focused on a sequence of teaching and learning, a connected series of lessons encompassed in a unit of work (a short-term programme of approximately five weeks' duration). The unit of work acted as a useful vehicle for considering a range of mediation practices over a teaching and learning sequence.

The process commenced with an initial orienting discussion with two of the teachers (and followed up with the third) to discuss the research focus and their roles. It was the beginning of exploring their conceptions of language and culture, and their understanding of mediation (see Appendix 1). The subsequent planning meetings were intended to capture each teacher's intentions for teaching and learning, and thereby either directly or indirectly, their conceptualisations of language and culture, and intercultural language teaching and learning. The teachers designed the programme objectives and learning activities, and developed related resources (see Appendix 2). The teaching phase was designed to capture the realisation of their conceptualisations in practice. The debriefing discussions were intended to capture each teacher's reflections on both her planning and teaching. The debriefing took the form of a semi-structured interview in which extracts from the classroom data were presented to each teacher to prompt her observations and reflections on mediation. This retrospective dimension was intended to elicit the teachers' observations, such as noticing patterns in their talk, opportunities (actual or missed) for making connections, and explication and clarification of concepts. This process enabled the teachers to reveal their rationales and any awareness they had of the relationship between their personal theories and practices. The reflective phase provided a basis for me to work with them individually and collectively to discuss key ideas and inform the next phase of the research cycle.

As mentioned previously, the assumption underpinning my involvement was that given the teachers' limited prior knowledge of intercultural language teaching and learning, it would be necessary to scaffold their learning along the way. I participated in the collaborative planning and debriefing sessions with each teacher by providing input and resources, probing and questioning the teachers' reflections and making observations of patterns and significant moments in their teaching. My role was that of a collaborator, providing a theoretical and research perspective on intercultural language teaching and learning and mediation, as well as practical suggestions and guidance in developing teaching materials. This dual role was based on my own background and identity. As a former teacher of Indonesian in secondary schools myself, I was known to the participants both as a teaching colleague and as a researcher. I had a particular relationship with each teacher that may have influenced how they perceived me, what value they gave to my contribution and the nature of their own involvement in the process. In the case of Collette, for example, her perception of me as her colleague, as an equal, enabled us to share expertise, create possibilities in the programme and reflect on interactions with students. There were, however, also moments where her perception of me as a researcher positioned me as somewhat removed from classroom reality, thus creating some distance and resistance to some suggestions. In the case of Kelly, her perception of me as her former teacher was influential in her decision to participate in the research. She regarded the research as an opportunity to learn more about her teaching practice from me. This orientation meant that Kelly was open to many suggestions, had a desire to experiment (together with a desire to gain approval from me) and actively sought support in designing the programme. Finally, in the case of Maria, her perception of me as a researcher meant that she regarded my position as someone with a specialised interest and expertise from which she was keen to learn. This resulted in her openness to suggestions, a desire to interact in new ways and a keen interest in reflecting on her practice. While Maria had some reservations about how to enact an intercultural orientation, she appreciated what she regarded as a collegial dialogue about her practice, particularly given her sense of being an experienced teacher of Italian but a novice teacher of Indonesian.

While the process was collaborative in design, there was inevitably an unequal relationship between the teachers and myself, given my varied relationships with them and my role as researcher. Conscious of this, and aware of the sensitivity and trust required for the teachers to 'open up' their classroom teaching practice, my contributions were often framed as suggestions or clarifying questions. No specific theoretical framework was imposed during planning and the discussions unfolded according to teachers' conceptions, questions and experiences; it was a dynamic and iterative process. My contributions were based on my own understandings of mediation and intercultural language teaching and learning based on my interpretations of the literature and my own teaching experience. The following were my recurring emphases in discussions (see also Appendix 1):

- Developing an intercultural stance and capability is a valuable goal in language teaching and learning.
- Intercultural language learning involves people, their entire linguistic and cultural make-up, interacting to jointly create meaning, interweaving their lives and world views.
- Language and culture are dynamic and symbiotic systems of meaning.
- Teaching and learning are social, cultural and linguistic acts.
- Mediation is a process of sense making with others, of creating new knowledge; it is a transformative process.

These understandings had some practical implications that were also emphasised in the discussions. The teachers were encouraged to consider how they could, for example:

- Connect new learning to students' own language(s), culture(s) and lives.
- Position students as makers, discoverers and interpreters of meaning.
- Deliberately attend to analysing language, culture and their relationship in constructing and representing meaning, such as through analysing authentic texts.
- Provide opportunities for students to decentre and reflect on language, culture and their own identities.

At the time, one of my key interests was in using text analysis, of authentic texts in particular, as a vehicle through which to consider the relationship between language and culture. The discussions therefore often focused on this approach, and as the data reveal, this emphasis was adopted by each of the teachers in her own way. Given the collaborative nature of the research, it is to be expected that the power relationship and perceptions of roles and expertise between the teachers and myself have influenced the research experience. I was aware of this and approached the data analysis with a certain degree of reflexivity and sensitivity, recognising that my own influence was part of the data.

The data gathering process concluded at the end of the school year having captured at least two complete cycles of planning, teaching and debriefing for each teacher. The process involved a degree of reflexivity in that there was a sense of doing action research for the sake of research and furthering knowledge, and doing action research for the purpose of taking action, in this case transforming and improving language teaching. This created a sense of mutual benefit and a transformation of each of us as participants through our learning and enhanced self-awareness. Each teacher commented on the value of her experience and her appreciation of the opportunity to engage in reflective dialogue. For me, the action research experience amplified my understanding of the role of the researcher not as a discoverer of truth but rather as 'seeing truth as growing out of the knower's encounter with the world' (Gouldner, 1970: 493).

Analysing the data

The data gathering process yielded two sets of data: video recordings of classroom interactions and audio recordings of professional discussions. The data were analysed in order to select a series of extracts that could be transcribed for detailed analysis (see Appendix 3.1 for further detail about the analysis process). From the video data, a number of extracts were chosen in which the teachers' ways of mediating were particularly evident such as through instruction or discussion. In relation to the audio data, the extracts were chosen that revealed the teachers' understandings of intercultural language teaching and learning, and their own linguistic and cultural biographies. Such moments included the teachers describing their experiences both as intercultural mediators and as language teachers, and discussing difficulties or challenges in the research process. The extracts were then labelled, dated and transcribed. They were then analysed in relation to the key ideas drawn from the literature. Initially, two pedagogical frameworks in the literature were considered as possible reference points against which the data could be analysed. It was decided, however, that while both provided worthwhile ideas that would inform the analysis, neither provided a completely satisfactory framework for the full analysis. Firstly, Byram's (1997) *savoirs* while extremely valuable in outlining dimensions of intercultural competence, did not attend sufficiently to language or to the mediation dimension of pedagogy. Secondly, the principles proposed by Liddicoat *et al.* (2003) while valuable for considering pedagogy in general, did not attend sufficiently to language and culture as content. Hence, it was decided that the concepts of language, culture and their relationship would comprise the framework for conducting the analysis. This was justified on the basis that these are recurring themes in the literature, representing the most fundamental or distilled conceptual underpinnings of intercultural language pedagogy. In relation to the classroom interaction data, the teachers' ways of mediating were analysed with reference to the 'enriched' understanding of mediation based on the key ideas drawn from both sociocultural learning theory and intercultural language teaching. The final process involved analysing the two sets of data in relation to each other. The aim was to examine the connection, if any, between the teachers' conceptions and their ways of mediating these in practice. A matrix (see Appendix 3.2) was developed to consider the two sets of data, with the teachers' views (based on the concepts of language, culture and their relationship) on one axis, and the teachers' mediation practices (in terms of both learning theory and intercultural language teaching) on the other.

While the research process was collaborative, I conducted the data analysis. This was largely due to the limitations on the teachers' time but also their primary interest was in collaborating on planning, teaching and resourcing. My dual role meant that my role as a researcher was not an objective one in a traditional research sense, but rather it was, as is increasingly acknowledged in qualitative research, inevitably subjective:

> ...there is no clear window into the inner life of the individual. Any gaze is always filtered through the lens of language, gender, social class, race and ethnicity. There are no objective observations, only observations socially situated in the worlds of – and between – the observer and the observed. (Denzin & Lincoln, 2000: 19)

Any contribution to a process of shared experience and the interpretation of that experience is bound by the knowledge, experience and position of the individual offering the interpretation. Thus, as the researcher in this case, I was a contributor to the process while also being the arbiter of what was included in the analysis and the significance attributed to that data. In analysing the data, I had to be cognisant of the fact that they had in part been influenced by me, hence I tried to adopt a degree of reflexivity and criticality, to take into account the power relationships between myself and the participants and our own values, assumptions and subjectivities.

About this Book

This book is an account of three language teachers as they develop and attempt to mediate an intercultural perspective on language teaching and learning in practice. It represents an exploration of both the conceptual and practical dimensions of language teachers' work, focusing on the relationship between the teachers' conceptions, practices and self-awareness in understanding what they do and why they do it. The main frame for considering their personal theories and practices are the key concepts that underpin intercultural language teaching, that is, language, culture and their relationship. The case studies are drawn from a foreign language teaching context because it is the most common programme type in the Australian schooling context and represents the primary experience through which students encounter additional languages and cultures to their own.

The book is organised according to theory and practice throughout, outlining aspects of each and bringing them together to make sense of the experience of the teachers involved. The Introduction outlines why this book matters and briefly locates it within the field of language teaching and learning, and in particular the literature related to culture in language teaching and understandings of mediation. The study upon which this book is based is outlined, including its research orientation and design features, the participants and their teaching contexts, as well as a description of the data gathering and analysis processes.

A substantial body of work exists which theorises culture in language teaching, hence rather than revisit such work in detail, Chapter 1 provides a schematic overview of it. The discussion briefly outlines understandings of language and culture, and highlights the major shifts that have taken place in theorising the relationship between language and culture and how these developments have led to an intercultural orientation in recent times.

Chapter 1 acts as a backdrop to Chapter 2 that presents the conceptual understandings about language teaching that are held by the teachers' in the study. The discussion is presented as three case studies, Collette, Kelly and Maria, based on extracts from the series of planning and debriefing discussions. Each case offers an account of the person, the context, the experience and its significance. The cases illuminate understandings and at times tensions for the teachers as their conceptual frames interface with their teaching contexts and practices. The chapter concludes with a number of themes related to the teachers' understandings and provides a sense of how theoretical understandings in the field may or may not relate to the teachers' personal theories.

Chapter 3 explores contemporary understandings of mediation and how these may be relevant to intercultural language teaching and learning. The discussion commences with views of mediation as understood in language teaching, particularly as a translation or problem-solving skill used in communication. Following this is a discussion of mediation understood from the perspective of learning theory, and in particular sociocultural learning theory. The chapter examines how each of these theoretical understandings of mediation provides distinctive and yet complementary views that enhance how mediation may be understood. It is argued that an intercultural language teaching and learning orientation needs to take both perspectives into account.

Chapter 4 details the cases of the three teachers through discussion of the ways in which they mediate an intercultural perspective in their teaching practice. The organisation of the discussion mirrors that in Chapter 2, using the concepts of language, culture and their relationship to discuss the teachers' ways of mediating that are evident in the episodes of classroom interaction. The commentary explores connections between the teachers' ways of mediating and their conceptual understandings. The chapter concludes with a summary of the teachers' ways of mediating an intercultural perspective and an argument for an enriched notion of mediation suitable for intercultural language teaching and learning.

The insights from this study overall are outlined in the final chapter. It begins by proposing that the concept of mediation, as it relates to intercultural language teaching and learning, be revisited and a broader understanding be adopted. The chapter highlights the divergence between the teachers' theoretical understandings and their teaching practices. As the teachers enact their understandings, tensions and challenges emerge, revealing that the very foundational concepts of language and culture themselves, and how they are understood for teaching and learning, need to be revisited. The study reveals that language teachers are engaged in a process of transformation: of their knowledge of intercultural language teaching and learning; of mediating such knowledge for and with their students; and of mediating themselves in the process. The insights in this book raise a number of implications for those engaged in theorising and practising intercultural language teaching and learning, and these are also presented in the final chapter.

The conclusion to the book foregrounds the need to understand the complex nature of language teachers' roles as mediators of language and culture in the foreign language classroom. It acknowledges that language teachers simultaneously stand between what is familiar and unfamiliar; both in terms of knowledge of language and culture and in terms of linguistic and cultural ways of being in the world. The conclusion emphasises the importance of enabling teachers to develop a reflective capability, to understand their role as intercultural mediators and to recognise themselves as integral to both the substance and experience of mediation. Indeed, teachers' awareness of themselves as mediators and of their efforts to understand the tensions they are experiencing is crucial to genuinely realising intercultural language teaching and learning in practice. This book offers a window through which to view and understand the lived experience of three language teachers as they attempt to mediate an intercultural perspective in practice.

1 Understandings of Language and Culture in Language Teaching and Learning

Intercultural language teaching and learning has developed from a long line of theorising in the field of language teaching about the nature of, and the relationship between, language and culture. Comprehensive discussions of these concepts and their relationship are well documented (Dasli, 2011; Liddicoat, 2002, 2011; Liddicoat & Scarino, 2013; Liddicoat *et al.*, 2003; Risager, 2006, 2011) and it is not the intention in this book to canvass such ideas in full but rather to provide a brief overview of the key understandings about language and culture in language teaching, including the emergence of intercultural language teaching and learning. The discussion will then serve as a reference point against which to consider the views of the language teachers in the case studies, including their emergent understandings of intercultural language teaching and learning, which follows in Chapter 2.

Language, Culture and Their Relationship

An intercultural perspective on language teaching and learning is premised on particular understandings of language and culture. Indeed, language and culture are the core concepts upon which more elaborated theories of intercultural language teaching and learning rest. The following section briefly outlines how these concepts, and their relationship, may be understood and how this relates to the emergence of an intercultural orientation towards language teaching and learning.

Language

Language is arguably the most fundamental concept within the field of language teaching and learning. Understandings of language vary, however, typically falling into two main categories: language as code or language as social semiotic.

Language as code

Language can be understood as a code or system for labelling the world. In this view, the code is comprised of forms: lexical and syntactical. The code is governed by rules, which are fixed and enable mastery of the code in set ways. Language exists as an entity in its own right and is largely detached from its users. This view of language is particularly associated with the field of second language acquisition. It is a view influenced by the work of Chomsky (1965) whose theory of generative grammar proposed the idea that the human brain was hardwired for language and its development was largely automatic or predetermined. Humans, therefore, have an innate capacity for language. When this position is adopted in language teaching, language development is regarded as a cognitive process first and foremost. Cognitive models of language development rely heavily on computational metaphors of acquisition involving input and output processes. Krashen (1982) argued a distinction between language acquisition and learning with the former preferred over the latter in terms of effective language development. Krashen's notion of 'comprehensible input' related to the idea that the unconscious process of acquiring language required a rich language environment in which the language learner would select what was necessary for the next stage of development. While this model was devised for 'natural' language acquisition and did not specifically relate to second language learning in a formal learning context, it created interest in 'input' in approaches to language teaching. There was an emphasis on the language teacher using native-speaker-like talk to simulate the acquisition process. Work since has also focused on 'output' (Swain, 1985) in an effort to acknowledge the benefits of learners' productive capacities and associated metalinguistic awareness to their language development. Following such work, knowing a language meant more than knowing how to use a language, it also meant knowing *about* a language, that is developing metalinguistic understandings of the specific language and awareness of language per se.

It has been argued that the view of language as code renders it 'static'; a self-contained body of knowledge which, in the context of teaching and learning, represents one 'code' that becomes replaced by another (Scarino & Liddicoat, 2009). The code exists devoid of contextual or social influences; it is objectified and separated from its communicative contexts and users. What it means to know a language, in this view, is to know the structural elements of the code.

Language as social semiotic

The theory of language as social semiotic views language fundamentally as a social and functional phenomenon (Halliday, 1975). Language is a system of signs that come to represent particular meanings according to how these are attributed by those who use them. These 'signs' have meanings, both given and 'potential' (Halliday, 1978), which are used and adapted by people as they carry out particular functions in their lives. Language represents a resource that provides interactants with options for how they will construct meaning according to the social context. Language does not exist separate from its users. Indeed, it exists to enable them to participate in their community, establishing and maintaining relationships and making meanings together with other users. In a semiotic view, language is shaped by, and shapes, relationships between people and the social world. This sense of social practice means that language can be seen as organic and dynamic (Shohamy, 2001, 2006). It is open to change and evolution that originate in its daily use. Language is as distinctive and multiple in its meanings, as its many users.

In this understanding of language, context is crucial in shaping how meaning is made, by whom and for what purpose. Context is comprised of the circumstances of use, the roles and relationships of users and the ideational content of the text(s) used or created (Halliday, 1975). Language, therefore, is not only dynamic but also permeable and malleable, shaped by its environment and users. Language, however, is not passive in this process and it too shapes its users and circumstances, it is 'energetic' (Shohamy, 2006). In this view, language is both shaped by, and in turn shapes, the social contexts in which it is used.

Language pedagogy based on a social semiotic view focuses on both active language use and knowledge of language as a meaning-making system. It involves analysing language to understand how it is constructed and interpreting language for personal meaning. The processes of analysis and interpretation are not restricted to the target language but apply to any language system and across language systems; that is, developing learners' metalinguistic understandings and their capacities for understanding the nature of language itself. It is the view of language as social semiotic that relates most directly to an intercultural orientation in language teaching and learning. This will be explored in more detail later in this overview.

Culture

Culture is the other major concept that, while viewed as important, has been varyingly understood in relation to language teaching. The ways in which culture is typically understood can be broadly grouped into two categories: culture as 'facts and information' and culture as 'social semiotic'.

Culture as facts and information

In this view, culture is commonly understood as the shared attributes of a particular group of people, located within a particular geographical area. Culture comprises the observable products and features associated with the group. There is no recognition in this view of cultures as internally diverse or subject to change. Rather this 'high culture' view focuses on static aspects such as iconic artefacts, a literary canon or great artworks (Crozet & Liddicoat, 1999a, 1999b; Liddicoat, 2005). Culture then is a 'static entity made up of accumulated, classifiable, observable... facts' (Paige et al., 1999: 176). Aligned closely with this view is a 'cultural studies' view, in which culture represents the history, geography, society and institutions of a group. To know a culture, therefore, is to know *about* it, through observation and acquisition of factual knowledge.

A further view of culture, strongly associated with the field of anthropology (Gumperz, 1982; Hymes, 1974, 1986), is that of culture as the practices and social norms of a particular group of people. According to this view, culture constitutes the observable actions of a social group such as their customs and traditions. It involves acquiring the valued ways of behaving and acting or the associated values and beliefs that are expected within the social collective. This view suggests that cultures have particular ways of acting and particular values associated with these. This view removes any sense of personal agency or variability within a national or collective group, and does not acknowledge how cultural practices and values change over time. It also positions the 'observer' as an outsider who is unchanged by his/her observations.

These views of culture, particularly as they relate to language teaching, have been criticised for being 'static' (Liddicoat, 2002, 2005) and limited to a national paradigm (Risager, 2007) that does not sufficiently acknowledge diversity within and movement across cultures. In language teaching, these views of culture result in a focus on the familiar (similarities) or the exotic (differences), both of which are problematic on their own and both of which need to be treated at both concrete and abstract levels (Demorgon, 1989). In addition, such views lack a coherent scope in relation to what gets included or excluded as culture in language teaching (Paige *et al.*, 1999). In viewing culture as products, behaviours or beliefs, it becomes equated with factual knowledge, which in turn distances it from the individual and from language, resulting in superficial learning (Liddicoat, 2005; Liddicoat *et al.*, 2003). The relationship that the learner can have with the target culture is that of an observer of similarities and differences, leading to a reinforcement of the learner's own cultural norms. The learner is not viewed as a creator and enactor of culture (Paige *et al.*, 1999) but rather as a detached observer of it. There is little sense in this view of culture that a learner has his/her own cultural identity that is integral to his/her emerging intercultural identity (Hall & Ramirez, 1993; Houghton, 2013; Liddicoat *et al.*, 2003).

Culture as semiotic practices

Another line of thinking about culture is that of culture as a symbolic system. In this view, culture is located in the daily lived experiences of individuals as they participate in processes of creating, communicating and making sense of their social system (Geertz, 1973). Culture represents a framework through which people communicate about, make sense of and interpret their worlds. Culture is a 'differentiated, changing and conflictual, actual and virtual, multimodal symbolic system or social semiotic' (Kramsch, 1993, 1998). Culture becomes associated with peoples' actions and motivations, the variability of these and the contexts in which these occur, and the varying interpretations that can be made by individuals. To belong to a culture, therefore, is to develop the resources necessary to participate in shared meaning making.

A view of culture as social practice focuses on the ways in which people conduct themselves and participate in shared practices, constantly creating and shifting their memberships, through their interactions with others. In this view, culture is dynamic, multifaceted and dialogic; continually being created and contested through the actions of individuals in their daily lives (Bhabha, 1994). To know a culture, is to access its resources and participate in its practices in context-sensitive ways to achieve a purpose. It is this view of culture that is most closely associated with intercultural language teaching and learning.

The relationship between language and culture

In various forms, culture has long been associated with language teaching and learning, dating back to the late 19th century and gaining greater prominence in the late 20th century (Risager, 2007). Nowadays, it has become almost unthinkable in the field of language teaching and learning to consider language without culture and *vice versa*. Attempts abound to describe the relationship between the two with terms such as language-and-culture (Byram *et al.*, 1994), culture-in-language (Crozet & Liddicoat, 2000), languaculture (Agar, 1994; Risager, 2006) and linguaculture (Friedrich, 1986) and expressions such as 'language expresses cultural reality' (Kramsch, 1998) and language and culture are 'two sides of the same coin' (Moran, 2001). Such efforts reflect contemporary views of language and culture as inextricably related, yet this has not always been recognised and there have been a number of key developments in language teaching in recent decades that have led to this understanding.

The emergence of 'communicative competence' (Hymes, 1972) was a key turning point in the acknowledgement of the role of culture in language teaching and learning. Models of communicative competence recognised culture as a dimension of language ability; it creates the context for language use and is part of the knowledge that a learner 'needs to know' in order to be an effective participant in a given speech community. Psycholinguistic models of communicative competence typically position cultural knowledge as secondary to the knowledge necessary to use a language. For example, Canale and Swain's (1981) model includes 'sociolinguistic competence', which focuses on knowing which language to use according to the given context, including politeness and register. Van Ek's (1986) model has six dimensions of communicative competence with three focusing on the social: sociolinguistic competence, sociocultural competence and social competence. Each is framed as knowledge about culture that assists in making suitable language choices. The model of communicative competence developed by Bachman (1990) and later Bachman and Palmer (1996) in the area of language testing, features sociocultural competence as part of an overall pragmatic competence and includes awareness of language use, particularly register, dialect and cultural references. This competence is described in terms of the knowledge necessary to select language effectively. Thus, in these models, culture is seen as providing a communicative context, about which certain types of knowledge are helpful in assisting overall communicative language ability.

The efforts of the Council of Europe during the 1980s to recognise the increasing mobility of people across the continent and therefore the imperative to prepare citizens to live, work and study abroad was a crucial factor in the move towards a more integrated view of language and culture (for a detailed account see Risager [2007]). The work of Zarate (1986) was influential in arguing that, due to a difference between acquiring a culture as a foreigner and acquiring culture as a native speaker, there must be a greater explicitness in teaching culture for the former. While significant in focusing greater attention on the connection between language and culture, Zarate's work did not explicate how the two are related and the pedagogical implications of their interrelatedness.

Soon after, Damen (1987) advocated a move away from viewing culture as a fifth skill (that is, in addition to listening, speaking, reading and writing). She proposed 'closing the language and culture gap', stating that 'to ignore the interplay between language and culture is to play the language game without knowing the rules' (Damen, 2003: 72). She describes the relationship as follows:

> In human contexts, specific languages and cultures, being mutually interacting and reinforcing, are inextricably bound. Cultural rules and values guide, mold, often control, and nurture the sense of community that defines personal identity and binds disparate individuals into families, villages, cities, and societies. In turn, these cultural givens are transmitted, articulated and practiced through language. (Damen, 1987: 72)

In this view, language and culture are coexistent and mutually influential in shaping and reflecting social memberships, values and interactions. Damen (2003) identifies a paradox about language and culture; that they are simultaneously universal and distinctive, and it is this that presents a challenge for teaching. She argues that there is difficulty caused by both the distinctive nature of language and culture and the ways of learning both that needs to be better understood in order to adequately attend to the interrelationship. Language, for example, can be isolated and studied as form. Culture, on the other hand, is changeable and highly subjective, involving stages of acculturation. Damen (2003) proposes that teachers need to develop specialised knowledge of language and culture as systems as well as 'the stages of acculturation, their relationship to language and culture learning and their influences in the classroom context'. Thus, Damen's work indicates that while language and culture may be understood as interconnected as a general principle, they each entail different kinds of knowledge that must be considered in language teaching and learning; a proposition taken further by Risager (2007).

Beyond declaring the interrelatedness of language and culture, Byram (1989) attempted to articulate a comprehensive theory of culture as related to language teaching. Evolving out of the British context of requiring trainee language teachers to study abroad, Byram's work considered the role of culture in language teaching as it relates to the processes of acculturation and socialisation. He argued that the connection between language and culture is a fundamental starting point for language teaching since 'language has no function independent of the context in which is it used, thus language always refers to something beyond itself: the cultural context' (Byram, 1988: 180). He does, however, suggest that language and culture can be justifiably separated for some pedagogical purposes, such as the teaching of literature. There is a tension in Byram's view at the time between, on the one hand, language and culture understood in general terms, and language and culture understood for language teaching. In fact, it is this conundrum that is addressed by others such as Risager (2007), whose work is discussed later in this section. Risager (2007) argues for a view of language and culture as both distinct and integrated, depending on the perspective being adopted.

Another key development that influenced understandings of the relationship between language and culture is the foregrounding of the notion of 'context'. Emerging from a linguistic, discourse-analytic perspective within foreign language teaching, Kramsch (1989: 10) regards language and culture as forged together in the 'integrating moment' of discourse. She argues that culture is a feature of language itself and that the two are in a dialectic relationship, with language use being 'indissociable from the creation and transmission of culture' (Kramsch, 1993: 9). She further describes the relationship as one in which language expresses, embodies and symbolises cultural reality:

> Language is the principal means whereby we conduct our social lives. When it is used in contexts of communication, it is bound up with culture in multiple and complex ways. (Kramsch, 1993: 9)

Kramsch's (2003: 32) highlighting of culture as 'dialogically created through language *in discourse*' strengthened the view that language and culture are inseparable. She does not attempt to differentiate language and culture in general and in language teaching, instead viewing one as a given for the other.

In an attempt to provide a conceptual framework for language teachers to consider the relationship of language and culture, Crozet and Liddicoat (1999a) offer a continuum of 'points of articulation' between culture and language in order to show that some practices are more 'cultural' and others are more 'linguistic', but that there is 'no level of language which is independent of culture and therefore, which is not open to cultural variation'. The continuum reflects their attempt to show, what they later refer to as, the 'language-in-culture' and the 'culture-in-language' (Crozet & Liddicoat, 2000). While the continuum depicts language and culture as intersecting at various points, and therefore supports teachers to make the interconnection visible, it does not explain how to teach language and culture as variable; a challenge that Crozet and Liddicoat (1999b) acknowledge that language teachers face in practice. They suggest that language teachers need to develop a perspective that integrates language and the variability of its contexts of use, and perceives ambiguity and complexity as normal. More recently, Liddicoat and Scarino (2013) have updated the continuum by expanding it beyond pragmatics to include the symbolic and interpretative nature of language and culture in communication.

Claims that language and culture are inseparable are not without contestation. Concerned with the rise of global mobility and how languages and cultures 'travel' and what this means for national and individual languages and cultures, Risager (2006, 2007) critiques the view that 'language is culture, culture is language' as naïve and problematic:

> There is an identification that implies that there is no 'culture' that is not 'language' – an absurd idea which is synonymous with denying the value of much of the research work that is taking place within the humanities and social sciences, e.g. in relation to Cultural Studies. (Risager, 2007: 153)

Instead, she argues that there are two levels of the relationship between language and culture that require consideration, what she refers to as the 'generic' and the 'differential'. At a generic level, language and culture are interrelated, and this is particularly the case in relation to first language learning. Yet at the more micro, differential level, they are separable and this is particularly pertinent for second and foreign language learning. Risager (2006) proposes the need for greater precision in theorising the complex relationship between language and culture:

> I often get the feeling that what [language and culture pedagogues] actually mean corresponds with the concept of *languaculture*. They use the concept of culture in a tacitly shortened way – and such an understanding allows the category of culture to be determined by that

of language. This I see as being one of the most fundamental problems of the linguistic way of dealing with the concept of culture. (Risager, 2006: 198)

According to Risager, the concept of *languaculture*, originally developed by Agar (1994), is valuable in distinguishing between language and culture as integrated in a general sense, and the kind of language-culture that develops on an individual, local level. It is at this level, she suggests that not everything that is linguistic is cultural and *vice versa*, and that the individual has the potential to choose from his/her *languaculture* to act in particular ways during communication. Risager challenges what she sees as linguistically determined views of culture, arguing instead for greater nuance in understanding how language and culture are related, at what level and for whom. Her foregrounding of the notion of *languaculture* has been adopted more recently by Diaz (2013) who, in developing case studies of curriculum planning and implementation by university lecturers, adopts the concept in exploring a critical language pedagogy in higher education, finding it particularly useful for considering culture-in-language. She does, however, criticise Risager's lack of attention to the curriculum and the pedagogical practicalities of her theoretical model.

In summary, the concepts of language, culture and their relationship, which are fundamental to an intercultural orientation in language teaching and learning, are understood in two main ways. On the one hand, language is seen as code and culture is seen as facts and information: a 'static' view. On the other hand, language and culture are seen as social practices or semiotic: a 'dynamic' view (Liddicoat, 2002). The relationship between language and culture is characterised variously as integrated, linked and inseparable, but it is also argued that this is too simplistic and a more nuanced understanding of the relationship is needed as the two should be considered as separable in some respects. These understandings of language, culture and their relationship provide a basis for considering how the case study teachers conceive these ideas, and intercultural language teaching and learning, for it is the mediation of this that is the central concern of this book.

Intercultural Language Teaching and Learning

The term 'intercultural' has its origins in the mid 20th century, building on the notion of communicative competence (Hymes, 1972) and later sociocultural models of communicative competence (Byram &

Zarate, 1994; Nostrand, 1991). The increasing dissatisfaction with prevailing models of communicative competence led to the emergence of 'intercultural communicative competence' that recognised the capability of the learner to move between cultures. This shift meant that knowing and using a language expanded to include the ability to negotiate meaning across cultures and to form an identity as a user of the target language (Buttjes, 1991). In order to perform this movement, learners need cultural knowledge, but not knowledge that is additional to linguistic knowledge but [knowledge] that is integrated with it in communication. The intercultural models viewed culture as central to language teaching and learning as they acknowledged the crucial role and impact of the social dimension on communication. Indeed, the social dimension is given equal status to the grammatical system of language such as in Byram's (1994) early model comprising four types of competence: linguistic, sociolinguistic, discourse and intercultural.

In addition, the shift towards intercultural communicative competence was intended to challenge the prevailing native speaker norm that was assumed in communicative competence. It was argued that such norms were no longer appropriate given multilingual communities and the global mobility of people (Kramsch, 1993, 1994). Instead, a new goal towards a 'plurilingual and pluricultural' person and an 'intercultural speaker' (Byram & Zarate, 1994; Crozet & Liddicoat, 1999b; Kramsch, 1993, 1999a, 2003), or a 'bilingual position' (Byram & Zarate, 1994) was regarded as more appropriate for second language learners given their particular identities and communicative needs. This goal foregrounded the learner's own linguistic and cultural situatedness in the learning process and highlighted a relationship of the learner to the target language and culture that had not previously been unrecognised in models of communicative competence where the learner was not understood as being transformed by his/her new knowledge and understandings. The move towards intercultural communicative competence highlighted language learning and use as an embodied process.

Recognition of the transformation of the learner was particularly captured in Kramsch's (1993, 1999b) notion of a 'third place'. She described the starting position of a learner as one in which he/she operates within the reality of the first culture, with perceptions of oneself and one's culture, while holding perceptions of the other culture, which itself contains perceptions and realities of itself and the learner's culture. Kramsch suggested that learners need to move to a symbolic position, a 'third place' from which they understand these interrelationships and where learners are both insiders and outsiders of both cultures, located 'between the cultures the learner grew up with and the new cultures he or she is being introduced to'. This kind of learning, according to Kramsch (1993: 236), requires a new 'critical' pedagogy that focuses on learners becoming participants in a 'systematic apprenticeship of difference', learning to understand and operate in new ways and developing awareness of one's own positioning and identity in the process. Her critical pedagogy model comprises different aspects of context: linguistic, situational, interactional, cultural and intertextual, which need to be made visible to foreign language learners such that they recognise how language both influences and is influenced by culture. Through a process of conscious observation, comparing cultural realities and perceptions, and decentring from one's own language and culture, one's world view and frames of reference are changed, leading to a new positioning and ways of seeing the world, 'in-between' both languages and cultures (Kramsch & Nolden, 1994).

In addition to theorising intercultural communicative competence, there were calls for the development of pedagogical models to support the teaching of it (Kramsch, 1993; Zarate, 1986). Arguably, the most influential of these was Byram and Zarate's (1994) curriculum and assessment framework. The framework represented a landmark achievement in articulating intercultural communicative competence as it related to curriculum, assessment and pedagogy. The framework comprises four types of knowing or *savoirs*:

- knowledge (*savoirs*) of one's own linguistic and cultural system and that of the target language, and of interaction in general;
- skills (*savoir comprendre*) of interpreting documents or practices from another culture and explaining them in relation to one's own;
- skills (*savoir apprendre/faire*) of applying knowledge of a new culture during real-time interaction;
- attitudes and values (*savoir etre*) of openness and curiosity towards 'otherness'.

Byram has since added a fifth type, critical cultural awareness (*savoir s'engager*) in recognition of the political dimension of learners' overall intercultural communicative competence. He has also explained a difference between intercultural competence, as belonging to native speakers who interact with non-native speakers of the language, and intercultural communicative competence, which is developed by foreign language speakers interacting with native speakers. The latter being a more deliberate, learned, conscious process than the former. While the model was a major advance in articulating the multidimensional nature of intercultural communicative competence, and led to more practice-oriented work to support language teachers in developing pedagogy, curriculum and assessment (Byram, 1997; Byram *et al.*, 1994, 2002), it attracted some criticism for not clearly articulating the linguistic dimension of intercultural competence (Liddicoat *et al.*, 2003), for being Eurocentric and not explaining how the *savoirs* work together (Risager, 2007).

One of the important contributions of Byram and Zarate's (1994) model is that it recognised the affective dimension of intercultural communicative competence. It has led to various efforts to acknowledge learner disposition in such models, including developing tolerance of other cultures, tolerance of ambiguity and willingness to engage with difference. Some also advocate moving beyond 'sympathy' and 'sensitivity' to actively using affective learning in 'doing' difference (Carr, 1999). Others propose an explicit mechanism for attending to such learning in the form of a pedagogic principle such as 'responsibility' (Liddicoat *et al.*, 2003). Despite these efforts, according to Zarate *et al.* (1999), the affective remains undertheorised due to a reluctance to deal with aspects, such as empathy, that are viewed as personal traits which are highly subjective and difficult to address in teaching and assessment. Instead, based on their study which found that 'successful' classrooms were those in which teachers employed empathic actions, Zarate *et al.* (2004) suggest that empathy can be learned through active teaching such as encouragement, apology, disapproval, error correction and suchlike. They recommend that language teachers be trained to explicitly teach their students how to practise empathy in order not only to acknowledge but also to genuinely develop the affective dimension of intercultural competence, which is seen as a necessary part of the capability to mediate across languages and cultures.

Following the work in Europe, and responding to the increasing number of study abroad programmes in the United States during the 1990s, Paige *et al.* (2003) proposed a framework for considering culture 'as the core' of language teaching. According to their framework, culture learning requires both culture-specific learning (knowledge and skills relevant to a particular group or community) and culture-general learning (for example, the concept of culture, the nature of cultural adjustment, stress and emotion in cross-cultural communication) within three domains (knowledge, behaviour, attitudes). Acquiring knowledge about a specific culture is not sufficient and instead one needs to understand what it means to participate in another culture, how it affects identity, emotions and the nature of communication itself. Thus, according to this view, the capacity to communicate effectively across cultures is not solely an experiential- or knowledge-based one, but one which requires reflection and abstracted understandings connecting experience to an underlying conceptual framework about the nature of culture in its own right. Their work highlighted an intention to consider culture as the starting point for language teaching, with a need to consider various kinds of culture learning. The work did not, however, explicitly articulate the role of language and it was somewhat taken for granted in the model.

In an effort to articulate a pedagogy not for teaching culture as part of language teaching, but for teaching with an intercultural orientation, Crozet and Liddicoat (1999a) offered a set of principles and implications for practice. They identified five principles: culture must be taught explicitly; the bilingual/multilingual speaker is the norm; conceptual and experiential learning are required; there are redefined roles for teachers as learners of language and culture; and there needs to be a process and product orientation towards assessment and language learning. Crozet and Liddicoat (2000) presented a pedagogical model comprised of four phases of teaching: awareness raising, experimentation, production and feedback. 'Awareness raising' is the input phase where students 'notice' something unfamiliar. 'Experimentation' is where students practise their new knowledge before using it to interact in the 'production' phase. Finally, 'feedback' involves reflecting on the experience and the students' cognitive and affective responses. Their work, based on a linguistic starting point and drawing on pragmatics and conversational analysis, emphasised that culture is part of language and that therefore intercultural communicative competence is the ability to use language in culturally appropriate ways with sensitivity to context. While their model signals the importance of an intercultural starting point, it does not explicitly attend to the content dimension of intercultural competence (Risager, 2007) and therefore the issue of 'what' is to be taught and learned.

Continuing the attempts to articulate a comprehensive guide for language teachers, Liddicoat *et al.* (2003) outline a multifaceted and principled-based approach, with the starting assumption that:

> Intercultural language learning involves the fusing of language, culture and learning into a single educative process. It begins with the idea that language, culture and learning are fundamentally interrelated processes and places their interrelationship at the centre of the learning process. (Liddicoat *et al.*, 2003: 43)

Rather than being a model or methodology, this work comprises five principles as its foundation. The principles (active construction, social interaction, making connections, reflection and responsibility) underpin the overall approach and provide a basis for outlining implications for curriculum, teaching and assessment. The principles draw heavily on sociocultural constructivist theories of learning, and are not of themselves specifically intercultural. Rather, they highlight the teaching and learning process, understood as both cognitive and social, and emphasise the highly individualised and developmental nature of both intercultural language teaching and learning. In particular, the principles of 'making connections' and 'reflection' are intended to promote the process of decentring from one's own language and culture, in order to consider one's own intracultural identity and situatedness, and how this may impact on intercultural engagement and mutual understanding. The principles are intended as a starting point for teachers to develop an integrated view of language, culture and learning, in order to construct programmes, teaching and assessment that cater for learners according to their local context. Their work foregrounds the need to recognise intercultural language teaching not as a way of doing language teaching, but as an overall orientation towards language, culture and learning, as they come together in language teaching and learning.

Part of the difficulty in developing a pedagogical framework for intercultural language teaching lies in the fact that by its very nature it is a highly individualised and developmental kind of learning. This point is particularly evident in the area of assessment. Early attempts to articulate a framework for assessing intercultural communicative competence focused on different types of knowledge (*savoir*) in preference to the term 'competence' as it was deemed to be more encompassing of knowledge, skills and dispositions (Byram, 1997; Byram & Zarate, 1994). Byram outlined a comprehensive model of intercultural communicative competence showing a relationship between 'locations of learning' (classroom, fieldwork, independent learning), *savoirs* and types of competence (with intercultural competence at the centre). He provided guidelines for curriculum and assessment, including suggested criteria for judging competence, but the model was less clear on the contribution of language. Sercu (2004) has suggested expanding Byram's model to include greater recognition of learners' metacognition. Risager (2007) adds also that the model should include transnational and plurilingual competence. More recently, Houghton (2013) proposes the inclusion of what she refers to as *savoir se transformer*, in recognition of learners' identity development and their reasoned reflection about whether to change or not in response to the 'other'. While attempts to articulate models for assessing intercultural competence have been criticised and remain elusive, they can offer insights into pedagogy, as assessment arguably represents the point at which the underlying construct of language teaching and learning is most under scrutiny. Tasks that are designed for assessment, for example, may reflect the kinds of teaching and learning required to perform them.

Assessment practice is generally aligned with one of two orientations: communicative behaviours and performance, or attitudes/dispositions and understandings. The communicative performance orientation may be conducted through simulated interactions or scenarios in which assessment may focus on interactional norms, cross-cultural mediation and pragmatic norms (Liddicoat, 2011). One attempt to develop a comprehensive framework of assessment tasks of this kind is provided by Sercu (2004). Her task typology framework includes five task types: cognitive, cognitive-attitudinal, exploration, production of materials and enactment tasks. The tasks may include, for example, empathising with others, reflecting on own cultural norms, and mediating in an intercultural situation through a mini-drama or simulation game. The tasks also require learners to adopt different roles and subject positions (e.g. insiders, outsiders and go-betweens). Sercu's framework does not address how the tasks are performed, how they relate to each other and in what respect they capture intercultural learning. Nonetheless, the framework is useful for considering aspects of pedagogy such as learner roles and positioning.

The other main orientation in the assessment of intercultural communicative competence focuses on changes in learners' attitudes and dispositions. This work includes attitudinal tests to elicit reactions to particular cultural groups, culture assimilator tests focusing on the ability to read context and cultural norms, and cultural awareness tests that capture one's knowledge about language and culture and feelings of empathy and self-awareness (Liddicoat, 2011; Liddicoat et al., 2003). While it is not clear how learners' attitudes and dispositions may play out in intercultural encounters, these tests indicate areas of explicit focus in teaching. That is, promoting the exploration of representations of language and culture and considering reactions to these, including how they may change over time, are important areas for pedagogical focus. In fact, both orientations towards assessment are insufficient on their own, and Scarino (2009) argues that what is needed is both performance and knowledge-based approaches. Liddicoat and Scarino (2010, 2013) advocate a new assessment paradigm, one in which the learner is understood as having dual roles: as performer and analyser. As such, assessment needs to include both communication- and reflection-oriented tasks and experiences. They encourage alternative assessment practices such as the use of portfolios and commentaries that elicit learners' capacity to act interculturally and to reflect upon their actions and their own transformation in the process. A reorienting of assessment to include analytic and reflexive learning means that these aspects need also to be part of pedagogy and the underlying construct of intercultural (communicative) competence.

In fact, recent work has focused on expanding the construct of intercultural (communicative) competence in a number of ways. Kramsch (2006a) and Kramsch and Whiteside (2008) advocate integrating the notion of 'symbolic competence'. They argue that the process of navigating linguistic and cultural diversity is not restricted to a foreign country or culture but occurs between peoples of diverse languages and cultures within a single national culture. They propose that, in contemporary times, language users have to navigate complex and unpredictable exchanges in which there may be multiple languages, 'cultural imaginations and different social and political memories' at work. Kramsch (2008) describes contexts as highly varied and interactions as multilayered with participants having dynamic identities, which change over time and place, and with language use that must be interpreted according to the immediate as well as hidden, or past, contexts and meanings. From this perspective, 'competence' involves the ability to 'read people, situations and events based on a deep understanding of the historical and subjective dimensions of human experience' (Kramsch, 2008: 390). Language learners not only participate within someone else's language and cultural context, but they also shape the language and its cultural context. They, therefore, need to understand their own subjectivities and historicities, as they interplay with those of others. Kramsch's work further highlights a multilingual norm in language teaching and learning, and the subjective and symbolic power associated with this.

In a similar vein, Liddicoat and Scarino (2013) advocate the need to recognise the interpretative nature of communication across multiple languages and cultures and of learning itself. They propose expanding the construct of intercultural language learning by integrating a hermeneutic perspective:

> ...an intercultural orientation to language learning involves communicating and learning to communicate in and through an additional language *and* learning to understand the process of communication itself across languages and cultures, recognizing the linguistic and cultural construction of the interpretation and creation of meaning. (Liddicoat & Scarino, 2013: 44)

In this expanded view, as mentioned previously from an assessment perspective, a language learner is both a performer and analyser. He/she constructs meaning during language use, interpreting another linguistic and cultural framework and developing an identity within this, while reflecting on the experience of learning in the process. Interpretation is embedded in each of the key concepts of language, culture and learning that underpin an intercultural orientation. Learners need, for example, to understand language as code, social practice and the interpretative nature of language itself. They need to understand culture as facts and information, social practice and culture as an interpretative lens through which people construct the world. In addition, learners need to learn new concepts and participate in learning, while reflecting on how learning is also constructed through language and culture.

Furthermore, the reality of globalisation, multilingualism, mass mobility and communication technologies has increased interest in a critical perspective in language teaching and calls to expand the construct of intercultural (communicative) competence. As early as Kramsch (1993, 1994), the need for a critical approach to language pedagogy has been recognised. Phipps and Gonzalez (2004: 168) argue that a critical perspective is needed in order to 'open up space for a fresh debate about modern languages', claiming that languages are a social justice issue, constructing, expanding and even limiting the ways and the worlds in which we can participate. Risager (2007) adds another dimension focusing on language learners as global citizens, participating in a multilingual and multicultural reality. She suggests that learners need to be prepared for greater complexity and fluidity of languages and cultures, understanding that they are not fixed to particular groups or nation states, but that they are in fact transnational. She outlines a multifaceted model of intercultural competence that includes 'knowledge of language and critical language awareness' as well as 'knowledge of culture and society and critical cultural awareness'. These dimensions are crucial, she argues, for a pedagogy that will develop language learners as critically aware participants in the global community.

Byram (2008, 2012) also proposes a need for an expanded construct, proposing a critical take on and approach to intercultural language pedagogy. He advocates making explicit the humanistic values that underpin intercultural language pedagogy such that the political dimension can be addressed more consciously in practice. He emphasises the need to go beyond awareness raising and empower learners to be active, responsible, intercultural citizens. Dasli (2011: 22) characterises interest in a critical perspective as a 'critical intercultural language pedagogy "moment"'. She perceives it as involving questions of cultural identity and ideology, with language students learning and unlearning through problematising their reactions and critically reflecting on their own identities in intercultural communication. The theme of identity transformation through intercultural language learning is gaining increasing focus with emergent notions such as *savoir es transformer* (Houghton, 2013; Tsai & Houghton, 2010). The very notion of an intercultural speaker is under question with i Sole (2013: 336) suggesting the need for an alternative nomenclature; the 'cosmopolitan speaker'. She argues that this term reflects a new sense of language learners as they 'meander' into other languages and cultures. These learners develop awareness of their existing cartographies (or personal identity maps) and take these with them into new, flexible linguistic and cultural spaces, learning to 'dwell' there in ways that do not differentiate between themselves and the 'other'. These suggestions for developing an expanded construct of intercultural competence have implications for intercultural language pedagogy and also for the role of the language teacher.

The shift from communicative competence through intercultural competence to symbolic competence and, most recently, to critical intercultural citizenship and critical intercultural language pedagogy, has necessarily required a reconceptualisation of the role of the language teacher. This is reflected in notions of the language teacher as a 'principal mediator' (Byram, 1991), a 'quintessential go-between' (Kramsch, 2004a), a 'teacher of intercultural communication' (Kramsch, 2008) and a 'teacher of meaning' (Kramsch, 2008). Language teachers are viewed as 'professional mediators' with a 'capacity, and responsibility, to help learners to understand others and otherness as a basis for the acquisition of cultural and communicative competence' (Crozet & Liddicoat, 1999a). Scarino (2001) argued a need to go beyond the notion of language teachers as 'intermediaries' (Byram & Risager, 1999: 58), who act as functionaries for communicating for others, to a view of language teachers as contributors to and shapers of meaning. In this view, language teachers are not simply a conduit through which meanings travel, but they actively create ideas and knowledge:

> Teachers' work involves integrating theoretical knowledge from a range of dynamic and ever-evolving disciplines (both in education and linguistics), their own practice, knowledge and pedagogic designs. Their decisions and judgments are based on their own educational experiences; their personalities; their philosophy of language and how languages and cultures are learned; their particular context, including social and power structures of school communities, as places that create and sustain meanings; their understanding of students, with collective

and individual needs – as persons, as learners, as developing language learners and users; and the social, cultural and political contexts which constitute their professional landscape. (Scarino, 2001: 6)

Understood in this way, language teachers act in complex, situated and subjective ways, ideas echoed by Kramsch (2004a) who describes the language teacher as:

...the quintessential go-between among people with various languages, and of different cultures, generations, and genders... someone who has acquired the ability to interact with 'others', be they native or non-native speakers, present or past writers; someone who has learned to accept other perspectives and perceptions of the world, to mediate between different perspectives, and to be conscious of their evaluations of difference. (Kramsch, 2004a: 44)

As such, she suggests that the language teacher requires disciplinary and professional knowledge, interactional competence, interpretative and relational competence, methodological competence, intercultural attitudes and beliefs, and a critical cultural perspective. Kramsch (2004a, 2008) provides examples of the kinds of knowledge, practices and dispositions that language teachers need to perform such a role. These include, for example, the need to understand culture as discourse and understand one's own and students' discourse systems. It means understanding meaning as relational and multidimensional and asking students to reflect on how their identity mediates meaning. Language teachers need to challenge linearity through revisiting texts or restructuring knowledge, or by creating and sharing diverse meanings of the same text, and encouraging variation. Kramsch advocates the use of humour and promoting a critical stance through encouraging subjectivity and exploring historical connotations of language. Teachers and learners also need to talk about the 'meaning of meaning' and how meaning is made according to linguistic and cultural identities. Finally, Kramsch says, teachers must be aware of how they model being a multilingual speaker to their students and the relationship that they help construct between students and the target language and culture. Her view, also shared by others (Liddicoat & Scarino, 2013; Papademetre & Scarino, 2000), is that language teaching should focus more on meaning than content, and is more a matter of 'being' than a matter of 'method'.

Concerns about how well equipped language teachers are for their reframed role date back a number of decades. For example, Hall and

Ramirez (1987) found that language teachers had limited understanding of the variability of culture, teaching it either as celebrated group differences (with no sense of the individual) or as a melting pot of individual differences (with no framework for abstracting beyond the individual). Kramsch (1993) questioned whether language teachers possess the meta-awareness of their first culture needed to engage students in analysis across cultures. More recently, Sercu (2005, 2007) found that language teachers value an intercultural approach to language teaching, but find it difficult to realise in practice, and Diaz (2013) found that tertiary language teachers also lacked a framework for understanding critical *languaculture* pedagogies and how to develop them through the curriculum.

Papademetre and Scarino (2000) suggest that teacher knowledge needs to start with teachers' own linguistic and cultural biographies, individual situatedness and conceptual frameworks as a basis for developing an intercultural language pedagogy:

> As teachers and mediators of language(s) and culture(s) living and working in a society, we should be constantly concerned with our own construction of the culture(s) we teach, because the implementation and application of our conceptual construction forms the basis of mediation of what we teach to our learners. (Papademetre & Scarino, 2000: 65)

Language teachers, they suggest, need to undertake an ongoing 'journey' of discovery, development and reflection in which foundational concepts such as language and culture are constantly encountered, contested and reinterpreted, in order for teachers to understand their own enculturation and its relationship to their teaching. The view that language teachers need critical self-awareness in order to understand and perform the identity dimension of their work, is supported also by Menard-Warwick (2008). In her study of two teachers of English in the Americas, Menard-Warwick found that each teacher's unique intercultural experiences and identity influenced his/her pedagogy and overall framing of language learning. For example, having returned from two decades of living in the United States, one Chilean teacher framed her teaching through the theme of 'cultural change'. While the teachers' experiences represented a resource for planning and connecting with students' experiences, Menard-Warwick cautions that decades of overseas experience is not the primary basis for an intercultural perspective but rather it is teachers' meta-awareness of identity as a resource for teaching and learning that matters.

A number of key developments have taken place in theorising culture in language teaching and in the emergence of an intercultural orientation in language teaching. Understandings of language and culture have shifted substantially, from language as code and culture as information, to language and culture as social semiotic practices. Views about the role and relationship of culture in language teaching have tended to fall into one of two perspectives: the cultural and the intercultural (Liddicoat, 2011). The former, associated with communicative competence, positions the learner as outside the culture, acquiring factual knowledge about the 'other' culture. The latter, associated with intercultural communicative competence, positions learners as actively involved in the culture, while decentring from their own culture and being changed in the process. This perspective most directly involves language, as it is through language that the learner enters into another world view. An intercultural orientation has expanded further in recent times to include notions of symbolic competence (Kramsch, 2006a, 2011, 2012) and intercultural citizenship (Byram, 2008, 2012), reflecting growing interest in the interpretative and political dimensions of this orientation towards language teaching and learning. Dasli (2011) offers a characterisation of the transition that has occurred over recent decades as a series of 'moments', ranging from cultural awareness to cross-cultural mediation and, the still emergent, critical intercultural language pedagogy.

The shift towards an intercultural approach has also resulted in efforts to develop pedagogical, curriculum and assessment frameworks, and accompanying these has been a reframing of the role of the language teacher, from being a 'teacher of language' to being a 'teacher of meaning'. While the challenge for language teachers of developing an intercultural orientation in practice has been acknowledged, very few studies have investigated language teachers' understandings of the key concepts underpinning this orientation and how these relate to their practice. The following discussion will endeavour to explore the conceptions held by the three language teachers in this study, referencing these to the key ideas in the literature, as the foundation for exploring how they mediate in practice later in the book.

2 Teachers' Understandings of Language and Culture and Their Relationship

This chapter is presented as three case studies, Collette, Kelly and Maria, drawing on the discussions held between the teachers and me. The data comprise extracts from both the planning and debriefing discussions in which the teachers considered their intentions for teaching as well as their reflections on previous episodes of teaching. There are moments in which the teachers' conceptions are explicitly elicited, particularly in the debriefing sessions, as well as moments such as in general planning discussions, where the teachers' tacit understandings are revealed. In addition, a number of the extracts reflect aspects of how the teachers' views changed during the course of the research, as they developed their understanding of an intercultural perspective in language teaching and learning. The cases illuminate the nature of each teacher's conceptualisation of language and culture, and the connections with their views of language teaching and learning, and their teaching contexts.

Collette's Understandings of Language and Culture in Language Teaching

Collette's goal in language teaching

How teachers understand the goal of language teaching provides a window on their understandings of language and culture in language teaching and learning. The following extract reveals the goal of language teaching as Collette understands it.

Extract 1: Collette – goals in teaching (March)

Participant	Dialogue
Me:	So, you have that (i.e. intercultural awareness) in mind for them as a goal?
Collette:	It's come about more for me as an issue that, out of these kids, if I'm lucky, about 1% will use their Indonesian professionally. So, what else is it that I'm teaching them? Yes, I'm teaching them the communication skills and dealing with the public and presenting in public and collaborative skills and other skills and one of them is...if we all have a bit more tolerance and appreciation of some of these differences, rather than regarding them in a negative sense, then we'd be better off.

In the early stages of the study, Collette is reflecting on, and questioning herself about, her goal in language teaching, which has to this point been the active use of the target language or a communicative competence view (Hymes, 1972). She is reflecting on the very basis of what it means to teach and learn a language. She perceives an 'issue' about the relevance of a language proficiency or communicative orientation for the majority of students who may never use the language in future, 'if I'm lucky, about 1% will use their Indonesian professionally'. This moment of reflection leads her to question her overall purpose, 'what else is it that I'm teaching them?'. The question is framed in exclusive terms, marking a division between target language learning and learning how to learn skills. There is an emphasis on the term 'skill' which she repeats, indicating that she views learning itself as skill acquisition, with 'tolerance' and 'appreciation' included in the 'other skills' (Damen, 1987). This suggests that Collette regards teaching and learning, whether it be target language or other, as having a utilitarian end: professional 'use', 'skills for dealing with the public' and producing a social benefit, 'tolerance and appreciation', 'we'd be better off'. Language learning, according to this view, is purposeful and socially significant.

There is a tension for Collette between what she considers is expected of language teaching, communicative competence, and what her experience and emerging sense of intercultural language learning tells her is relevant for many students, intercultural awareness and empathy. There is conflict at the very basis of her position as a language teacher. This tension is borne out further in the following extract where Collette reveals her macro purpose for language teaching.

Extract 2: Collette – goals in teaching (group meeting, April)

Participant	Dialogue
Me:	These are almost your reasons for teaching culture.
Collette:	Yes. And you know the other reason behind it is you want some world peace and tolerance. That's my value, but if we could achieve some understanding of difference, wow!
Me:	What do you want them to understand about the nature of culture?
Collette:	I guess that it's adaptable and it changes. There are things that will come and things that will go.
	If they never use their Indonesian, *that* they will forget. If they are going to use it in a professional context their language will be reinforced by spending time in Indonesia. So this is more what the majority of our high school educated kids will need. Because that's the big justification I use with Year 8 and 9 level.

Collette is clear in articulating her personal values or 'reason behind' language teaching (i.e. 'world peace and tolerance'). In doing so, she is expressing a macro view of language teaching and learning and of education in general. This sense of purpose, of societal transformation, influences Collette's goals for language teaching, creating high expectations for what language teaching and learning can achieve. Her sense of purpose, however, creates a difficulty for her in that she acknowledges that her position is value laden, 'That's my value', yet she feels discomfort with values in teaching, 'You don't want to impose your own (values)' (Extract 7). She recognises that she holds values that underlie her teaching and this is, for her, what makes it 'hard to teach'. This tension relates to her distinction between learning and acquisition, with a sense that school language learning is partial and that genuine communicative competence will only develop *in situ*. These extracts portray a teacher with a number of tensions at a macro level: between communicative competence and intercultural awareness; between learning and acquisition; and between wanting to instil certain values for intercultural citizenship and a discomfort with teaching values. These tensions interact also with her views of language and culture.

Collette's views of language

The ways in which Collette conceptualises language vary according to how she understands its nature, role and relationship to teaching. She experiences a tension between how she understands language per se and how she operationalises it in teaching. The first extract, drawn from the initial group meeting, reveals her understanding of the nature of language in language teaching.

Extract 3: Collette – views of language (group meeting, April)

Participant	Dialogue
Collette:	Grammar. Sentence structures.
Kelly:	Yep, sentence structures.
Collette:	Understanding nouns and verbs. If we're going to do it...you know...your *me-* verbs and *pe-*verbs, the intransitive, vocab.
Kelly:	Also getting them to realise it's not a word-for-word translation.
Collette:	I guess you break it down into speaking, writing, reading.

Collette interprets the question of 'key notions' and 'what needs to be taught' as asking about content and she responds by itemising linguistic structures and features. She moves from general descriptive grammar items such as sentence structure, nouns and (intransitive) verbs to the specifics of how such structures are manifest in Indonesian, listing '*me-* verbs and *pe-* verbs'. In this way, she is 'break(ing) it down' which reflects a taxonomic, structural view of language in language teaching. In fact, Collette states, 'But we do that (separate language from culture) because language has a list, it's easy to separate'. The predominant view here is that language is primarily lexis and grammatical structures; a body of knowledge which can be separated from culture. It is a view of language as code.

Collette's understanding of language as code is reflected also in her comments about the purpose and function of language.

Extract 4: Collette – views of language (March)

Participant	Dialogue
Me:	How did you feel about the mix of target language and English?
Collette:	I guess that's my big question for myself with this project is, I find to get to anything meaningful, I then don't use Indonesian. You can apply it to the immediate differences but then for the why there are those differences, I think it's harder to apply it. I think to go deeper, it removes pure language and how important is that? To go back to the 1% and think, how important is pure language, Indonesian only, and how important is the other stuff for most kids who are not continuing?

Collette experiences a tension (a 'big question') between language viewed as code and language for expressing meaning. She explains how she aims to use Indonesian for communication with her students, but this is insufficient for meaningful communication and she reverts to English ('I then don't use Indonesian'). By doing so, she constructs language in exclusive terms, either language for use (i.e. the target language) or language for learning (i.e. English). She considers that learning which requires complex cognitive demands (i.e. reasoning) is not achievable using the target language. This is problematic for her as her goal is communicative competence and this, in her view, requires 'pure' language use; 'Indonesian only'. Collette is aware of a tension as she wants students to have 'meaningful' learning yet finds it difficult to reconcile this with her communicative orientation, thus she separates conceptual learning (using English) and 'pure' language learning (using Indonesian). This kind of separation of languages is closely aligned with a monolingual view of language learning and use, a view seen as inappropriate for learners within an intercultural orientation (Byrnes, 2006; Kramsch, 1993).

The notion that language (the target language) cannot be used to express substantive meaning is also evident in the following extract.

Extract 5: Collette – views of language (September)

Participant   Dialogue

Collette: There are millions of resources around but it's having the time to pull, to find things that are at a language level that are relevant for kids, that bring out those concepts and those ideas and in some ways I think that's probably the biggest challenge with it (i.e. intercultural language teaching). At senior level I don't think it's difficult. The kids have a reasonable level of language that they can be given anything and extract the meaning out of it but at junior or middle level there are some great things around but then you look at it and think how am I going to make sure by the time they get to senior level all the bits have been connected and joined? It makes you realise how rich some language pieces are too. Sometimes I would start on a particular issue and then I think 'OK well it's got this in it and this and how do I modify it or simplify it'?

There is a recurring idea in this text of 'level', in the sense of communicative competence and of phase of schooling ('junior', 'middle' and 'senior'). This notion impacts on Collette's concern for how to marry target language use and conceptually demanding content, something she describes as 'probably the biggest challenge' in an intercultural orientation. These senses of level are related in that together they form a barrier to meaningful language use. Students have limited proficiency in the target language and their stage of cognitive and social development restricts her expectations. The notion of 'level' connects with Collette's view of language as forms and skills that are accumulated over time and which can, once sufficient, be activated for meaningful communication. There is a sense also that ideas and meanings are somewhat fixed, 'they (senior students) can be given anything and extract *the* meaning out of it' (my emphasis). Thus, meaning is something that is made once a high level of proficiency is obtained, once sufficient target language has been assembled at a senior level. Moreover, language is depicted as something that is predetermined ('it's got this in it and this') and must be known by the teacher *a priori*. Combined with her notion of 'pure' language, there is a sense that language must be familiar and made ready for teaching. There is a tension here in her view of language as language in texts is described as 'rich' while language in teaching must have reduced complexity, 'how do I modify or simplify it?'. Language, for language teaching, is described as 'bits' that require 'connecting'. Her view of language for teaching is enmeshed with the educational culture of curriculum and the compartmentalising of 'content', which constrains, separates and stages content. The need for Collette to consider what can be taught as language results in her viewing language as items to be covered and accumulated. Her sense of dissecting and then gathering 'bits' over time is commensurate with Collette's sense of responsibility as the language teacher to ensure that the parts are assembled, 'how am I going to make sure by the time they get to senior level all the bits have been connected and joined?'. The extract reflects a view of language as a body of knowledge; what Liddicoat (2002) describes as a 'static' view.

The final extract similarly reflects this view and her sense of struggle that language provides structure and sequence in her teaching and while culture may provide relevance, it is unruly and less well defined.

Extract 6: Collette – views of language (September)

Participant	Dialogue
Me:	And where does that fit in with your notion of sequencing language?
Collette:	Yes, and I think that's a challenge that would put a lot of people off doing it and I guess it's easier to walk into a classroom and

(Discussion continues)

know the pathway that you're taking and what you want to achieve this year. But if you threw a few things away and just said, 'Let's see how we go', I think your motivation of the kids is quite high but it's a lot of work to get it all complete and that's what you want to explore at all levels.

Language, as presented here, provides the 'pathway' for teaching. There is a sense of linearity and security in that 'knowing the pathway' is related to a sense of 'ease' and 'achievement'. There is an association between language and certainty, in contrast with culture and uncertainty (i.e. 'if you threw a few things away and just said, "Let's see how we go"'). Having uncertainty associated with culture may lead to improved student engagement, but according to Collette it also means increased demands on language teachers (i.e. 'put people off doing it', 'it's a lot of work' [for the teacher]). Unlike language, culture is difficult to manage, 'to get it all complete'. When the focus is on 'pure' language, the teacher can be the holder of knowledge and provide clear direction in learning. It is a view of the teacher as a 'teacher of language' more so than a 'teacher of meaning' (Kramsch, 1993).

Collette's views of culture

From the outset, Collette's conceptualisation of culture is closely related to her own life experiences and connection to the target language culture. Her understanding influences how she views culture in language teaching and the tensions that it creates for her as it appears far removed from her own experience and understanding of culture. This view is apparent in the following extract in which Collette considers the nature of culture and its purpose in language teaching.

Extract 7: Collette – views of culture (April)

Participant   *Dialogue*

Collette: I guess you make the comparison yourself naturally. Now if we're looking at Indo, we have to be looking at diversity. Indo is a beautiful example of how to blend in and values. And that's what makes it hard to teach is because you don't want to impose your own and say, 'Well this is what I think'. We want them to work out their own values, understand why someone else values something and make a decision themselves. That's that concept of, 'You don't have to go to the mosque and pray to fit into Indonesian society'.

Culture is depicted here as belonging to a national group. It reflects what Risager (2007: 3) refers to as a 'national' paradigm, 'conveying a uniform image of the various national states, of the language, the literature, the country and the people'. Indonesian culture is characterised as 'diverse' and a 'beautiful example of how to blend in'. There is a strong association of Indonesian culture with internal diversity and the value of tolerance. It is close to what Liddicoat and Scarino (2013) refer to as a 'cultures as national attributes' view; a sense of culture as residing within a particular geographical place and people located in that place. Furthermore, culture is viewed as a carrier of values and practices of a particular group, some of which may be accepted or rejected by the learner, 'We want them to work out their own values'. She is describing a process of decentring from one's own cultural position, developing empathy and accepting difference (Crozet & Liddicoat, 2000; Zarate *et al.*, 2004). Her statement, 'You don't have to go to the mosque and pray to fit into Indonesian society', encapsulates her view that culture may be national at one level, but it is also highly personal at another level. She is acknowledging the impact of culture on identity transformation and the complexity of what it means to 'belong' to a culture. The idea of 'blending in' echoes the literature related to study abroad experiences and notions of sensitivity (Bennett *et al.*, 2003) and tertiary socialisation (Byram & Alred, 2002). It also resonates to some degree with Kramsch's (1999b) notion of 'thirdness' and the experience of accommodating two linguistic and cultural realities. It reflects a view of culture as practices, 'as a framework within which people live their lives, communicate and interpret shared meanings' (Liddicoat & Scarino, 2013: 22). The motif of 'blending in', of choosing which practices and values to adopt as part of one's own framework, mirrors Collette's own experience, and resonates with the notion of *savoir se transformer* (Houghton, 2013; Tsai & Houghton, 2010). She has converted to Islam but has not adopted all of the practices associated with it. Collette brings this view into her teaching, constructing culture as a reference point, a basis upon which students can 'work out their own values' and 'understand why someone else values something and make a decision (for themselves)', determining their own position on otherness.

Collette is particularly concerned not to represent culture as homogeneous and instead aims to show students the internal diversity within a national culture.

Extract 8: Collette – views of culture (March)

Participant	*Dialogue*

Collette: I guess I wanted them to understand some of Indonesia's past and what (traditional houses) were like. I didn't want that to colour their understanding of the present and because they'd all done research on a traditional house, I didn't want them to go along and think all Indonesians live in houses like this. I wanted them to get an understanding of the variety that is in Indonesia and be aware there are different houses that have been around for a long time and a bit of an understanding of what was important and significant in that house and in those presentations a lot of things came out about extended family and a community living together in one long house as opposed to having your own private house with just mum, dad and the kids. I was fearful that would colour their perception of Indonesia and they'd think that everyone lives in a long house, community dwelling. So, I wanted them to have an understanding of the history, the past and be aware of the present.

For them to relate to this they have to think 'well, in Australia I come from a fairly well-off background and my house is probably not the average house for Australia either', so we looked at that... 'Is mine a typical house and if I went to Indonesia and met up with someone of the same financial background would it be different and what adjustments would I need to make to fit in there?'

Me: It's the kind of topic that would be done at a fairly descriptive level, but you want to take it further.

Collette: Yes, I guess. Just looking at the daily routine, it's just because the way you do it here it's not going to be like that in Indonesia and why isn't it? So you try to prepare the kids to understand how an Indonesian person would feel if they come here. It could be a little different or confronting and they need to understand where it comes from and why when you go to Indonesia you're going to be asked *Sudah mandi?* (Have you bathed?) three times a day... and why and the reasons behind that. I guess we are getting to Year 9 and 10 and we do get exchange students and there are a lot of issues raised just with accommodation.

Much of this extract frames culture as artefacts, behaviours and societal norms, focusing on housing and bathing. It also depicts culture as internally complex and dynamic. Collette sees culture as a vehicle through which to challenge stereotypes ('I didn't want them to go along and think all Indonesians live in houses like this') and particularly to destabilise a sense of culture as 'typical' ('the way you do it here it's not going to be like that in Indonesia'). She understands culture as internally diverse in terms of norms, 'I wanted them to get an understanding of the variety…' and social class, 'would it be different', 'not the average'. Culture is viewed as dynamic (Liddicoat, 2002), 'the history, the past and …the present' with both 'traditional' as well as 'modern' aspects. Collette sees culture as general and specific, and as national (Indonesia) and individual (student' own culture), akin to a transnational view (Risager, 2007).

This conceptualisation of culture underpins Collette's view of culture in language teaching. Culture acts as a counterpoint, offering an alternative world view and norms to one's own. While it may appear to be a view of culture as societal norms, it goes beyond this and frames culture as permeable and potentially transformational, 'if I went to Indonesia' and 'what adjustments would I need to make?'. Part of its transformative nature rests in its potential for affective impact ('understand how an Indonesian person would feel'). The focus on developing empathy through understanding culture reflects Collette's notion of 'fitting in'. She uses culture to raise students' awareness of their own culture, and prepare them with skills ('when you go to Indonesia') to act as intercultural intermediaries (Buttjes, 1991) and intercultural citizens (Byram, 2008).

Collette understands culture as belonging both to the target language being studied and to students themselves. She juxtaposes the two and invites students to observe similarities and differences as a way of enabling them to consider their own 'fitting in'.

Extract 9: Collette – views of culture (March)

Participant	Dialogue
Me:	You talk in there at the beginning about 'fitting in' and how would you accommodate …so your language is very much… rather than just what's similar and what's different, you then move to applying it for them in terms of 'fitting in'. Tell me more about 'fitting in' and why you introduced that?
Collette:	Mmm, good question. I guess they sort of…when you learn about Indonesia it's one thing to be told, 'this is different and this is the same' but if they're going to Indonesia who cares

(Discussion continues)

if this is similar and this is different. They can list off, this is going to be similar and this is going to be different but that's not really meaningful for them. So, I guess 'fitting in' can make it more meaningful for them so I try to relate back to your experience and have you had someone from overseas or has someone in the class had that and what is it that you take or you think you take for granted? I guess I'm trying to open them up to that and there are some things that you'd do and you're going to be happy to do because that's normal for you and there are some things that you're going to have to question 'Do I want to do that just so that everybody accepts me and I look like I'm doing the right things and everyone else thinks that I'm normal?'. Or do I feel strongly enough that despite the fact that that's what most people do in Indonesia that's not something that I will do and a path that I will take. I can still do that without being culturally insensitive. You want them to be sensitive. Teaching kids that it's OK not to take on board everything. Be sensitive towards others and be respectful of difference and you don't have to adopt all of the differences to make yourself the perfect person going in to Indonesia.

Me: So, for you where does that idea come from because you don't get that in textbooks?

Collette: Well, that's life experience, I think. I guess when I first went to Indonesia I'd read a lot of different things. I guess the year I went back to Indonesia I lived in Yogya but I chose to live in a *kos* (dormitory) with other Indonesian students. We had such a blend of people from different religions and cultures and it was my eye opener that we had all these different people with all these different religions but we all got on. So, I guess that's where it came from and I had to think 'Well, how much do I want to fit in?'. Then I went a step further and married a Moslem and had to consider 'Well, how much do I respect his family and values?' and 'How much do I allow that to influence my values?' and consider 'Well, am I a Moslem?' and for the benefit of his relationship with his parents, I am. But me as a person, no, I'm not. So, for me that's a conflict in my values and I've modified things and I guess I've adopted something from another culture that's not 100% me so I guess in some ways I feel like I live a lie but why am I doing that and how acceptable is that? And I guess for kids if they're going to Indonesia they should think about that.

Through this discussion, Collette becomes conscious of her notion of 'fitting in', in part developed through her experiences of living in Indonesia and marrying an Indonesian, as a driving force in her teaching. Culture is acting as a pedagogic device that frames her aims in language teaching, 'Teaching kids that it's OK not to take on board everything. Be sensitive towards others and be respectful of difference'. She recognises the limits of a comparative, observer perspective in language teaching ('who cares if this is similar and this is different') and uses the theme of 'fitting in' to provide greater relevance ('I try to relate back to your experience'). She draws on her own experience of living in another culture to encourage students to decentre ('what is it that you take or you think you take for granted? I guess I'm trying to open them up to that'). This kind of learning resembles what Byram and Zarate (1994) refer to as *savoir etre*, that is developing openness towards otherness. Culture represents knowledge that, for Collette, cannot be taught but is acquired through direct experience ('it's one thing to be told... but that's not really meaningful for them'), as has been her own experience ('when I first went to Indonesia I'd read a lot of different things ...I lived in Yogya ...and it was my eye opener'). In the absence of direct experience in the classroom, Collette uses hypothetical scenarios of intercultural encounters and connections to equivalent experiences in students' own culture to give a sense of relevance and validity for students. Culture is, therefore, a stimulus for teaching an empathetic disposition towards the target language culture.

The final extract highlights Collette's understanding of culture as quite distinct from that of language and other programme 'content'.

Extract 10: Collette – views of culture (April)

Participant	Dialogue
Collette:	Part of me says to really understand culture you've got to experience it. You can't experience it in a fifty-minute class with a group of Year 9 students. And there are things which are good for them to discover when they go there. I don't think you can define culture whereas everything else you teach you can say 'these are the rules and this is this', whereas really it's a sharing of opinions and understanding of some values. So I don't know how deep you can go with it.
	I think part of it too is that I've got Year 9s and I don't think they've got the same maturity level. I think you could have a better conversation with kids. They seem to become more

(Discussion continues)

serious when they're in senior school, not just in terms of language but in terms of discussing some of the differences.
And I guess we haven't really seen a good example of how to do it (intercultural language teaching) yet. You go through teachers' college and you look at this and role model that. Where is there a good example of how you teach culture? Well, I learnt it when I went there.

Collette sees culture as something that is best experienced and which, therefore, is at odds with classroom language teaching. Culture, in her view, requires conditions that enable 'discover(y)' and depends on cognitive 'maturity'. Her orientation towards communicative language teaching and the need to use the target language in classroom interaction, impacts on her sense of what constitutes culture teaching and learning. She considers students' limited proficiency in the target language as unsuited for culture learning, hence she is unable to reconcile culture within her communicative competence view. Culture learning, therefore, is reserved for higher year level students who have developed sufficient communicative competence, in her view, to cope with the conceptual load associated with culture. Collette perceives the nature of culture itself as problematic for teaching ('everything else you teach you can say, "these are the rules and this is this"'). She defines culture as 'a sharing of opinions and understanding of some values', with a fixed body of knowledge such as language, 'everything else'. The amorphous and undefined nature of culture contributes to Collette's reservation about the degree of culture learning possible in a classroom ('I don't know how deep you can go with it'). Culture, therefore, is a problematic concept for Collette in that it does not conform to her communicative orientation towards language teaching and her beliefs about how culture is best learned. Her final comment highlights this tension as Collette reveals a desire for exemplification that will show how culture might be integrated in language teaching. Her interest in examples of 'how to do it' reflects her struggle with on the one hand, a strong interest in culture, and on the other hand, the challenge it presents to her view of language teaching. Thus, Collette constructs culture as indefinable, experientially acquired and not fully realisable in language teaching and learning. Her way to incorporate culture into her understanding is to offer it as content for comparison and decentring, as a basis for developing students' disposition towards another culture, thereby preparing them for 'real' experience in future.

Collette's views of the relationship between language and culture

Thus far, Collette has constructed language and culture for the purpose of language teaching as quite distinct; language is seen as a 'pure' body of knowledge and therefore can be taught and learned, and culture is seen as behaviours, practices and values that cannot be taught and learned but must be acquired through experience. How language and culture relate to each other, particularly in language teaching, is the subject of the extracts and discussion that follows.

Collette has a strong sense of language and culture as inseparable at a generic level (Risager, 2006).

Extract 11: Collette – views of language and culture (April)

Participant	Dialogue
Collette:	Well, I just don't have the view that they're separate at all. See that's something I find hard. How do you teach it? Part of it is your value system, part of it is your awareness and understanding of some of the differences which you don't always know until you spend time there. You just can't say they're separate. This is what I find hard.
	I guess you're very careful with it (culture) too because with that video I was thinking 'I don't know enough about these offerings to be able to share with the kids' and I'm either going to be making assumptions. I haven't researched it further and I don't have enough knowledge. With Islam, I think I do.
	But we do that (separate language from culture) because language has a list, it's easy to separate. In separating culture we put part of ourselves on the line, we define what it is and we bring in our own values. And I guess we're brought up in a society where freedom of expression is valued but you don't want therefore to put too much of your own influence on it. That's why, whereas grammar, easy! That top part (i.e. language structures and vocab), is easy, you remove values and you can teach that but it's that language awareness and meta-awareness that's more...

Collette understands language and culture as inseparable, individually shaped, influenced by one's values and part of one's understanding and gained through experience. She expresses a tension between her understanding of language and culture at conceptual and experiential levels, and how to move this into a language teaching frame ('how do you teach it?'). In fact, she explains that language and culture are separate in teaching because of the nature of language and culture themselves. Language as she describes it 'has a list', 'a grammar' and can be removed from 'values', therefore making it 'easy'. Culture, on the other hand, is 'hard' because it involves 'put(ting) part of ourselves on the line', it is a personal process involving values and experience that cannot be readily taught and is less readily available than linguistic knowledge. She evaluates her own knowledge of culture as sufficient in some areas ('With Islam, I think I do') and insufficient in others ('I haven't researched it further and I don't have enough knowledge', 'I don't know enough about these offerings to be able to share with the kids'). There is a question of legitimacy in relation to culture for Collette that is not evident in relation to language. Culture is problematic for her in language teaching as it is not a discrete body of knowledge that she feels she can fully know, as she feels she does with language. Furthermore, culture is value laden in Collette's view and she is concerned that her own values come into her teaching of it. At times, she recognises the influence of her own enculturation on her view of teaching (Papademetre & Scarino, 2000), such as her secular education with its value of 'freedom of expression'. She considers it important for the teacher to 'remove the values' and not 'put too much of your own influence on it'. For Collette, language represents values-free, objective content in teaching, whereas culture does not. It is difficult for her to reconcile culture within her conception of language teaching as communication oriented, and therefore as something that must be 'doable'. This emphasis on usability means that culture, a more conceptual and experiential kind of learning in her view, cannot be readily related to language.

As the study progresses, Collette explores an intercultural orientation in language teaching and recognises some possibilities where language and culture may be more closely related in practice.

Extract 12: Collette – views of language and culture (June)

Participant   *Dialogue*

Collette: You know what I reckon, 'My ideal marriage partner'. My ideal lifetime friend. Because kids have got lots and lots of... What makes a perfect partner? And what doesn't? And then you could look at you know Nicole Kidman and Tom Cruise. Is that the perfect match and why...

(Discussion continues)

Me: What I'd love to do and it's probably more a Year 10 unit is to do something proper around *Ada apa dengan Cinta*? (What's up with Love?) [an Indonesian film]

Collette: Well, I'd work with that because I like that text. It's there to excite them isn't it and it ties into the... It might even be 'relationships and partners'. I actually like that and so it can bring up all of the things...even when the exchange kids come here and the Indonesian females are not used to really going out...and separate families. And I think that's the stuff that kids are really interested in.

Me: And then their final task might be some descriptions of qualities in a person or a relationship who they admire.

Collette: OK. Now we've got a text to start with because that's what I like. I mean if I've got something to start with and I'm happy to explore what I think comes out of it and then see what the kids see in it before I start.

Collette expresses enthusiasm for the plan unfolding in this discussion, 'I like that text', 'I actually like that', 'that's what I like' and 'I'm happy'. Her interest relates to her concern for relevance and target language use as she recognises through the use of an authentic text, the opportunity to explore culture in language (Crozet, 2003; Crozet & Liddicoat, 1999a). The authentic text represents an instantiation of culture which can be experienced in the classroom context while still meeting the requirement of teaching to focus on language skills (in this case, primarily listening). She outlines other points of connection such as, 'What makes a perfect partner?' and 'My ideal lifetime friend', building connections to students' lives and opportunities for them to personalise their learning. She relates learning to real-world experiences, 'that's the stuff that kids are really interested in'. Collette believes that relevance influences students' engagement and she views culture as providing relevance in language teaching and learning.

Collette's eagerness in using an authentic text with which she is familiar, 'Now we've got a text to start with because that's what I like' is not only due to her personal interest, 'I like that text', but also to its linguistic nature. That is, the text represents a fixed body of linguistic and cultural content that she can know *a priori* to teaching it, 'I'm happy to explore what I think comes out of it and then see what the kids see in it before I start'. The film text offers Collette the potential for language and culture to become more closely related in language teaching. By using an authentic text as the stimulus, she is able to focus on language use while also exploring cultural practices and values depicted in the text, as created by native speakers. There is no question of legitimacy of cultural content for her, nor is there a question of relevance for language teaching, hence language and culture can coexist.

While this extract shows Collette's developing sense of what may be possible with an integrated view of language and culture at the textual level, she remains concerned overall that culture detracts from language in language teaching.

Extract 13: Collette – views of language and culture (September)

Participants	Dialogue
Collette:	The teaching I found was in some ways frustrating because I didn't feel things were linked all the time and I guess you're used to going through a progressive stage and having really developed in your mind the links that should be there. And I guess most of what I've done culturally has been very teacher driven and very teacher directed and this different approach can allow for students to discover it more. And it brings up issues that second time around I would teach differently but things you hadn't considered to be relevant but that the kids themselves raised. Like the clothing topic was a good one, where there were certain things that the kids wanted to say and things I just hadn't thought were relevant and it brought out all the cultural issues. And I guess usually you'd start with 'this is appropriate in Indonesia and this is appropriate here'.
Me:	And tell them?
Collette:	Whereas this way they discover some of that themselves and then they have to consider why.
	So, how to get them thinking about why they do the things they do without it being English rich. Really, every time it went to a really serious, good, meaty discussion on something, you'd tend to go back to English and I think that...you know, my teaching wasn't as good as my teaching is when I'm ...I'm...
Me:	Language driven more so?
Collette:	Yes. I guess I feel I've got more control and I can...

(*Discussion continues*)

Me: Do you think…you know, it's a balance thing. Wanting them to understand and go deeper but knowing they can't do that in the target language…

Collette: It doesn't hurt to sacrifice some language.

Me: Do you see it as a sacrifice? Do you see a way that perhaps even over the longer term… Do you think over a five-year programme, it would be sacrificed?

Collette: I think towards the end no. But I think in the first three years I've found myself using more English than I would normally use to try to get them thinking about these concepts. I guess it's hard to know because as you become more experienced at teaching in a different style and get more resources and you can know what some of the uses are going to be, you know, some of the issues raised that you hadn't pre-empted then you probably could be more language…I don't think at the end of Year 12 it would make a scrap of difference because if a kid's going to learn the vocab and then they've got the tools to explore things further and if they're not motivated then I guess that's the difference. I guess if you can't motivate them then you're not going to get them to a level where they can discuss it or use Indonesian to discuss it.

Collette expresses frustration that an intercultural orientation means that 'things were (not) linked all the time' leading to a lack of 'progress(ion)' in learning. She considers culture to be incidental content, 'it brings up issues…(that) you hadn't considered to be relevant'. It is a view of culture as contextual information to support language use, 'there were certain things that the kids wanted to say…and it brought out all the cultural issues'; a sociocultural competence view (Damen, 2003). While Collette sees some value in relating language and culture more closely, her reference point for judging the quality of language teaching is native speaker target language use. She has a clear sense of expectations about language teaching and what constitutes valid content, 'you're used to going through a progressive stage and having really developed in your mind the links that should be there'. For her, language structures and skills provide the 'typical' content that underpins coherence in her teaching, 'things (are) linked all the time'. When culture becomes more closely aligned to language, there is a danger for her that target language use decreases. An increased use of English does not equate with her view of good language teaching as communication in the target language, 'my teaching wasn't as good'. Language structures and skills provide clarity and purpose in her teaching, 'I feel I've got more control', unlike culture that raises 'issues raised that you hadn't pre-empted'. She associates cultural content with an increase in students' motivation, 'if you can't motivate them then you're not going to get them to a level…', but it poses a dilemma for her in that she perceives it as unpredictable content and feels that it detracts from target language use and therefore is not 'good' language teaching.

In the final debriefing discussion, Collette articulates her understanding of an intercultural approach and the relationship between language and culture.

Extract 14: Collette – views of language and culture (September)

Participants	Dialogue
Collette:	I guess it's a method…the perspective has changed slightly for me with the approach or model where you take the relevant cultural thing as your basis and then build the language around that rather than a structure and a set of language which you then build a topic around and then you consider what cultural things should I introduce into that. So I guess in a way its working backwards or the other…
Me:	So, you feel like it's more that you start with a cultural…
Collette:	You start with a cultural point and build the language around it whereas I've always done it the other way around. I've always had the topic and the structure of the language and then considered what cultural elements should be included in the teaching of that particular area. So I guess that's the learning curve that I've gauged from this.
	Rather than take a pure language structure, language rich first and break down the cultural bits that come from that, try looking at it from the other perspective first and build up with Indonesian. How do they build their language? Well, they start in a sense from the culture and they build up the model of language they can use from that basic concept.

Collette's language reflects a degree of uncertainty in her thinking, starting with 'I guess' and then characterising intercultural language teaching and learning as a 'method', 'perspective', 'approach or model' and using terms such as 'thing' and 'things'. While she is unsure about how to talk about it, she articulates an understanding of the relationship between language and culture that has 'changed slightly' as a result of her experience. Collette previously privileged language in her planning and teaching and she explains that this is now 'the other (way around)' with culture being her starting point. She contrasts the 'other' perspective with her previous process of considering 'pure language structure, language rich first' and 'building up' the target language as her priority. Language is referred to only in terms of structure, 'build the language', 'structure', 'set', 'pure language structure', 'build up with Indonesian', 'build up the model of language'. Culture is referred to in a number of ways as 'thing', 'point', 'elements', 'bits', 'other perspective' and 'concept'. Language is described in very specific terms in contrast with culture that is described using varied and vague terms, reflecting her overall understanding of these concepts. What dominates this extract is Collette's view that teaching is a process of dissecting knowledge into 'topics', 'area(s)' and 'bits' and reassembling or building them up again in students' minds. Language, conceived as structure, fits into this frame whereas culture, despite her attempt to label it as 'bits' and 'elements', does not fit neatly. Collette does not see language and culture in the same terms, and her exploration of an intercultural perspective has resulted in her changing their positioning in her conception more so than in how she understands the concepts themselves. The concepts of language and culture as content in language teaching remain largely unchanged, but rather it is their importance for planning and teaching that changes.

The extracts in this section reveal how Collette experiences a number of tensions as her frames of conceptualising language and culture and their relationship come together with her conception of language teaching and learning. Her framing of 'good' language teaching as focusing on communicative competence acts to separate language and culture in her teaching; a view which runs contrary to her understanding of their relationship in general.

Collette's views of intercultural language teaching and learning

An intercultural orientation in language teaching and learning poses a challenge to Collette's orientation towards communicative language teaching together with a structural view of language. In debriefing about her experience in this study, Collette reflects on the impact on her conceptions and overall orientation, including her increased awareness of her own linguistic and cultural identity in her teaching.

Extract 15: Collette – views of intercultural language teaching (September)

Participant	Dialogue
Me:	One of the things you mentioned was that this draws on your own values and beliefs a lot more explicitly than normal teaching and you are very much connected to Indonesian through your marriage and those experiences. So, tell me a little about that and how that's part of what you bring to this.
Collette:	Wow! I try not to judge too greatly I guess.
Me:	What's it given you and made you aware of?
Collette:	That tolerance...that need for... I guess the main thing it's given me is I've sacrificed some of my beliefs and my values in order to achieve harmony because I think that balance and harmony and family are more important. So some of my own personal values and beliefs I've sort of... sometimes I feel like I live a bit of a lie but I feel it's important to maintain a good relationship with (my husband's) family. And kids ask questions about things about that too.

I really push that I want kids to have tolerance and understanding and the need for that is even more important. And I felt that there wasn't that tolerance and understanding with certain things in Indonesia especially with religion and I see the world's politics and problems and part of that is because people don't want to give and take. So I guess that's the main thing that my marriage has brought out.

I think the understanding and not judging but wanting to find out a little more. They're the kind of things I'd like them to understand and become more aware of. People may have intentions and their beliefs and views, and you may disagree with their beliefs and views but there's good intentions behind it. It doesn't necessarily mean that it's something that you're going to take on board but try to work out why they're trying to follow that path. And I guess I try to...with world issues and terrorism, is try to take away the fear factor and let them know that there are so many wonderful people out there. And don't judge a Buddhist because they're a Buddhist or a Moslem because they're a Moslem, and you can live in harmony. Doesn't mean you have to kowtow to everything but be willing to share your knowledge and find a level ground.

(Discussion continues)

Me: Do you see a way through this kind of teaching that that can happen perhaps more so than the more traditional approach?

Collette: With some things because the dilemmas appear naturally and then the kids have to think, 'Well what would I do?' and they have to question it.

Me: Or you can actually frame the programme that way.

Collette: Yes, well 'beliefs' could be one (topic). 'Lebaran' if you're not a Moslem. Or just the *Hari Raya* (Holidays) or 'celebrations'. And not from 'this is what a so and so does' but 'if you were in Indonesia and it was Easter what would happen?'

Me: Yes, working from those as topics that already have those dilemmas and allow those questions within them.

Collette: Yes, it's certainly an avenue in and it's certainly something that hasn't been explored from a text basis at all.

In considering an intercultural orientation in language teaching, Collette recognises that her personal identity, values and experience are embedded in her teaching. She shows awareness of how her own experience shapes her aims in teaching her students, beyond target language use, and she recognises this as legitimate learning. She perceives that by reframing her orientation towards culture, she can legitimately address her aim to increase students' acceptance of others, 'take away that fear factor', 'let them know', 'become more aware', 'find out a little more'. She is aiming to develop students' dispositions towards otherness and prepare them to become intercultural citizens (Byram, 2008). She begins to move culture to the centre of her teaching frame, suggesting that it could shape content such as a 'topic' on 'beliefs' or 'celebrations'. This would enable her to position students as participants in culture, 'if you were…what would happen?' and critically reflect on their reactions, 'they have to question it?'. Collette can see the value of culture for making language learning relevant for students, to personalise their learning and develop their *savoir s'engager*, their critical cultural awareness (Byram & Zarate, 1994).

Despite the opportunities for relevance that Collette feels it offers, an intercultural orientation in language teaching also presents difficulties for her.

Extract 16: Collette – views of intercultural language teaching and learning (September)

Participant	Dialogue
Me:	What has it (i.e. intercultural language teaching) made you consider about your teaching? What about questions for you in grappling with it?
Collette:	I think one of the hard things is you don't have your views and opinions to colour everything the kids do and it's hard not to take too much control there. So it's how to get them asking the right questions without them having…also wanting to find out themselves and discover themselves rather than just asking and wanting you to just give them all the answers.
	Because my perspective on Indonesian culture would be very different to…it's something you can't just dot point and I mean yes, there are certain things everyone should know and be able to pass on but it is informed by your own beliefs and values and culture and upbringing and all that. At what age are kids really old enough to understand that and I guess that's really a question for me also. I don't think I ever really understood that until I was removed from my own culture which then makes you so much more aware and it's hard for you to remove a kid from their own culture. So, the kids that get the most out of it from what I've seen tend to be the kids who have had a bit more exposure elsewhere.
Me:	Can you envisage ways to keep language and culture together so that students have that experience of the two things together?
Collette:	That's what we've been trying to do. You probably need to have a group sit down and brainstorm the avenues into it but there are definitely ways into it. I think you really need to have some models to show and say 'have a go at this and see how powerful it is and see what your students responses are like'.
Me:	Has there been anything about these interactions that have been helpful in your own thinking?

(Discussion continues)

Collette: The drawing attention to the interaction and whether or not
it's deliberate. And how to pass on that information and that
most things culturally are a given and it's going to come up but
getting the kids to question without providing them with the
answers but giving them the encouragement or the structure to
want to know or to understand that. And thinking about how
I can get them to do that and explore their own and to work
out their own answers to acknowledge it might be different to
what the next person's (view) might be.

Due to the variability of culture, intercultural language teaching and
learning is, in Collette's view, associated with a discovery approach to
learning, 'discover themselves', 'wanting to find out themselves'. While
culture provides some factual content, 'there are certain things everyone
should know and be able to pass on', culture learning is largely personal
and experiential, 'your own beliefs and values and upbringing and all that',
'it's something you can't just dot point'. This view of culture influences
Collette's understanding of intercultural language teaching, seeing it as
focused on developing students' skills and disposition to engage with
otherness, along the lines of *savoir etre* (Byram & Zarate, 1994). An
intercultural orientation challenges her communicative orientation, but
she remains of the view that culture learning, including decentring, is
best done through direct experience of the target language culture, 'I
don't think I ever really understood that until I was removed from
my own culture which then makes you so much more aware'. This is
something that she feels her classroom language teaching cannot provide.
Also, despite her increased awareness of her own experiences and values
in her teaching, such as her meta-theme of 'fitting in', Collette's own
enculturation and expectations of language teaching restrict her explicit
use of these in her teaching, 'one of the hard things is you don't have your
views and opinions to colour everything the kids do and it's hard not
to take too much control there'. She is also uncertain how to approach
such personal content in her teaching and indeed about how language and
culture can be more integrated, 'have a group sit down and brainstorm
the avenues into it', 'you need to have some models'. She finds it hard to
envisage an alternative approach to language teaching asking, 'how I can
get them to do that (question and understand) and explore their own and
to work out their own answers'. She values the potential learning that an
intercultural orientation may offer but is uncertain about how to realise
this in practice.

Concluding comments on Collette

Collette's case study provides insights into her conceptualisation of language and culture and their relationship in language teaching. It reveals her view of language as largely structural and her view of culture as social practices (Liddicoat *et al.*, 2003) within a national paradigm (Risager, 2007). The case also shows a teacher struggling to reconcile her view of language and culture as inseparable in her life experience and yet quite separate in language teaching. She is able to separate them in language teaching due to her focus on communicative competence as this constructs her view of language as rules of language use and culture as contextual information for effective language use. An intercultural orientation challenges this view and Collette experiences tensions as she attempts to create an alternative conceptualisation of both the nature and relationship of language and culture. She reveals some change in her conception of the relationship between language and culture towards the end of the study, as she repositions culture from being peripheral to language, to culture being at the 'core' (Paige *et al.*, 2003). This reorienting reflects her sense that culture provides relevance for students but it remains problematic for her as she ultimately retains a native speaker norm and focuses on communicative language use as her primary goal in language teaching.

Kelly's Understandings of Language and Culture in Language Teaching

Kelly's goal of language teaching and learning

Kelly's perception that her students are largely monolingual and monocultural influences what she sees as her goal for language teaching. In the following extract taken from early on in the study, she explains her thinking for the immediate teaching sequence and for the teaching programme more broadly.

Extract 17: Kelly – goal of language teaching (March)

Participant	Dialogue
Me:	If you were to summarise your agenda for the sequence, what would it be?
Kelly:	I guess the cultural relevance and religious relevance of places.

(Discussion continues)

Me: Do you think that's important because it sounds like you haven't done that sort of questioning and probing much before?

Kelly: I just think it would open up their ideas a bit more and they would get more of an understanding and tolerance for other cultures also and that's something with students at this school, they lack tolerance.

Me: And do you see it as part of the place of the languages curriculum to do that?

Kelly: I think we have a role to play to change…not change their attitudes, but to show them the other side. Like the case with the Moslems and they're all terrorists and that's the fundamentalists and show them the other side.

Me: To show them the diversity?

Kelly: Yes.

Kelly conceives that the aim of language teaching is to expose students to alternative views that they may not be aware of or hold. In particular, she is aiming to 'show' diversity and significance, 'cultural relevance and religious relevance of places', that exist in the target language culture to counter perspectives students may have such as 'they're all terrorists'. She constructs cultural understandings as somewhat binary, what students do and do not know and whether or not they are correct in what they know. She modifies her original statement that the place of the languages curriculum is to 'change' students' attitudes, instead reframing it as offering alternatives, suggesting that such learning is a matter of personal choice and reflecting a sensitivity to not imposing her own values, a sentiment which may have been derived from her own secular education (Papademetre & Scarino, 2000). Hence, a major influence in Kelly's motivation in language teaching and learning is to raise students' awareness and appreciation for difference by exposing them to an alternative view, as she says to 'show them the other side'.

Kelly's views of language

Similarly to Collette, Kelly's conceptualisation of language and culture and their relationship in language teaching and learning alters somewhat as she develops her understanding of an intercultural orientation in language teaching. Early in the study, Kelly explains how she plans to operationalise an intercultural orientation as she understands it.

Extract 18: Kelly – views of language (June)

Participant	Dialogue

Kelly: What I had planned was just getting them into small groups and giving them an advert and having some questions for them to answer. So like 'What words do you already know?' and another one, 'What are the words that you don't know?' And then I thought that could link up with using a dictionary and maybe a dictionary exercise. Then I thought looking at the purpose of the food adverts and who it is aimed at so I guess some of those English (i.e. the Learning Area) questions they get asked.

Me: Yes, some critical literacy type stuff.

Kelly: Yes, in the (Year 12 external) exam sometimes they get asked what is the purpose of the text, who is it aimed at, what do the food adverts tell us about Indonesian society. Then we could get a couple of ads in English and do a comparison of the similarities and how are they different and then linking food tastes. I guess an example could be vegemite and Indonesians think it's salty so bring in words like *asin* (salty) and then think about 'Why do Australians like vegemite so much?' and look at it from that perspective. And look at the persuasive language and what type of language is used to convince people to buy the product.

Me: So that's a lot of what you want them to do and some language stuff. But what do you want them to think about in terms of language and culture here? What do you actually want them to come away with, a new concept, or some sort of new perspective...?

Kelly: I hate these questions! I guess maybe looking at the use of formal and informal and an understanding of when you use formal and informal in texts...I also thought maybe I could go to the market and get some actual products and look at the language on the products or actually have an ad of a product like *Indome* and actually have the product and see how it's different.

Me: So what's the actual learning here for them? What are they learning? I'm trying to think myself.

Kelly: Do you mean from a language perspective or a culture...?

(Discussion continues)

Me: Well, both language and culture. OK, take a step back. What's the new learning here for these kids and yes, there are a lot of purposes of advertising and the power of advertising to persuade people.

Kelly: That ties back to the types of language used too isn't it like the describing...I guess it brings in adjectives. Actually I brought a couple of PowerPoints they did from the last unit of work. They used words like *ramai, sepi* and *sibuk* (crowded, quiet, busy/occupied) and they couldn't really go beyond that and I thought well maybe that's my fault for not spending time going through that and I thought well this will bring in more of those adjective describing words. So that could be the main focus and build up their vocab that way.

Kelly refers several times to 'words', familiar and unfamiliar and the aim to 'build up' students' vocabulary. At this point, language is equated with words and language learning is a process of accumulating words; a view of language as code (Liddicoat, 2002). During the discussion, Kelly explores notions of critical literacy which she associates with Year 12, 'in the exam', and the English curriculum, 'the purpose of the food adverts...some of those English questions'. She introduces the idea of comparing texts across two languages, Indonesian and English, and invites students to reflect on 'persuasive language'. The notion of persuasive language reflects a genre or critical literacy orientation towards language. The example that she provides, however, focuses on a single word, 'salty', indicating a dominant view of language as lexis. She refers to 'formal and informal' language, indicating her awareness of register and understanding language in context. This is reinforced by her statement that students need realia in order to 'see how it's (i.e. language) different'. There is a sense that language is 'real' or 'unreal' and that real language exists outside of the classroom and does not reside with herself. Kelly responds to questions about learning with reference to language structures and features. Kelly views language primarily as a body of lexis and structures that are built up and that once sufficient can lead to broader meaning.

Kelly's conception of language as words and structures relates particularly to the target language that she views as having a purpose that is quite distinct from students' first language, English.

Extract 19: Kelly – views of language (August)

Participant	Dialogue
Kelly:	Looking back I would get them started into the Indonesian side of it sooner because I think they were more settled. I know one of my hesitations myself with this was 'How much English do I use?'.
Me:	Do you see a way of doing it that doesn't rely on so much English?
Kelly:	I would like to start using questions in Indonesian but I don't think the students would have the confidence maybe to answer in Indonesian or at that level of vocab.
Me:	If it's a question they were used to seeing such as *dibandingkan* (compared to) there's no reason you couldn't use it in the regular interaction of reading through the passage, 'What does this mean?', brainstorming in Indonesian. What stopped you using so much Indonesian or was it a typical level anyway?
Kelly:	I think another concern was that if I gave them too much Indonesian at a complex level that would turn them off as well. Because they'd see all this new vocab and say 'What's she doing? I don't understand all this'. They'd be thinking 'This is Year 12 stuff'.
Me:	So can you see a way to use more at a suitable level?
Kelly:	I think adapting Indonesian sources to get an idea or issue across. I do think it relates back to the time factor and I've started looking for *jamu* (traditional medicine) stuff. It would take time to read it, and simplify it so I don't think it can't be done, I just think it's how and when. This (research) has really made me think about how I can change the topics because obviously the kids want topics they can see relevance to. You look through the textbook and think 'How am I going to use that?'. It's finding the sources that are suitable for that level.

For Kelly, language is equated with the target language. She separates Indonesian, as the target language, from English, treating Indonesian as an object of study and English as the medium for instruction. This presents a conundrum for Kelly as she works with her understanding of an intercultural orientation, because she would like to increase the use of the target language as a medium for interaction, 'I would get them started into the Indonesian side of it sooner', but her teaching to this point has restricted the target language to content. In her view of language teaching, the target language and English have distinct uses and she feels this is challenged within an intercultural orientation, 'How much English do I use?', 'I would like to start using questions in Indonesian but I don't think students would have the confidence...'. Her view that language is an accumulation of vocabulary and forms means that she perceives students as having a limited resource to use the target language for genuine communication, '(students would) see all this new vocab and say "What's she doing? I don't understand all this"'. Her students, therefore, have yet to accumulate a sufficient body of vocabulary to use language meaningfully. She has a view of language as code within a monolingual framing of language that keeps Indonesian and English separate, with one reserved for simulated use and the other for 'real' use. Such a separation reflects the native speaker norm underpinning communicative language teaching, which has been critiqued as inappropriate for emerging bilingual language learners (Byrnes, 2006; Eisenchlas, 2010; Kramsch, 1993) as it focuses on target language use with little connection to the languages and cultures that learners bring to their learning.

For Kelly, the target language not only represents the content to be covered but also contributes to constructing the learning culture of her classroom. She perceives students to be 'more settled' and 'confident' when the focus is on language, words and grammar. The target language is both a force for managing and is itself something that needs to be managed. Kelly is sensitive in selecting and presenting the target language in ways that render it manageable for students, 'finding the sources that are suitable for that level'. She is concerned that 'too much Indonesian at a complex level' will lead to a negative affective impact and result in disengagement, 'that would turn them off'. In Kelly's view the Indonesian language is curriculum content that needs to be 'adapted' or contained and simplified to render it teachable. She expresses interest in incorporating authentic language texts, 'I don't think it can't be done. I just think it's how and when', to provide greater relevance, but she is uncertain about how to manage the linguistic complexity that using such materials would entail. Thus, language as presented in authentic texts presents a problem as it may be more engaging in terms of ideas but may result in disengagement due to linguistic demands. It is this latter view of language as lexis and linguistic structures and rules, and the correlation of this to her manageability of classroom interaction, that dominates Kelly's conception at this point.

As part of engaging with an intercultural orientation, Kelly begins to explore meaning in text and begins to expand her view of language.

Extract 20: Kelly – views of language (August)

Participant	Dialogue
Me:	(Viewing extract from classroom interaction) What do you notice here?
Kelly:	The number of kids who didn't actually translate the whole text. I was really happy with that because it was good to see the number of words they knew and could get the meaning without needing every word. I could now see where I'd have a grammar lesson or a *'ber'* lesson now when I do it again. There's lessons I'm thinking I could have had.
Me:	Normally what would be your basis for choosing what words to focus on?
Kelly:	It would depend on what I wanted to teach. Normally it would be like *'ber-'* words, 'so this is a *"ber-"* word' and then identifying it.
Me:	So has doing this made you more aware of those patterns?
Kelly:	It's made me more aware of those patterns and choosing a text just for the sake of it and then what language point can I pull out of it. Now, I'm looking for certain words. I'm more conscious of the link of certain grammatical features with certain texts.
Me:	What about their engagement with the learning and language?
Kelly:	I think they became aware of the importance of the language involved because they could read those articles, so it boosted their confidence a bit more.
Me:	I guess what I saw was they were learning the language to get at the ideas. They're wanting to know what this means because 'I might have some ideas about it'. Do you usually ask 'What does that mean?'.
Kelly:	Yes. It's more or less telling me what they've read rather than this is what this sentence translates to which is what I've done in the past.
Me:	Do you feel you're letting go a little bit?
Kelly:	Yes. I think I'm not prompting them as much, trying to get them to think 'What's the main idea of the whole sentence?'.

(Discussion continues)

Me: Is that important to you as a language teacher?

Kelly: I find it more important that they understand the idea of a sentence rather than word for word.

Me: What's your overall impression of the tasks and the impact on their language and culture learning in this unit?

Kelly: I'm happy with the texts. It's provided an opportunity for them to see if they've got a broad vocab they can use those words in any situation. And to understand there's no stereotype in Indonesia because before this there was that stereotypical image and that comes through as a different cultural side of it. Having a greater understanding of the culture. I'm happy with the level of language. I initially thought they would think 'It's all too much, too overwhelming' whereas I think they saw it as a challenge and were happy to give it a go.

Kelly's sense of satisfaction, 'I was really happy with that', relates in part to her judgement that students are engaged in worthwhile language learning because they are demonstrating knowledge of words and are reading for gist, 'could get the meaning without needing every word'. This awareness of meaning beyond the word level is a priority for Kelly yet she experiences difficulty because she has hitherto presented language to students as code, 'so this is a *"ber-"* word' and 'this is what this sentence translates to'. She observes that previously she has focused on grammar 'just for the sake of it'. By focusing on whole language in texts, Kelly develops a greater sense of the target language as a system, 'It's made me more aware of those patterns', and understanding language in context, 'I'm more conscious of the link of certain grammatical features with certain texts'. Kelly remains committed to lexis and structure, 'I could now see where I'd have a grammar lesson' and 'it was good to see the number of words they knew', but she is somewhat reframing her view of language, focusing on gist and meaning beyond word level to sentences, 'important that (students) understand the idea of a sentence'. She expresses pleasure with a focus on language in context through texts, observing the positive impact on students' learning, '(students) saw it as a challenge and were happy to give it a go', and 'more or less telling me what they've read'. This extract reveals how Kelly begins to engage with a conception of language beyond words and structures to that of language as contextualised meaning (Kramsch, 1993; Moran, 2001).

As the study continued, Kelly's conception of language began to include a focus on meaning and language use in context.

Extract 21: Kelly – views of language (September)

Participant	Dialogue
Me:	What have you noticed about your classroom language? Like what you're saying? Who with? Whether you're mixing Indonesian and English?
Kelly:	I think with Year 10s there's a bit of both. But one thing I've noticed is that they're more confident. Like if I give them a reading piece they're actually more confident with reading it now without having to go word for word, as I think seeing those bigger words in the newspaper article they might have thought, 'Oh, my God. This is too much' but now they're thinking, 'Well, hang on I don't have to understand all of it to get an idea of what it's about'.
Me:	So, has that changed the way you see you can teach language or what language can be for them?
Kelly:	I guess now I see that they can do a few more challenging texts rather than the structured sentences that are really easy for them to work out. That's something I've thought about more and more because at Year 8 and 9 we spend a lot of time doing the word-for-word translation and even now with my Year 9s I'm saying, 'Well what's the meaning of this? You don't need to know everything to get an idea'. So, I'm now even starting to change how I teach it at Year 9 getting them to think about it more rather than 'This is what the sentence means' and not giving them an opportunity to see if they understand what's in front of them.
Me:	Do you see a way to use the target language more or differently? If you can, characterise how you have used language and how you might do it more so.
Kelly:	I guess I haven't really looked at the texts. I just thought, 'That's sort of got something to do with the topic and there's language in there they should know' rather than finding texts that are related to the topic that they'll see as relevant. Not just going to a textbook and flipping through, 'OK, that's going to be useful' but thinking 'If I'm going to use this, are they going to get anything out of it?'. I'm trying to be more selective. Also, just giving the simple language that's quite repetitive whereas now I'm looking at things that can challenge a few kids.

In this extract, Kelly reflects on her evolving view of language as she understands it in teaching. She reports increased confidence of her students (and herself) resulting from a focus on reading for meaning and analysing language in context. She comments on how her own emphasis in interaction has shifted towards meaning beyond individual words, 'What's the meaning of this?', 'think about it more', 'see if they understand'. She explains how by focusing on language in texts she has become more critical about content in her teaching, choosing texts not just for familiarity of vocabulary or topic, but content that students value 'as relevant', 'are they going to get anything out of it?'. In addition, Kelly has increased her expectations of students and the level of language they can manage, 'now I'm looking at things that can challenge a few kids'. She observes that she is questioning her previously held views stating, '[going beyond sentences] is something I've thought about more and more', and she is becoming more aware and critical in what she considers as meaningful content, 'I'm now even starting to change', 'I'm trying to be more selective'. Thus, Kelly reveals that her view of language as content has expanded from words and structures to include meaning and ideas embedded in language. While the extent of language presented to students has increased (from words and sentences to text) and her pedagogy includes greater analysis and focus on meaning, Kelly's fundamental view of language as teachable content for communicative language use remains strong with increased attention to textual awareness.

While Kelly's expectations of target language use in the classroom increase, she experiences a tension in how she understands the role and use of students' first language and the target language, as she has treated them separately to this point.

Extract 22: Kelly – views of language (September)

Participant	Dialogue
Me:	What are you asking them to notice?
Kelly:	I wanted them (students in the Year 12 class) to talk more in Indonesian and I gave them each a picture and gave them five minutes. Then getting them to think about what does that tell us about Indonesian society and what does it tell us about Australia?
Me:	Are you needing to provide different target language?

(Discussion continues)

Kelly: Not at Year 12 because they already have lots of language but if I did at Year 8...I guess the reason I don't go overboard with language at Year 8 and 9 is I don't want to get them off side. In the past at Year 8 it was an issue because numbers would be down if you give too much language. I guess that's one reservation I have with doing something like this, cultural studies, is making sure the language resources and materials are not going to be overboard for them and they feel they can't use them.

Me: What about language for classroom interaction?

Kelly: I guess I'm not asking the same questions over again. Junior kids, I seem to think of as little kids, so I'm prompting them but senior kids, I guess I'm asking about their thoughts and values.

Me: But are you doing that in English or...?

Kelly: No, in English. Today I actually spoke half of the lesson in Indonesian and I surprised myself at how I could cope. It would only be Year 11 and 12s that I'd even contemplate asking in Indonesian. I think there are certain things that I would change. Especially if I did it from the start. I don't think at Year 8 I use enough of it (the target language). There are times when I could use more Indonesian. It also depends on the time of the day after recess and I had Year 8s before that...So, with my Year 12s it worked really well. Trying to use it more in context also.

Kelly's conception of language is interwoven with her focus on communicative competence, primarily comprising linguistic and grammatical competence similar to early models (Canale & Swain, 1981). Her exploration of an intercultural orientation highlights for her the potential to use the target language for classroom interaction, 'I don't think I use enough (target language)', 'I could use more Indonesian'. She feels, however, that students need to accumulate sufficient words and skills in the target language before they can engage in substantive content, particularly that related to culture. There is a tension for her as she wants to use the target language for instruction and interaction, but perceives that students' linguistic competence is insufficient to do so. She therefore separates the target language out, using it predominantly at the junior levels as static content and once students have accumulated sufficient language, then using it during classroom interaction, 'It would only be Year 11 and 12s that I'd even contemplate asking in Indonesian'. The target language, therefore, remains somewhat devoid of substantive ideational content, including cultural content, as this is perceived as beyond students' target language repertoire and therefore outside of manageable language learning.

Kelly's views of culture

Kelly's conception of culture in language teaching mirrors her view of language in that she regards culture as a source of content. In the initial stage of the study, she perceives culture largely as facts and information that can enrich language but that need to be kept manageable so as not to detract from language.

Extract 23: Kelly – views of culture (March)

Participant	Dialogue
Me:	Do you think (intercultural language learning) asks (students) to think a bit more than they normally would?
Kelly:	Yes, we don't normally have these sorts of questions that make them question why they study the language or these places. In the past, just learn them and their cultural relevance and leave it at that. It's more tourist information than why it's relevant.
Me:	Yeah and not knowing what they (i.e. students) are going to say. There's a level of discomfort with that and also you really start to get to see what they're thinking and when we talk about building on students' learning...that's really the place where you start to do that.
Kelly:	Yes, this is the thing also because I didn't know how far to push it because I would have got a bit more worked up and she would have got more worked up and I thought I'd back off. I was frustrated because she wouldn't realise there were other reasons why Moslems might not want to go to the Barossa [wine region]. I don't think she understood that they follow their religion and beliefs regardless of where they are.
Me:	So you didn't want to push that?

(Discussion continues)

Kelly: No, because I know what she can be like and I didn't want it to be a conflict in the class because she would either get upset or storm out of the room. And the same for Sarah. They are both headstrong and have outside issues that they often bring and when school issues and outside issues mix…to try to manage that within the size of the classroom. I'd just rather avoid that if I can.

Kelly characterises her understanding of culture in language teaching as 'tourist information' and factual knowledge, 'just learn them (i.e. the places) and their cultural relevance and leave it at that'. Up to this point, she has typically held a static view of culture as facts and information (Liddicoat, 2002) that provide background information for target language use and a view of culture as belonging to a particular group and place within a national paradigm (Risager, 2007), 'they follow their religion regardless of where they are'. This view of culture as information to support appropriate language use is challenged as Kelly engages with an intercultural orientation in language teaching. She begins to conceive of culture as practices and values that relate to a particular world view. She associates culture with exploration, 'questions that make them question why' and going beyond observable features of culture (Lo Bianco, 2003). For Kelly, however, this view of culture offers greater uncertainty in language teaching, 'I was frustrated', 'she wouldn't realise', 'I don't think she understood'. In this extract, she is trying to convey a sense of Islamic values in relation to drinking alcohol, 'there were other reasons why Moslems might not want to go to the Barossa', but in doing so, she presents an essentialised view of culture that her students challenge. In opening up her sense of culture, and her pedagogy in relation to it, Kelly enters into unfamiliar territory of diverse perspectives and personal views, an affective dimension of teaching and learning with which she is not comfortable. At this point, culture represents a challenge to Kelly's knowledge and control of teaching and learning; it represents a source of conflict, 'I'd just rather avoid that (i.e. conflict) if I can'. Kelly expresses a tension in that, on the one hand, she considers culture as providing insight into language, 'why it's relevant', but on the other hand, it involves inviting personal views and understandings that are not easily contained. She is uncertain about how to manage such exchanges, 'I didn't know how far to push it', and recognises her own personal investment in the interaction, 'I would have got a bit more worked up'. Kelly has a view of culture as providing relevant information in language teaching but that it also potentially involves a personal dimension that challenges her desire for containment of content and interaction.

For Kelly, culture represents a vast body of knowledge that cannot be readily known by her students and herself.

Extract 24: Kelly – views of culture (April)

Participant	Dialogue
Kelly:	You get put on the spot by the kids a fair bit and for me I like being prepared and having something detailed down so I guess it's...
Me:	Does that make you feel uncomfortable?
Kelly:	Yes and no. I just like to make sure I know everything before I go in and teach.

I've shown that video with my Year 10s and students say 'Why are they putting food and flowers there? Don't people come and steal them if they're poor?' and trying to explain to them the purpose behind it in a language they can understand. I think it's important for them to understand it but I would have preferred to have done some background knowledge first.

We have really short terms and only seeing them three lessons a week, I don't really have time and this was one of my concerns with this culture stuff. I don't think our school has enough time for it to actually work successfully because having just one lesson I think it needs to have a couple of lessons to see if the kids are absorbing what you say.

Kelly perceives culture as phenomena and practices that have a 'purpose behind it'. Culture is a body of knowledge about a particular group of people that can be researched and presented as content in language teaching, 'I would have preferred to have done some background knowledge first'. Kelly imagines teaching as a matter of coverage and feels comfortable when the scope is known *a priori*, 'I just like to make sure I know everything before I go in to teach', 'I like being prepared and have something detailed down'. Kelly feels uncomfortable when teaching culture because she views it as not fully knowable, 'You get put on the spot by the kids a fair bit'. There is a tension for Kelly because teaching involves breaking content down into knowable (and teachable) units within the time and conditions available, and she feels culture is not suited to this, 'I don't have enough time' and 'I don't think our school has enough time for it'. The constraints on culture that exist, in Kelly's view, are also due to its nature; it requires time to acquire such knowledge, 'it needs to have a couple of lessons to see if the kids are absorbing what you say'. Culture is also seen as additional to the target language and therefore should be minimised so as not to detract from teaching language, 'having just one lesson'. Hence, culture is viewed as problematic; it is background information (facts about practices and values) for language use but it is uncontained and unfamiliar content that may pose a threat to the focus on language.

As the study continues, Kelly draws on her own experiences of Indonesian culture as a way of understanding the potential that culture might have in language teaching, and in doing so, she reveals an emergent sense of culture as social practice.

Extract 25: Kelly – views of culture (June)

Participant	Dialogue
Kelly:	I thought *gotong royong* (mutual cooperation) was a good cultural element we could…there's also something here in Indonesian about it as well. Then I thought maybe I could focus on the *ber-* verbs because there are a few *ber-* words in here and use it for reinforcement and the *me-*. The second topic was *Kesehatan* (health) and I thought we could look at the role of the *Puskesmas* (community health centre) or *jamu* (traditional medicine), the traditional medicine and then have that against modern views of medicine and what our views of medicine are and Indonesian views towards modern and traditional. Because when I was over there my impression was they were more inclined to go the *jamu* side of things than to actually go to a doctor or even I had a couple of people in my *kos* (dormitory) who… Is it cupping? …and I thought why don't you go to a doctor and get some medicine and I thought just look at perceptions of medicine.
Me:	That's still kind of a bit of a micro level. If you pull back a little, what will this contribute to how they think about language and culture? Do you want to look at …just off the top of my head now…things like the way these global companies have influence. Maybe look at the techniques they use. The place these foods have in an average person's life…

(Discussion continues)

Kelly:	Can it also relate to things like social class and divisions within society as well?
Me:	Yes.
Kelly:	Like, who would be inclined to eat at these places like McDonald's, it's not the average person on the street...Could you look at it from a social status, prestige sort of...?

In this extract early in the study, Kelly is beginning to question her existing view of culture by considering practices such as *'gotong royong'* (a community value related to mutual assistance and exchange of labour) and *'jamu'* (alternative medicine). While she conceives of these as cultural 'elements', she is expanding her view of culture to include social practices and values. She also includes a sense of contestation, traditional 'against' modern, and differences in social class, 'who would be inclined to eat at these places'. Kelly is recognising variability within Indonesian culture, expanding her sense of culture by including multiple perspectives and social class. By reflecting on her own experiences in Indonesia, Kelly considers differing views on cultural practices, 'I thought why don't you go to a doctor?' and uses this to frame cultural content, 'I thought, just look at perceptions of medicine'. In connecting her experience to her teaching, Kelly abstracts her 'impression' and creates teachable content, 'perceptions of medicine'. Experience, therefore, becomes a source for identifying culture as content, which she frames within a contrastive perspective (Indonesia and Australia). The scope of what counts as culture for Kelly has broadened but her underlying view of culture at this point largely reflects a cultural studies orientation (Liddicoat, 2011).

For Kelly, culture provides the context in which the target language can be understood, and it is through culture that language learning can be made relevant to students.

Extract 26: Kelly – views of culture (July)

| *Participant* | *Dialogue* |
| Kelly: | What does the food advertising tell us about Indonesian society and how does that compare to Australian society? And I guess the main one, What issues emerge from food advertising? So that's linking it up to obesity, diabetes. And then that would link into the articles that we're going to read from there. |

(Discussion continues)

Me: Just one question going right back to the start. How are you going to introduce this?

Kelly: The whole concept?

Me: Mmm. I know you're going to start with that example but have you thought about the key messages and ideas you want to set up from the start?

Kelly: What I thought was structure it similar to what they need for lesson two, with an example and talk about 'What do you think this advert is telling us?' and go through the main words and go from there.

Me: I'm kind of asking the 'Why do it?' question.

Kelly: Why do it? And I guess...OK link it up to 'So would this ad influence your eating habits?' and make them reflect on how ads influence their choices.

Me: ...What's going to be some of the key input from you?

Kelly: I really just see myself there as support and just really... if they're having trouble with the language rather than telling them the answers for everything, I'd rather help them a little bit by giving them a clue. I'd rather get them rather than the 'chalk and talk' sort of stuff. Get away from that and get them to actually be a bit more responsible. I actually see myself as doing limited input and getting them to...just giving them a couple of prompts and I think that's one of the things I've done a lot in the past and maybe that's to the detriment of them. Just giving them all this information and they just revise it and then regurgitate it rather than them actually thinking 'Why am I doing this, how is it...?'. So this time I'd like to see how much they actually learn for themselves rather than me saying 'OK, this is the structure, just learn it'.

Me: Yes, it's a risk isn't it?

Kelly: Yes, but I guess it's only three weeks and it's only Year 10 so it's a good chance to experiment and if it works you can think of how can I use it further on down the track. I don't do a lot of group work in Year 10 because I feel it's a year when they should be building up their language but then I also want to make it fun and this is a topic that I think will interest them a bit more and they probably see the relevance behind it. It's

(Discussion continues)

that whole issue of relevancy because it's really hard for them because most of them haven't been to Indonesia before...the penny will drop for quite a few of them if they go (on the school trip). It would just make a bit more sense to them and I think this is a topic that gets them thinking about their lives a bit more. So, I guess more group interaction and how they work together outside their friendship group and outside of their comfort zone.

Kelly's notion of culture is broadening to include social practices and issues and she observes connections within culture, 'food advertising... that's linking it up to obesity and diabetes'. She then uses these to compare to students' own culture, 'How does that compare to Australian society?'. She perceives a link between content and teaching focus that draws on students' opinions and experiences, 'that would link into the articles that we're going to read' and 'link it up to, "So, would this ad influence your eating habits?"'. While Kelly can identify cultural content and comparison, she is uncertain about how to sequence and guide the learning so she returns to a focus on structure, 'structure it similar to what they need for lesson two, with an example', 'go through the main words', marking the dominance of language content in her thinking. Culture offers relevance in language teaching, 'this is a topic that I think will interest them', 'It's that whole issue of relevancy'. For Kelly, relevance of topic is a means of parcelling culture for teaching in the absence of direct experience of it, 'it's really hard for them because most of them haven't been to Indonesia before'. Thus, culture is viewed as belonging to the target language country and providing background for understanding the target language, 'it would just make a bit more sense to them'. Culture is associated with positive affective learning and represents an alternative to the difficulty associated with learning the target language, 'if they're having trouble with the language', 'It's a year when they should be building up their language but then I also want to make it fun'. Culture is perceived as an adjunct to language; it has value as meaningful content that enables students to make comparisons across national groupings and also invite an element of decentring from students' own culture. Kelly equates culture with more personalised and independent learning, 'actually thinking', 'how much they actually learn for themselves', 'actually be a bit more responsible'. She formulates probing, open-ended questions for discussion and interpretation, 'What do you think this advert is telling us?', 'Would this ad influence your eating habits?' to encourage students to reflect on their own values and practices. She sees culture as less fixed than language, and therefore more aligned with student-centred learning, 'giving them a couple of prompts', 'help them a little bit by giving them a clue', 'limited input', and greater social interaction, 'more group interaction', 'how they work together', 'outside of their comfort zone'. At this point, therefore, Kelly's conception of culture has expanded to include knowledge of how to learn, similar to *savoir comprendre* (Byram & Zarate, 1994), processes such as noticing, comparing and reflecting (Crozet & Liddicoat, 1999a) as well as general learning principles of social interaction, making connections and taking responsibility (Liddicoat *et al.*, 2003).

In the final extract, Kelly reflects on how her understanding of the nature and purpose of culture in language teaching has changed during the study.

Extract 27: Kelly – views of culture (September)

Participant	*Dialogue*
Kelly:	I think what I've learned is how you can break down stereotypes and give kids knowledge as to why cultures are different and how all cultures aren't the same. I guess for me also I thought culture was just the shadow puppets or the islands. I didn't think it was about the society or attitudes towards junk food. I didn't see that as a cultural thing. So, it made me think a little more about what I could include as culture.

Kelly notices a contrast between her previous (cultural studies) view of 'shadow puppets or the islands' and her current view, 'about the society or attitudes...'. Her conception of culture in language teaching has expanded to include social issues, values and attitudes more akin to a 'culture as practices' view (Liddicoat, 2002). She perceives the value of culture as being that of representing an alternative world view, and therefore increasing students' cultural awareness and appreciation of diversity 'why cultures are different and how all cultures aren't the same'; to develop an openness towards otherness or what Byram and Zarate (1994) refer to as *savoir etre*. Kelly uses culture to challenge stereotypes by exploring practices and their associated values and world view, 'give kids knowledge as to why'. Culture is largely viewed by her as homogeneous, belonging to separate groups, 'us' and 'them' within a national paradigm and therefore providing a point of difference and contrast. Culture also presents a difficulty in language teaching for Kelly as, on the one hand, she sees culture as information and somewhat a distraction from communicative competence, yet on the other hand, culture is essential to her overall purpose and sense of relevance in language teaching.

Kelly's views of the relationship between language and culture

From the outset of the study, it was apparent that Kelly held a strong view of language and culture as quite distinct, with culture providing relevant background information to support language learning and use.

Extract 28: Kelly – views of language and culture (March)

Participant	Dialogue
Me:	How do you feel about linking the language and culture stuff?
Kelly:	I think it's a good idea and it makes it more relevant for the kids to see how the language is used in a cultural setting but once again because I haven't done a lot of it; it was new for me too. I guess with that 'How much of the language do I incorporate into the culture lesson' making it more of a language lesson than a culture lesson?
Me:	I was saying to the group last night that I see this intercultural stuff or part of it, as mining the language rather than teaching culture not as an add-on or even something that sits alongside language but something that sits deeply within the language and you pull that stuff out. How is your thinking about language and culture shifting in this process?
Kelly:	I think I need to do a bit more language stuff before I teach the cultural unit so they're more familiar with words and phrases that are related to that cultural element.
Me:	What have you been thinking about for the next sequence?
Kelly:	Maybe I could go down the path of street traders or roadside sellers. We don't have them in Australia. I was just thinking it's something that's not in Australia. I came up with why because it's employment for the uneducated and unskilled labourers, and cheap food for poorer families and it's just a way of life for Indonesians and it brings in like a social aspect... I thought I

(Discussion continues)

could bring in the different *pedagang kaki-lima* (street traders) and the types of things they sell and also how they have different sounds to represent what they sell. So, then I thought well what am I doing this for?

Me: Yes, because it's separating language and culture.

Kelly: Yes, so there's this email and it's still language that relates to the *pedagang kaki-lima* and I thought that might help them with the language.

Me: Yes, the life of a *pedagang kaki-lima* is more interesting too. It starts getting into 'Well, what does this man do and how does it affect his family?' and then you get into those issues about people's lives.

Kelly: Then I thought about how I could link it with the cultural element and make it into an assessment task. Maybe put a presentation together about the role of the *pedagang kaki-lima* and why they are important and think a bit more about their purpose rather than what they do.

Me: Yeah, yeah that's good.

Kelly: I was even thinking maybe for the assessment task they could do like a text analysis where they have to write a response to an email and then maybe compare what's in their street and start using *dibandingkan* (compared to) and things like that.

Kelly declares her uncertainty and inexperience in dealing with language and culture in her teaching. She views culture as increasing the relevance in language teaching as it provides contextual information to support appropriate language use, 'to see how the language is used in a cultural setting'. She is concerned with the dosage of each and their relative contribution to teaching, 'How much of the language do I incorporate … making it more of a language lesson than a culture lesson?'. She questions how best to treat language and culture as she is committed to coverage of the target language, 'a bit more language stuff', 'words and phrases' and sees this as a precursor to culture learning, 'before I teach the cultural unit'. Kelly treats language and culture as separate, in her thinking and structuring of teaching, 'the culture lesson' or 'a language lesson'. There is a tension in Kelly's comments in that she sees culture as providing the contextual information necessary to understand language, yet she sees that language should precede culture so that students are familiar with the language associated with cultural content. Her view of culture as 'difference' among national groups is evident in her choice of 'street traders' as a cultural focus as, she explains, 'We don't have them in Australia', 'it's just a way of life for Indonesians'. She recognises a disconnection between language and culture that she attempts to counter with a suggestion of the inclusion of a text, 'there's this email and it's still language that relates'. Kelly has identified cultural content and is attempting to draw language into it, 'that might help them with the language'. She recognises that culture has become the focus and language is separate, 'I thought about how I could link it with the cultural element'. At this point, she understands language and culture as connected in the sense of a link that joins two discrete things. Her description of the text analysis task indicates a degree of integration of language and culture as students will explore the significance of cultural practices, 'why they are important... rather than what they do'. She is attempting to explore culture in language or *languaculture* (Risager, 2006); however, on the whole, language and culture remain largely parallel, occasionally linked through text analysis.

For Kelly, texts offer instances in which language and culture coexist and where they can be explored simultaneously in teaching, and therefore are valuable for intercultural language teaching.

Extract 29: Kelly – views of language and culture (August)

Participant	Dialogue
Kelly:	I've really made a conscious effort to find stuff for this next unit. I can just see there's potential to use texts that are more relevant and are actually used in Indonesian society. Whereas now I want to find texts that mean something to them and they can get involved and feel like they're included in it. To be honest I went to the textbook and I can't believe I wanted to use it and I wasn't keen on doing this. And now I think I don't want to use the textbook.
Me:	Do you think (authentic texts) made you more interested in the unit?
Kelly:	Yes, I was looking for texts and it gave me a bit of a buzz to think I can actually understand this and it gave me a bit more confidence to adapt the texts. So I have really enjoyed doing it because it made me aware of more options I can do in the class.

Kelly makes a distinction between authentic texts, those from 'Indonesian society', and the commercially produced 'textbook' for learning Indonesian in Australia. She values the former as they represent language that is 'actually used', thus addressing two of her priorities, the target language in use and what she describes as 'relevance'. In her view, such texts are valuable for language teaching as they comprise both language and relevance (meaning); they are 'texts that mean something to [students]' in which they 'feel like they're included in it'. In this way, texts become a valid experience of the target language and culture in which '(students) can get involved'. At this point, Kelly perceives texts as more than vehicles for grammatical structures and vocabulary but as a stimulus for personal engagement for her students. Kelly is aware of a change in what she values as content for language teaching, 'I can't believe I wanted to use (the textbook) and I wasn't keen on doing this' and she evaluates the textbook as inadequate, 'I don't want to use the textbook'. She perceives authentic texts as presenting substantive linguistic and cultural content, 'I was looking for texts', 'I really made a conscious effort to find stuff', that although they require effort to transform into teachable content, they offer meaningful content and affective value, 'it gave me a bit of a buzz to think I can actually understand this', 'it gave me a bit more confidence'. Thus, language and culture are more closely related when Kelly considers them both through analysis of authentic texts, resonating with Kramsch's (1998) view of discourse as an 'integrating moment'.

Kelly's dominant view, however, of the relationship between language and culture is that culture provides contextual information for teaching language.

Extract 30: Kelly – views of language and culture (September)

Participant	Dialogue
Me:	Tell me about how you see the relationship between language and culture.
Kelly:	I can see how important, well, not important but a lot easier for students to grasp certain concepts when you're teaching them about certain aspects of culture in the target language. I think they understand how it's different and why it's different to Australia when they can put it in a context they feel is relevant. I guess it makes students more aware of the differences between each culture. So, I think in future it would work better at senior level because they have got more language so they can read the in-depth texts but it's something I'd think about for Year 11 and 12s now I can see how you can incorporate culture and actual realia into your lesson and units plans.

(Discussion continues)

Kelly: And that's something I noticed when I asked reading comprehension questions. They were just reading straight from the text rather than trying to put it into their own words or in Indonesian whereas I think we did that piece in English first and then we did the Indonesian and they were able to make the connection. I think it made it easier for them to pick up the language because we'd already discussed the ideas...They could actually see how it was all connected.

Kelly regards a focus on culture in language as beneficial for language learning as '[it's] a lot easier for students to grasp certain concepts', 'easier for them to pick up the language'. Culture is seen as providing the relevance 'put it in a context they feel is relevant' and authenticity 'actual realia' in supporting language use. Culture comprises 'ideas' that are 'incorporated' into language, and this connection is evident in text. She sees a role for students' first language in engaging with cultural 'ideas' prior to exploring texts in the target language. That is, culture is associated with 'in-depth' ideas and is therefore detached from the target language, unless the ideas are explored initially in the first language and then connected to the target language. Culture, therefore, is of a different order to the target language and is more closely aligned with English as the language of instruction. Thus, language and culture are primarily seen as different but complementary, each constituting unique content towards the main focus on communicative competence.

Over time, as Kelly develops her understanding of an intercultural orientation in language teaching, she constructs a somewhat different view of the relationship between language and culture.

Extract 31: Kelly – views of language and culture (September)

Participant   Dialogue

Me: If you had to tell someone in a nutshell what intercultural language learning is about, for you anyway, what are the key ideas?

Kelly: I would say the key ideas for me would be trying to teach the culture through the language but using different types of culture... of how you incorporate certain ideas and values of a particular society or culture and comparing that to your own and see how that is different to your own. I guess getting them to think more about the 'whys' rather than just saying 'this is

(Discussion continues)

the culture in Indonesia, we don't have that in Australia', and just leaving it at that. But actually going into the why it's different and 'what does that tell us about our own society?'.

Me: Do you feel you have more of a framework for thinking about culture?

Kelly: I guess I have a bit more of an understanding of intercultural language learning and how you can incorporate it into the classroom because at the start of the year it was like, 'Oh, God. This is going to be too hard'. But now I can see the benefits of it. I guess the layers of it and not having it in the target language but getting the ideas across, it can be in either.

Me: Anything else?

Kelly: I just think the whole way of linking culture with the language. In the past I just did culture in English and didn't bring the language into it whereas it's made me think a bit more about the language I could bring into the cultural aspect. And, like I've mentioned throughout, the differences in the culture and it's not just the religion, there are other parts to it so just broadening my ideas about what culture actually is.

Kelly's opening statement summarises how she perceives the relationship between language and culture in language teaching, 'teach the culture through the language but using different types of culture'. Culture is framed as diverse, 'different types of culture', 'why it's different', with multiple aspects, 'ideas and values', 'not just the religion', 'there are other parts to it'. Thus, she has come to understand culture as internally varied. She sees culture as providing depth of ideas in language, the 'whys', and sees the two as related, 'linking culture with the language', 'language I could bring into the cultural aspect'. Culture largely remains associated with the target language country, with some comparison to learners' own culture although little if any connection to their first language. Kelly's references to 'not having it in the target language' and 'it would work better at senior level because they have got more language' indicate that the target language has become framed as supportive of students' learning of culture. Thus, Kelly understands the relationship between language and culture as more connected than previously, 'I just did culture in English and didn't bring the language into it', and now feels that she has a more integrated view of both culture in language, and language as a resource for understanding culture.

Kelly's views of intercultural language teaching and learning

Kelly's initial conception of language teaching is one of coverage of language structures and vocabulary with associated skills for language use. As such, she is concerned with issues of manageability and teachability of content.

Extract 32: Kelly – views of intercultural language teaching (August)

Participant	Dialogue
Kelly:	I really enjoyed it. At first I was really hesitant but I am really pleased how it turned out. At first I wasn't sure how well they'd work in groups. I was concerned if they didn't do it then it would affect lessons down the track. For me, the turning point was when we did the (newspaper) article. For them then they could really start to think it was real because they could see the picture related to the article and then things started to click. I think the group work was structured really well. (Researcher shows extract from class interaction) I think the line of questioning is very repetitive.
Me:	Why is that?
Kelly:	That's the point I want them to get. I think if it's the political or economic side of it then that would totally lose them. But if it's anything to do with people, I think it's easier for them to understand or get into a debate about these issues. In some ways I was conscious of the questions I was asking. If I went too much in depth with it they would just switch off.
Me:	Did you find it hard to ask those questions?
Kelly:	Yeah, because some of them I'm thinking up on the spot and some I think 'I've already asked that'. It frustrates me a little when you know what you want them to know and you give them all these clues and ask the same questions but in a different way but they're still having trouble to get your point.

Kelly understands intercultural language teaching as involving greater uncertainty about which she is 'hesitant' and uncertain, 'I wasn't sure', 'if they didn't do it'. She worries about coverage of content, 'it would affect lessons down the track' as well as engagement, 'if I went too much in depth with it, they would just switch off'. Kelly has a planned pathway of learning for students, 'that's the point I want them to get' and 'you know what you want them to know', which she feels is less structured and clear with an intercultural orientation, 'you give them all these clues and ask the same questions but in a different way but they're still having trouble to get your point'. Kelly experiences difficulty with an intercultural perspective in her teaching as meanings are less clear and the control that she associates with teaching language structures is not immediately available. She expresses relief when the group task of analysing the newspaper article was successful, 'then things started to click' and she could see the value in social interaction and interpretation of language associated with an intercultural approach.

For Kelly, an intercultural orientation is associated with risk, to her linguistic, cultural and pedagogical knowledge and skills, as well as foregrounding the affective dimension of language teaching and learning.

Extract 33: Kelly – views of intercultural language teaching (August)

Participant	Dialogue
Me:	(Shows another extract) How do you feel about the discussion that went on in this lesson?
Kelly:	I thought it was productive in parts because they were all having a say. I think it provided discussion for those people who in the past would sit back.
Me:	What do you think contributed to that?
Kelly:	I think it's something they can identify with and I think that whole issue just brought things a little bit home to them. When it picked up on the discussion I thought 'Oh my God, it's going to cause a huge thing and if it gets out of hand, how on earth am I going to bring it back in' because once they start expressing what they feel, it just comes natural for them and I'm thinking 'How am I going to manage it?'. So, next time I'll have to think about certain questions to ask and which ones not to ask but then I thought some of that the kids just brought up themselves and picked up from what they thought.
Me:	What do you think was going on for them?
Kelly:	I think they were getting excited. Well, not excited but obviously it was a way of them venting their feelings because it's not often they get to do that even in other classes they can't express opinions without it being something from what they've read. This gave them an opportunity to actually say what they felt. I think if you asked that to Year 9s I think their level of maturity…you don't want them to venture too far off so you've

(Discussion continues)

	got to keep it structured but I think with senior kids you can have those sorts of questions where it's open to interpretation.
Me:	What do you think that kind of discussion did for their learning?
Kelly:	It opened up their eyes that it's an issue for the region. It gave them an insight into something... they thought everyone in that area was skinny and lived on healthy food.

After initial concern about her ability to manage the discussion, 'I thought, "Oh my God, it's going to cause a huge thing"', Kelly perceives benefits in terms of student participation, 'it provided discussion for those people who in the past would sit back'. There is a sense of ambivalence for Kelly as she values students' opinions, 'they were all having a say', 'venting their feelings', 'an opportunity to actually say what they felt', but she feels anxious about her ability to manage these, 'How on earth am I going to bring it back in?', 'How am I going to manage it?'. She values interaction and personalisation, which she understands as integral to an intercultural approach (Liddicoat *et al.*, 2003), and considers it necessary to challenge students' assumptions and world view, 'it opened their eyes', 'it gave them an insight'. She recognises that an intercultural orientation in language teaching and learning may be unpredictable and personal, but this creates a tension in that she values this for learning yet wants to contain it in order to manage teaching. She wants to set limits in order to keep within her view of language teaching, 'you don't want them to venture too far off', and her desire to cover planned content, 'you've got to keep it structured'. Kelly contemplates how she might keep it manageable, 'I'll have to think about certain questions to ask and which ones not to ask', and attempts to create order, previously done through grammar, through structured questioning in relation to culture in language. Kelly's experience reflects the kinds of difficulties experienced by other teachers in integrating culture in their teaching (Sercu, 2005, 2007).

Kelly's understanding of intercultural language teaching and learning also presents a challenge to her view of the role of the language teacher.

Extract 34: Kelly – views of intercultural language teaching (September)

Participant	*Dialogue*
Me:	What do the concepts of mediation and interaction mean to you?

(Discussion continues)

Kelly: I guess, looking at my involvement in the classroom. At the start of the year and before all of this I was more teacher directed and at the end, it's turned to be more student directed with me just assisting them. So, not giving them ideas but just trying to point them in the right direction of where they should be going.

Me: How did you see your role before that?

Kelly: I guess, not really thinking about it. I think it was more me at the front, writing on the board, teaching it to them and not really getting them to have any input. The only time they really had an impact was when we started a new topic and we did a brainstorm to find out what they already knew about that topic. And now they're forming opinions on certain issues and expressing what they feel. And in the first two terms I was just like, 'I don't want to know about it', oh not 'I didn't want to know about it' but I didn't think about using that to generate discussion to try to get them to think about why we do things and why we learn about different cultures and the language and that sort of thing.

Me: So, do you think you're involving them more in their learning?

Kelly: I think because they had an active role, I think they felt they got more out of it because they were involved in the discussions and I felt happy because it wasn't just me talking for 40–50 minutes and then either having their own little social groups or only 3–4 listening. I think that topic really engaged all of them and when they were talking by themselves they were talking about what we were learning.

Me: What kinds of ways of mediating led to better learning for them?

Kelly: Having a set of focus questions so they could see where I was coming from and where we were headed with the whole unit of work.

Me: And what kinds of questions? How would you characterise them?

Kelly: I guess the 'why' or 'your opinion' sort of question and steering away from the factual questions. Also generalising as well sort of general questions which make them think a bit more…

Kelly reflects on her perspective towards language teaching as 'teacher directed' with the main focus being '(the teacher) at the front, writing on the board, teaching it to them'; the 'it' presumably being the target language. She comments on the level of input from students, 'the only time they really had an impact was when we…did a brainstorm…to find out what they already knew', 'I was just like, "I don't want to know about it (i.e. students' views)"'. In this view, teaching and learning are constructed as a process of covering set content, with minimal involvement by students except to state their existing knowledge. On reflection, Kelly views students' opinions and perspectives as beneficial to their learning, 'they got more out of it because they had an active role' and teaching and learning are viewed as a process of active knowledge construction (Liddicoat et al., 2003), 'they were involved in the discussions'. She emphasises the different nature of questioning, 'the "why" or "your opinion" sort of question', noticing the interpretative and critical perspective of an intercultural orientation. Kelly perceives such questioning as requiring students to 'think a bit more' and engage them personally in language learning, 'forming opinions on certain issues', contributing to an overall sense of purpose in language learning, 'why we do things and why we learn about different cultures and the language'. An intercultural orientation for Kelly foregrounds students as participants taking more responsibility for their learning with the teacher acting as a guide, 'it's turned to be more student directed with me just assisting them', 'trying to point them in the right direction' and in contrast to her previous view of the teacher as the holder of knowledge, 'it wasn't just me talking for 40–50 minutes'. Her view of language learning and learning itself has expanded from a paradigm of acquisition to that also of participation (Sfard, 1998).

Kelly explains how an intercultural perspective on language teaching has prompted her to consider her pedagogical approach and the culture of language learning in her classroom.

Extract 35: Kelly – views of intercultural language teaching (September)

Participant	Dialogue
Me:	Do you feel it was a more connected chunk of learning?
Kelly:	I think it was more continuous. Rather than you're going to learn about this today and then the next lesson is a language lesson and you're not going to go over that same language. Also, the lessons seemed to flow into place as well. Not saying

(Discussion continues)

that some units of work, you're all over the place, but you're just going from the textbook whereas you've got your own resources now. There was the start of what you wanted them to achieve and then the end point of that goal at the end.

Me: Did you like doing the reflection at the end?

Kelly: Yes, I did because it made me realise that in some cases I need to change my teaching methodology.

Me: So, did you feel like, not just your role, but the way you interacted with them...

Kelly: I didn't feel like I was a teacher. Whereas when you're standing at the front of the lesson you feel like, 'Just listen to me, I'm the teacher', whereas this one I made an effort to go around and see what their opinions were and just do some one-on-one.

Me: What does an intercultural approach now mean for you?

Kelly: I guess using authentic material because just trying to explain it doesn't really connect but using an example helps to explain an idea or concept for them. I'm starting to look at more Indonesian resources and how I can incorporate that into lessons. I'm also starting even with my Year 8s moving up and down the aisles and having a chat to kids along the way. I've noticed this with my Year 8s because I'm moving around the room more and they're actually asking questions.

Kelly's understanding of language teaching and learning has been driven by her structural view of language and preparing students to use Indonesian with native speakers. Her exploration of culture and her expanded view of culture as multifaceted have increased the connection between language and culture, particularly through 'Indonesian resources' that she wants to 'incorporate...into lessons'. What comprises legitimate content has broadened for her to the inclusion of authentic texts drawn from the target language culture and adapted for her students. She continues to associate language with control and manageable content, 'it was more continuous', 'the lessons seemed to flow into place', but she also values authentic texts as they enable her to focus on culture in language. Kelly's reflection on her previous practice, 'You're going to learn about this today', shows her growing sense of the value of involving students in social interaction and personalising learning. This shift has enabled her to work with students individually, 'just do(ing) some one-on-one' and increase her engagement with them, 'go around', 'moving around the room', 'moving up and down the aisles'. She perceives increased engagement with students, sharing 'their opinions' and 'actually asking questions'. Kelly contrasts her former understanding of teaching with her sense of an intercultural orientation, critiquing the performative nature of the former, 'you're standing at the front of the lesson', 'Just listen to me, I'm the teacher', with the somewhat liberated sense of the latter, 'I didn't feel like I was a teacher'. Her conceptualisation of the relationship between language and culture has prompted her to focus on meaning, and in doing so, has provoked a reflection on her pedagogy. Kelly's final comments reflect an emerging shift in her stance from being a teacher of language, to becoming a teacher of meaning (Kramsch, 2004a).

Concluding comments on Kelly

The case study of Kelly demonstrates a close relationship between her conceptualisation of language and culture and their relationship, and her understanding of language teaching and learning. She refers to language and culture predominantly through a teaching lens, as though they did not exist as concepts outside of this frame. Initially, she holds a structural view of language and an informational view of culture; however, she expands these understandings as she engages with an intercultural orientation, broadening her view of language to the level of text and the relationship to meaning, and her view of culture to social practices and values. She considers language as a priority and regards it as unproblematic in teaching, and indeed it provides structure and a basis for sequencing her teaching. Culture, on the other hand, is viewed as additive and difficult to render in teaching. While her conceptualisation of culture expands, it remains within a national, comparative paradigm in the main. Kelly perceives culture as enriching language, providing understanding of the cultural context of language use, and therefore relevance for language learning. Culture also acts as a point for personal engagement, for student-centred learning and an affective dimension of learning, which Kelly finds both confronting and valuable. Her initial separation of language and culture, with culture providing background information about the target language context, becomes a more integrated view over the course of the study, with culture taking on greater significance and with language being a means to understanding culture. Overall, Kelly has expanded her views of language and culture, and brought the two into a closer relationship particularly through textual analysis. She has also increased her expectations of target language use in the classroom and continues to perceive the use of students' first language as problematic, revealing her prevailing orientation towards communicative competence as the goal of language teaching.

Maria's Understandings of Language and Culture in Language Teaching

Maria's goals of language teaching and learning

As an experienced language teacher, Maria has clear goals for her students comprising, for this class, the requirements of the mandated curriculum and assessment framework for senior secondary students of Indonesian and her personal theory of language teaching and learning. She explains her goals as follows.

Extract 36: Maria – goals of language teaching (February)

Participant	Dialogue
Me:	Tell me about your teaching style? What would I see if I came into a few lessons? How would you characterise what you do?
Maria:	I endeavour primarily when I can...because there are times when I can't because of the calibre of the vocabulary, I endeavour to exemplify the target language in spoken form. Like you said, we are the guitar, the instrument, and if they don't hear it from us where are they going to hear it from? I reinforce that with video, native speakers and interaction. So, it's not just me talking but asking questions about what they've understood. It's a little bit of a text analysis at times, however, getting that interaction from them and really pushing that they answer in Indonesian as well. You are a primary resource for them and also a guiding force for them. I endeavour to be truthful and when I can't answer their questions I try to guide them to where they can get the answers. I want them to think globally, rather than locally, and to tap into their other subjects that may help them in their understanding or further their knowledge of the topic.
	And the boys will tell you that (interviewing native speakers) has been the most rewarding time when they're actually interacting...because that's what language is for, for communicating.

Maria begins her response with a qualification ('when I can'), marking an awareness of a likely difference between her intentions in teaching ('I endeavour', 'I try', 'it's a little bit of') and the reality of it. Maria's explanation conveys a strong commitment to use of the target language in

interaction as her primary focus in language teaching. She talks of her aim
to model target language use in the classroom ('I endeavour to exemplify
the target language in spoken form'), seeing herself as a primary 'resource'
and driver of the expectation that students will also use the target language
in classroom interaction ('really pushing that they answer in Indonesian').
Oral interaction with native speakers of the target language, 'when they're
actually interacting', is a priority for her, 'that's what language is for,
for communicating' and is associated with affective benefits, 'the most
rewarding time'. She aims to create situations that require target language
use, resembling authentic contexts of use. In this, the language teacher acts
as a *de facto* native speaker interlocutor, 'we are the instrument' and model
of target language user.

For Maria, using the target language is related to her aim to broaden
students' understanding of the world and their appreciation of diversity.

Extract 37: Maria – goals of language teaching (March)

Participant	Dialogue
Maria:	I guess what I was trying to say is this is happening in Indonesia (i.e. liberal attitudes towards sex) but we must keep in mind there is that officialdom in Indonesia that most [Indonesian] kids are aspiring to.
Me:	So, again in terms of your teaching aims, what are you trying to get across to them?
Maria:	Again, the diversity...of values systems in Indonesia. Like Australia it is a melting pot. It doesn't mean all Islamic girls are like that...I'm trying to throw on the plate not just one aspect...and there are many gaps and there still are gaps of course but I'm just trying to fill some of them.

Maria aims to highlight cultural diversity within the target
language culture. The teaching topic referred to in this extract relates
to contemporary values and attitudes in Indonesia towards relationships
and sex, but her emphasis is not just on the attitudes themselves but
on their range, 'this is happening but we must keep in mind...'. She
reinforces this emphasis stating that she sees Indonesia as a 'melting pot'
(seeing its similarity in this regard to Australia) and hence aims to show
its multiplicity, 'not just one aspect'. Maria views culture as internally
diverse, explaining that any representation of it will be incomplete, 'there
still are gaps'. The target language culture is associated with infinite
possibilities, 'I'm just trying to fill some of them'; it is multifaceted

and dynamic (Liddicoat, 2002). This understanding of culture features prominently in her overall aim in language teaching of encouraging students to appreciate diversity.

Maria's views of language

Maria's understanding of language in language teaching and learning is closely related to her concept of language in general. She views language as dynamic and multifaceted, including both standardised and highly individualised forms.

Extract 38: Maria – views of language (March)

Participant	*Dialogue*
Me:	Why did you want to focus on slang?
Maria:	All the language in here (the textbook) is standardised and as soon as you leave the textbook, you pick up any recent literature for young people, the language is quite different.
Me:	So, why is it important for them to know that because you could argue that it is important for them to learn the standardised form?
Maria:	Yeah, I know exactly what you mean. As a teacher I think it's my role, too, not to just teach to the exam, it's how to teach them the different registers which aren't so pronounced in English or many other languages. I was thinking the other day about my own native tongue; there isn't the stark significant difference between teenage, city language or the language in the country, for example, or older or younger generation whereas in Indonesian, I just wanted to bring it to their knowledge, awareness... we could use some of that language, which they didn't because it's difficult, maybe I could give them a bit of vocab...but it certainly makes them aware of formality and informality. They don't think that way because in English there isn't that massive difference.

In explaining her intentions while designing a teaching episode, Maria reveals her view of language as internally diverse and contextually sensitive. She recognises the political dimension of language, evident in standardisation, as well as its variability, contrasting Indonesian with her first language Italian and with English, both of which she perceives as less variable than Indonesian, 'in English there isn't that massive difference'. Maria views the colloquial form of the target language as additional to the requirement that she attend to the standardised form in preparation for the Year 12 examination, 'I think it's my role, too, not to just teach to the exam'. She understands language as linguistic forms, 'I could give them a bit of vocab', which are context dependent. Maria conceives language as plural, contrasting Indonesian, English and Italian, 'my native tongue' and 'many other languages'. She describes language as internally diverse and associated with subcultures, 'teenage, city language or the language in the country…or older or younger generation'. It is a differentiated view of language, primarily focused on language as a resource for communication.

In relation to the target language within a teaching and learning frame, Maria holds a largely structural view.

Extract 39: Maria – views of language (June)

Participant	Dialogue
Me:	So what have you seen or what have you noticed in their talking about language?
Maria:	In their talking I think they're becoming more accustomed… maybe it was happening before and I just didn't pay much attention to them. What I've noticed is them paying much more attention to looking at how structures can convey different messages.
Me:	Because they said after a little debrief after the exam that they did and they said 'Oh, the exam is OK if you know the vocab. If you know lots of vocab'. And I said to you, 'That's interesting. I wonder what they're meaning by vocab?'. And it would be interesting if they thought that was lots of words and now they're sort of starting to think that, you know, you need to focus on the structures. And that's kind of what's powerful in the language.
Maria:	Absolutely. And looking at….you can never escape that because you're studying the structure of what's being used.
Me:	You need the repertoire.
Maria:	That's right. You need the repertoire and I've always done that in my style of teaching. I've always said, 'OK, we just looked at the word *lahir* (born) yesterday' and I said, 'Boys can you think of the ways we have seen this root word used?' and they come

(Discussion continues)

up with *dilahirkan* (was born) and *melahirkan* (to give birth). And then there was another one *tempat lahir* (birthplace) and I said, 'Look at this language, you know, it's building blocks, building blocks'.

Me: Word families I call them.

Maria: Yeah. I always draw the example of you know… your brick and then you add a brick and you add a brick. So yeah, we've always done that and I'll continue to do so. But this certainly has made it more emphatic. You know the video you gave me? … to say, 'OK, What sort of language is she using here compared to the tradesperson or the, the factory worker?' or, 'What structures are more evident to you and why?'. So there again the use of language to convey, not just meaning but underlying…

Maria is concerned with language structures and how these impact on meaning, 'how structures can convey messages'. She views the structural dimension of language as inevitable, 'you can never escape that because you're studying the structure of what's being used', but structures are not an end in themselves but are necessary to understand what is 'useful'. Maria frames language in structural terms for her students, 'Can you think of the way we have seen this root word?', 'What structures are more evident to you?', reflecting her own view of language as comprising 'building blocks'. She sees language as forms that are built up and assembled over time, 'your brick and then you add a brick and you add a brick'. The house building analogy indicates Maria's understanding of structures as forming the fundamental base of language, a view to which she is committed, 'I'll continue to do so'. It is a view that accords with an understanding of language as code (Liddicoat, 2002).

As Maria engages with an intercultural orientation, her focus on structure and target language use shows increasing attention to meaning embedded in language use.

Extract 40: Maria – views of language (September)

Participant   Dialogue

Me: Do you think your questioning or your actual interaction around these texts in the classroom has been any different?

(Discussion continues)

Maria: From an understanding language stance yes. From an understanding culture strand, I think, it needs a little bit more…when, for example, you're looking at some pictures, or you're looking at an article, looking at its source, or looking at what is it saying, 'What does it want to say to its reader?'. And I don't think we often do that enough when we're teaching the language. Is that, 'Yes, we understand the language and we've picked up the *di*-s and we've picked up the passives' but have we looked at what stance that this article is taking? And it was interesting when Jaxson mentioned, 'I think it's a female writer'…

Me: When you probed further he gave his reasoning for it.

Maria: Yes, those sorts of questions, I always feel I cut them off their answers because I'm conscious of … 'Oh, we're speaking too much English we've got to move on now'. But they're the questions that they love to answer.

Me: And they're the points of connection really. That's the reason why they thought that.

Maria: You could do it in the target language, '*Mengapa, menurut pendapat Anda, penulis artikel ini seorang perempuan?*' (Why, in your opinion, do you think the author is a woman?).

Me: Do you feel that the role of the target language has changed in all of this, or the place of it or the use of it?

Maria: Oh, sure has. It sure has. It almost…this is the feeling I get. It's almost like it's us and them. When we're speaking we're using our language, and it's almost…

Me: We get the proficiency?

Maria: Yes, we get the proficiency. And then when we hone in on the resources. That's when it changes completely, and we almost become like um …what's the word? We're analysts. We're analysing quite regularly now whereas I think before it doesn't seem to pick that up that much.

Me: So, how has the target language use for both of you changed? Like, what were they doing with the language before?

Maria: First of all the language was simpler. It was regurgitating a lot of… Whereas I think with this sort of topic, you can't really regurgitate. You take expressions, you take words out, and they're quite sophisticated words, and then you elaborate into a sentence and make an opinion.

Maria perceives language structures as essential, 'Yes, we understand the language and we've picked up the *di*-s and we've picked up the passives'. However, she recognises that structure alone is an insufficient view of language, 'but have we looked at what stance that this article is taking?'. Her comment reflects a heightened awareness of language as constructed and contextually bound (Kramsch, 1993). Maria views language as an object that can be analysed and examined for meaning beyond surface comprehension or recognition of grammatical structures. Her interest, in both grammatical structures and analysis of more extended texts, is in language for a purpose, whether it be language use according to rules, or manipulating chunks of language, 'words', 'expressions' in order to express an opinion. She views the target language and students' first language as having different roles in interaction, expressing her discomfort with using English for discussion and showing her preference in using Indonesian for this. This reflects Maria's view that 'proficiency' is the primary goal of language teaching and she recognises a shift from this, 'it changes completely...We're analysts' (Liddicoat & Scarino, 2013). She relates 'simple' language with communication (and regurgitation) and 'more sophisticated' language with analysis (and opinion), revealing a sense of different kinds of language for different language learning goals.

While Maria conceives of language in structural terms, she also views it as contextually bound and situated, as socially and politically imbued.

Extract 41: Maria – views of language (September)

Participant	Dialogue
Me:	Thinking about your use of language in general, not just this unit, but you know, in the signs and the whole sort of travelling of all of these things, what did you notice about your use of target language, use of English, the mix, the way you're using them? Like are you using them for different purposes now to what you would previously or how is language featuring in the general approach, not just in that lesson, or that unit?
Maria:	Oh you can never, never separate the two. And even might I say that it's more analytical in the signs and with these articles. We looked at language for purpose. It wasn't just, 'Oh, that's a passive, that's an active'. It's 'Why is an active being used there?' 'Why is a passive being used there?'. Not, 'Is it a passive?' or 'Is it

(Discussion continues)

an active?'. So that, that I think worked really well. So there's a lot more incidental...it just didn't stand as, 'This is going to be a language lesson. This is going to be an understanding culture lesson'. The two were intertwined all the time. And they permeated the whole unit. So I think in summary...

Me: Did you find your own language use had to change in what you were asking them?

Maria: Yes. It had to be more succinct. It had to be a lot more focused. I had to sort of also explain to them that because the genre here was mainly journalistic, that we were going to go into a higher level and to expect obstacles along the way. See I'm saying that now, but I don't know I really said it convincingly at the beginning. And now looking back, I would say 'Now guys, this is what, we are going to be looking at, quite a different type of language' and maybe draw examples of, in English you might say tabloid-type language and journalistic language and then bring it in and say, 'Well, this is what happens in the second language too'. And so the high level...

Me: So it (the textbook) doesn't have the interest of 'Well, who is this for?' and you know, that has a genuine interest in itself because it's not just created for Year 9 students learning Indonesian.

Maria: Absolutely, absolutely and it links into other subjects. It's, it's co, sort of co-curricular. So I would say I think it's been successful from a linguistic point of view because it's certainly introduced a lot more sophisticated language. It's introduced the concept of skimming through, but getting the gist of it. And that's really important too as a second language learner. And introducing language that is real. Language that is fresh. It's, it's alive. It's not dead. It's not dead. And it was interesting and I said to you before when we go back to (the textbook) that language sounds dead in comparison to this. Although it takes a lot longer.

In addition to forms, 'that's a passive, that's an active', Maria focuses on 'language for purpose', examining the functions that aspects of language, particularly grammar, serve: 'Why is an active being used there?'. She refers to 'genre' and 'type(s) of language', 'tabloid', 'journalistic', reflecting her understanding that language is politically and ideologically shaped (Byram, 2008; Phipps & Gonzalez, 2004), 'I had to sort of also explain to them that because the genre here was mainly journalistic…'. Maria values contextual knowledge as important for understanding how language use and meaning are shaped, 'we are going to be looking at quite a different type of language'. The language is seen as grammatically complex, 'a higher level', 'obstacles', 'a lot more sophisticated', 'it takes a lot longer' because it is an authentic text. This sense of complexity is seen as expected and a necessary part of dealing with authentic language. In fact, Maria distinguishes between the target language as captured in textbooks and authentic texts, characterising the former as 'dead' and the latter as 'real', 'fresh' and 'alive'. This sense of the life in language being provided by culture echoes Risager's (2006) notion of *languaculture*. Maria regards language as varied and dynamic, a semiotic resource for expression of meanings, and also a code with fixed aspects such as structures and textual features. Thus, she uses Indonesian in classroom interaction as a medium for communicating, and as an object for analysis, mediating its meanings through English.

Maria's views of culture

Maria attributes her sense of life in language to culture. She considers culture to be complex, multidimensional and rather difficult to operationalise in language teaching because of its dynamic nature.

Extract 42: Maria – views of culture (February)

Participant	Dialogue
Maria:	Religion is such a complex thing in Indonesia. I'm still perplexed about how to do this. I thought I might do *Tanah Toraja* and maybe do Islam and then compare like animism with a major religion and maybe a little of the history of Islam in Indonesia but religion is such a complex thing. (*Discussion continues*)
Me:	A lot of our resources are very informational, very descriptive and I guess that's kind of the old static view of culture.
Maria:	Yeah, that's tradition, that's not …Like the *Tanah Toraja* are so fascinating but in here there is just a lot of information.
Me:	And it's kind of hard to do anything with that.
Maria:	Yes, that's…with religion. I'm in a bit of a bind…because we're in a Catholic school it would be interesting to …I don't know if compare is the right word…
Me:	It kind of depends on what you want them to come out with? What do you want them to understand about religion?

(Discussion continues)

Maria: The most important thing is to get them aware of the fact that when we talk about Indonesia as a united country from a religious stance, not that it's not united, but there are many, many differences depending on location, you know, It's the most populous Islamic country but is Islam in Indonesia similar to Islam in Saudi Arabia or in the Middle East? Or you could look at the role of women, but for boys that's not as interesting, and fasting, the period of fasting. I've got articles on fasting but they're really information based. And that's where the interview would have to balance it...

...You want to get them into something that's meaty, rather than me just handing out information... From a linguistic... there are two things that tie us too. You've got that culture and that's really important and that's the interesting part but you've also got to teach them the language too and how to read it...

Maria refers to culture as multidimensional and having a number of aspects, including 'religion', 'history', 'the role of women' and 'the period of fasting'. She has difficulty transferring her understanding of culture as 'complex' into teachable content, 'I'm still perplexed about how to do this' and indicates her uncertainty, 'I might', 'maybe', 'maybe...but'. She struggles to see a way within her current understanding of language teaching to deal with culture as she understands it. Similarly to previous studies (Kramsch, 1987; Sercu, 2000; Zarate *et al.*, 2004), Maria considers that her current textbook resources are limited as they offer only a facts and information view of culture ('in here, there is just a lot of information', 'rather than me just handing out information', 'I've got articles...but they're really just information based'). Maria conceives of culture as internally diverse, 'there are many, many differences', and situated, 'when we talk about Indonesia as a united country from a religious stance, not that it's not united but...it depends on location'. Maria refers to using ethnographic approaches (Paige, 1993; Papademetre, 2000; Roberts *et al.*, 2001; Sobolewski, 2009) such as interviews with native speakers of Indonesian to provide greater authenticity in relation to culture. In her final comment, she reveals a view of culture as 'meaty', 'interesting' and 'important' and a priority alongside language, 'there are two things that tie us', 'you've also got to teach them the language'. Thus, culture is seen as vital in language teaching, together with language, but it is seen as problematic in terms of how to represent its variability (Crozet & Liddicoat, 1999b).

Maria views culture as highly individualised, both reflecting and challenging assumptions and generalisations about social norms.

Extract 43: Maria – views of culture (March)

Participant	Dialogue
Me:	So, what do you hope they've gained as a result?
Maria:	It's really to give them insight into the different views that are prevalent in Indonesia and to give them some insight and that we can't stereotype it very easily and we shouldn't stereotype. We have the religious view and the more conservative view from those Islamic girls and here it's, 'It's my life Mom' (the title of the article) and there it's 'No, it's my parents who are telling me how to lead my life'. So, you've got this contrast and how language falls into that as well. The idea of perhaps the class distinction and the different language used in the city with the younger generation. They need to find out their background (of the person they are interviewing) where they're from…find out about the ethnic group, did they go to a religious school…and how you come to a conclusion, you can't, but present it in an oral form. It was interesting in 'Swapping Lives' (a video watched in class) that the Australian girl had no qualms in asking personal questions whereas the Indonesian girl felt very uncomfortable in asking that (i.e. questions about sex) and then you have the rap singer saying, 'We're all into drugs and open sex'. And you could see the boys thinking 'Wow, how does all this fit into it?'. So, you get all these overlapping views so that kaleidoscope that we talk about is in here (points to the text) and then this is stereotyped as well (i.e. the textbook) because we're teaching the standard Indonesian.
Me:	In contrast there was a language point and you used technical language with them.
Maria:	Oh, temporal markers.
Me:	Yes, so you went straight to the technical language but with culture you…

(Discussion continues)

Maria: It's hard to define. It's very hard to define. What is easy is in the abstract with this kaleidoscope, there is something tangible. But it's tangible from different angles so I have to draw on different examples. I think that's why I do it. With language there are specific terms. If it's a temporal marker I can define that but when it comes to culture, and I think also because I'm not of that culture, I find it necessary to draw on different resources in the way I teach it.

Me: Why is it important that you're not of that culture?

Maria: Because I don't think I'm a true reflection. I really don't think I'm a true reflection in my teaching.

Me: So, do you have to be of that culture to have the authority to speak about it?

Maria: Not the authority but the experience. I truly believe that. Or having lived there, having tasted, not just tasted but having extended time there...if I were teaching Italian I can really get into the shoes of that even though there are differences between regions there too.

Me: Is that because it's something to do with your identity?

Maria: Yes, I do draw on my experiences...there are times when we might even start the lesson with a prayer in Indonesian and that's another resource and another cultural thing, another angle. I find it difficult to define culture. Culture is very difficult...it's not difficult, it's so broad and you've got to be really careful.

Me: So that's why if you use an example...

Maria: I feel like I'm pretty safe because this is a sample of what can happen...

Maria sees culture as internally diverse with 'different', contrasting perspectives and subgroups including 'religious', 'conservative', 'class' and 'sex'. She understands it as varying depending on people and place, 'ethnic group', 'the younger generation'. One of the factors with which culture varies is also language: 'language falls into that as well', 'the different language used in the city'. Language is part of her view of culture: a language-in-culture view (Crozet & Liddicoat, 2000). Maria uses an analogy of a 'kaleidoscope' in describing culture, referring to it as indefinable, 'It's hard to define', 'It's very hard to define', 'I find it difficult to define culture', 'Culture is...so broad'. 'Culture is highly variable because it is connected to people and their individual lives', 'They need to find out their background'. Even within a person, culture is not seen as something that is fixed: 'how you come to a conclusion, you can't'. She views culture as embodied and experiential ('the experience', 'having extended time there', but 'not just tasted') and therefore considers herself, with limited experience in Indonesia, as an outsider, 'I'm not of that culture', in contrast with Italian, her first language, 'I can really get into the shoes of that'. With her sense of being an outsider to Indonesian culture, Maria attempts to convey to her students the dynamic nature of culture itself, through her experiences and examples, 'I have to draw on different examples'. She is sensitive to generalisations about culture, 'we can't stereotype it very easily and we shouldn't', and critiques the textbook on this basis. In fact, she draws a connection between generalisations about culture as being related to teaching the standardised form of the language, 'because we're teaching the standard Indonesian', both of which she views as restrictive and not doing justice to the variable nature of culture and language. She recognises that language does not conform to national boundaries or particular groups, but that it is fluid, uncertain and transcends borders; there is a sense in Maria's discourse that she views culture within a transnational paradigm (Risager, 2007).

Maria does not hold a view of culture as norms or practices belonging to the target language country only, as she explains in this final extract, it also belongs to her students and their own experiences and identities.

Extract 44: Maria – views of culture (September)

Participant	Dialogue
Maria:	And drawing the links, because if you're just giving them a series of articles, like polygamy or, 'And now we're going to see this film…'. I'm hoping that they will draw from what we've done in the unit to further understand where Indonesia is at, at the moment.
Me:	(Recaps on the discussion) Anything else?
Maria:	Another one was… and I did this again without the depth that in hindsight now could have been done, is drawing examples with our own community, what's happening in our own backyard. We drew the example of Shane Warne. That would have been a perfect time to get them to read the article and 'What stance is this? What does it tell you about our society?'. Another one was…once you've shown *Inul Daratista* (an Indonesian singer),

(Discussion continues)

	show them the Video Hits and say, 'Well, um are we being a little hypocritical?'. So that would make it a successful part of the unit… and draw comparisons with Australia.
Me:	That comparative perspective is another kind of mediation.
Maria:	And you have to do that because they have to hone in on their own experience.
Me:	And you did that when they had to do the oral. That was an attempt to get more of their individual selves involved.
Maria:	That was good that one. I thought that was successful. It would have happened earlier and then finish off with an essay or a broader….
Me:	…social issue, with that individual perspective.
Maria:	Yes, how does where you were born, with whom you were born, affect your life? Because the schooling came up, how that shapes the personhood… And then bring it in a broader perspective, how is a country's identity affected by its secular or religious or non-religious stance on issues?

Maria understands culture as layered, including both national and individual dimensions. She holds a macro 'broader' view related to socialisation and national identity, 'how is a country's identity affected by its secular or religious or non-religious stance on issues?'. She also holds a micro view, belonging to individuals including her students, 'drawing examples with our own community, what's happening in our own backyard', 'hone in on their own experience'. She recognises the importance of one's primary socialisation (Byram & Alred, 2002) in shaping cultural identity, 'how does where you were born, with whom you were born, affect your life…how that shapes the personhood'. Maria conceives culture in general as textured, dynamic and related to one's own enculturation (Papademetre, 2005). She attempts to render this in language teaching through multiple examples, decentring from one's own enculturation, and through developing a critical stance (Byram, 2008; Phipps & Gonzalez, 2004).

Maria's view of the relationship between language and culture

Maria understands language and culture as integrally related in general and in language teaching, particularly focusing on culture in language.

Extract 45: Maria – views of language and culture (June)

Participant	Dialogue
Me:	So, almost what you set out to do is what really you feel they went away with?
Maria:	For example, that sign that I just mentioned outside the pub. I want them to pick up, hopefully, and if they haven't, I'll bring it to their attention. I wanted them to pick up something about our culture. In that, management is… 'takes the responsibility, reserves the right to', how would we say that sign or would that sign appear in Indonesia? How would we word it, keeping in mind those cultural innuendoes? So that's something that I'm looking for. Not the fact that they can use imperative at the drop of a hat, because that comes. That's not easy. But even if they are approaching a class…and giving them encouraging language. They need to know the structures that they could use, keeping in mind that unit of how to be encouraging in language, rather than, 'If you don't do this, you're going to have this'.
	I really tried to hone in on the idea how language can have underlying meanings that often as a second language speaker we don't always grasp. And that's when the tutors come in and explain to me that that sentence came up. That often the language that's used *dilarang* (it is forbidden) is an exception. OK, we use that as an exception. But even that one is not as hard as I think 'trespassers prosecuted' and so on. But I tried to hone in on the idea that the language that's used in the signs that we looked at is not necessarily punitive. And does that in some way highlight a cultural system or a cultural mentality that is prominent in Indonesia? And how our language differs. Of course, differs in the underlying mentality or culture behind it. I think it worked from that perspective, because I can hear them now using the words 'It's encouraging', 'It's the language that's not in any way punitive'. So they are recognising signs in the language that make it more polite *lebih halus* (more refined) and I thought that worked. I thought that worked.
Me:	It's interesting, because it's only really in five lessons.

(Discussion continues)

Maria: I know! I feel they have got a lot out of that. (It was) more intense. We looked at culture a lot more. Now, you might say, 'How can you not look at culture in your other units?'. But you're not really doing a lot. It's basic fact. Really it's facts. Whereas, when you're looking at culture, it's not necessarily facts. It's looking at patterns and making those patterns evident to your students and then not actually answering for them, but them coming to that conclusion, so, I came to that conclusion myself by teaching it. I hadn't thought of it right at the beginning. It came to me as I was teaching it. OK, hey, wait a minute, this language is quite more refined than that. And what grammatical structures have been used to infiltrate that or to convey that? And I think that, as I said, I think that worked well and it was more intense, yes.

Maria refers to language as containing aspects of culture, 'something about our culture', 'innuendos', 'a cultural system' and 'a cultural mentality'. Language is seen as the vehicle through which cultural values and meanings are expressed, '[the] culture behind it', 'signs in the language that make it more polite'. Language is seen as comprising structures which serve a purpose and have a particular impact on people, 'the structures that they could use...', 'what grammatical structures have been used to infiltrate that or to convey that?'. These structures are reflective of 'difference' that arises due to cultural difference, 'different' world view, 'And how our language differs'. These meanings are not immediately evident to those who do not share the particular cultural mindset, 'meanings that often as a second language speaker we don't always grasp'. Language and culture, therefore, operate together to create particular meanings, 'how would we say that sign or would that sign appear in Indonesia? How would we word it, keeping in mind those cultural innuendoes?'. Maria is aware of static views of culture, 'But you're not really doing a lot. It's basic fact. Really it's facts' and contrasts this with her dynamic view, 'When you're looking at culture, it's not necessarily facts. It's looking at patterns and making those patterns evident to your students and then not actually answering for them, but them coming to that conclusion'. Maria perceives culture as providing the underlying meanings in language, that is a 'culture-in-language' view (Crozet & Liddicoat, 2000), and it is this relationship that she wants her students to appreciate.

Maria's consciousness of the cultural meanings embedded in language frames her orientation towards her treatment of culture in her teaching.

Extract 46: Maria – views of language and culture (June)

Participant	Dialogue
Maria:	There's an understanding language and an understanding culture and that goes back to what you said 'What do you want them to achieve by the end of the unit?'. And it may be a simple unit on greetings and times and so on. But there's culture *jam karet* (time is rubber). What does that mean, being late? Um, and sometimes you've got to be very careful what you're actually saying. If it's correct or not, because again you're making general statements about different people of different islands of different ethnic groups, so you've got to be extremely careful. But yes, I think ...even before you came on board, um, I was very conscious of that. But with your intervention, I think, and the way you address questioning, I think yes certainly, it's made me more conscious of it. Much more conscious of it. And I would endeavour to use that much more and not panic if I feel that I haven't covered the language as much as I should be. Because I think that sometimes you don't want to spend lessons and lessons talking about, 'and what does this mean?' or 'What does that mean?'. Well, not that way, but sometimes it's just something that's not even planned. You're talking about it, it comes through.
Me:	Do you feel you can plan it more now?
Maria:	Yeah, I have certainly. Certainly I would say yes without, um, without a doubt.
Me:	OK and you don't see that as incompatible or going to take time from the language or anything like that?
Maria:	No. No. I don't see, whether it takes time, that's another story but incompatible? No way. Incompatible? Certainly not. It's just finding a happy medium, a harmony between the two. Um, because I'd hate, I hate....
Me:	Because when you're teaching a language....

(Discussion continues)

Maria: You've got to put it into a context. It's hard not to put it into a
context. So um, whether it be language of signs, public language,
whether it'll be *agama* (religion). All of it has a context.
I think film is a wonderful means for culture. Because it depicts
so much visually. It's rich and it has so much in such a short
time. And kids nowadays are... they're impacted by visual
stimuli. I find that extremely... but we don't do enough of it.
Again, time restrictions and so on. But I often think, look, how
many are going to go on with it? So you might as well make it
enjoyable and find as much as you can and then hopefully, you
start really focusing the Year 10s and Year 11s on the language
and you know, you, I'm not saying you don't do language in
any way, of course you do, but...

Maria refers to language and culture using the terms 'understanding
language' and 'understanding culture' from the state-based curriculum
and assessment framework that has been adopted in the school. This
framework has three strands (communication, understanding language
and understanding culture) that are designed to be interrelated when
developing teaching and learning programmes. Maria has clearly adopted
some of this framing and draws on it to reference different aspects of
language teaching. She explains that culture provides the meaningful
context for language use: 'You've got to put it into a context. It's hard not
to put it into a context'. This interdependence is a given for Maria, but she
questions how to represent it in her teaching, '...incompatible? No way.
Incompatible? Certainly not. It's just finding a happy medium, a harmony
between the two'. While language and culture are interconnected, they are
seen by Maria as distinct in nature with varying importance depending
on the teaching programme, with more culture at lower year levels, 'not
panic if I feel that I haven't covered the language as much as I should be',
and more language at senior levels, 'you start really focusing the Year 10s
and Year 11s on the language'. Culture is seen as 'rich' and 'enjoyable' and
requiring sensitivity to represent its variability, 'sometimes you've got to
be very careful what you're actually saying', 'you've got to be extremely
careful'. Culture is also likely to emerge incidentally in language teaching,
'sometimes it's just something that's not even planned. You're talking
about it, it comes through'. Thus, language and culture are unique in their
contribution, both necessary and both challenging in their own way,
language in terms of grammatical complexity and culture in terms of
representational accuracy.

Maria's view that culture provides meaning in language is particularly evident when she works with authentic texts.

Extract 47: Maria – views of language and culture (July)

Participant   *Dialogue*

Me: Did anything feel different to the normal kind of teaching you were doing?

Maria: Yes, because we were actually examining specific language. We were examining underlying meanings behind structures that we had seen in other chunks of language. We were looking at those chunks of language but in other contexts. So, there was a greater examination of language. And not large pieces. Normally what happens you're not looking at particulars, not really, you're getting the gist of it because of the length, whereas in this type of work, you are really examining at length something that is quite succinct. And there's the contrast, whereas something that's quite elaborate we're not spending the time on the particulars. In this type of piece, we're actually looking at all the innuendos, from a suffix to the *kami* (we, exclusive) or the *kita* (we, inclusive). And that was a very useful tool.

Me: And what do you think the impact on their learning was?

Maria: Well, just an example of this (students' work) and some of their responses prove to me that… I really think they've understood it. I believe that it has made an impact on their understanding of the examination of language and how in different cultures how we word things is different and the way we word it reflects our interaction with people.

At first initially I think they were a little bit startled by it. And because in the past… it really has in some ways impacted on me also as a teacher keeping in mind how students learn. I've certainly used more English. But I had to because I had to draw comparisons. Often in this sort of unit, I wouldn't do as much of it.

Me: And you don't see that as a problem if it's across a programme?

Maria: Perhaps I could have…in future, if I were to do it again, I could write a comment in Indonesian and say write a paragraph and discuss this.

Me: There wasn't time. It was like a mini…

(Discussion continues)

Maria: Yes, because really it was a trial… and I have often wanted to do that (focus on signs), because language is powerful and advertising is another fantastic means as well… It certainly captivates, I think, your audience. It is an excellent way to hone in on snippets of the language that mean so much.

Maria views language and culture as comprising a world view that influences interaction, 'in different cultures how we word things is different and the way we word it reflects our interaction with people'. Words have 'underlying meanings', 'snippets of the language that mean so much' which are subtle and not immediately evident, 'all the innuendos', but which can be revealed through close examination of language, particularly when focusing on authentic texts. Her understanding that culture provides the meaning in language results in her close attention to their interrelationship, 'It certainly captivates…your audience', providing an affective benefit in learning. With the focus on analysis of culture in language, Maria notices her increased use of English for instruction and discussion. While she is somewhat concerned about this, as it challenges her communicative orientation, she perceives it as necessary, 'I had to because I had to draw comparisons', and beneficial for learning, 'keeping in mind how students learn'. Hence, she associates the emphasis on meaning that is required to explore culture in language with use of English as a medium for instruction, viewing this as different from her usual orientation but as necessary for students' learning of culture.

The extracts reveal Maria's view that language and culture are distinct in nature, yet interrelated both in general and in language teaching. Language comprises forms that are definable and knowable whereas culture comprises a world view that is indefinable and acquired primarily through enculturation. For Maria, culture provides 'life' and meaning in language that can be interpreted differently depending on one's own enculturation and world view; it resembles a semiotic view of both language and culture (Liddicoat, 2002; Liddicoat & Scarino, 2013).

Maria's views of intercultural language teaching and learning

Maria's conceptualisation of language and culture as interrelated in general and in language teaching strengthens as she develops her understanding of intercultural language teaching and learning. She becomes increasingly aware of her own enculturation and how this relates to her identity and orientation in language teaching.

Extract 48: Maria – views of intercultural language teaching (February)

Participant	Dialogue
Maria:	It just really struck me...it (choosing an Asian language) makes more sense. It really was never a choice because Indonesia is our closest neighbour. It just made sense. The alphabet is the same. I could do in-country study if required...
Me:	So, why did you then do the School of Languages Year 12 [course]?
Maria:	It's very interesting isn't it? I felt my knowledge of pedagogy in the area required enhancement, required further knowledge and programming. My strength is not programming. I might be quite confident in the language but I don't feel confident in my programming.
Me:	So, you felt you didn't have that teacher headset in relation to the language?
Maria:	Yes, exactly. I felt I was still a student. So enrolling with the School of Languages helped me a great deal. I was on the right track but it was just collating resources, building up that... and I'm still on the journey. And I'm not content yet. I still feel there's something, even if it's spending a year there. That's what I tell the kids all the time, 'We can't turn our backs on someone so close'. Because we see it in our faces every day. That's why to me it makes more sense to me now to teach Indonesian than it does Italian.
Me:	So, you feel it in your bones more passionately than Italian?
Maria:	Yes, and I never would have thought that. Also, because it's a new language. Even when you're teaching a *me*- verb, it's not clear in my head either but I think, 'How can we get around this?' and you compare languages too. And also having tasted a little bit of culture, just a little because Sumatra is different to Kalimantan...that's (the diversity) the beauty of it.

Maria's choice to study Indonesian as an adult is a reasoned and deliberate one ('it makes more sense', 'we see it in our faces every day'). She is conscious of being a second language learner and novice teacher, 'I felt I was still a student', and considers herself to be on a 'journey' of understanding a language and culture within which she has not been directly socialised. She feels closely aligned with her students in this exploration ('it's a new language') and believes it to be important to find ways into understanding it, 'it's not clear in my head either'. Maria considers her linguistic and cultural identity as a resource for her teaching, problematising it and working with students ('How can we get around this?') and drawing out connections wherever possible ('you compare languages too'). She sees a clear rationale for teaching and learning Indonesian due to the country's geographical proximity yet cultural distance from her students' own cultural context. Maria's multilingual and multicultural experiences and identity highlight for her the need for students to engage in exploration of diverse languages and culture; an intercultural orientation in language teaching makes sense to her.

Maria is not initially aware of the degree of influence that her own background and identity has on her teaching and she begins to reflect on it during one of the early debriefing discussions.

Extract 49: Maria – views of intercultural language teaching (March)

Participant	Dialogue
Me:	(Discussing extract from classroom interaction) There was a bit about...it got onto sex and masturbation and you were going to avoid that whole section. Why was that?
Maria:	That's my cultural background. I didn't feel comfortable with that.
Me:	Because they were bursting to get to that.
Maria:	Really, were they?
Me:	Yes, especially Jaxson because he had read ahead and seen it.
Maria:	See, that's my background.
Me:	Then I thought maybe it was because you were in a Catholic school.
Maria:	I don't know how far I can go sometimes...My issues are there.
Me:	You talk about Paris. Do you remember that?
Maria:	That had been my experience in France. I had learned French for so long and then I went to Paris and it's all this Parisian. It's a bit like Jakarta. Jakarta is always being seen as the heart of trade, culture, business and anything that comes out of Jakarta is OK so Indonesian youth are influenced by that.
Me:	So what were you trying to point out to them about that?

(*Discussion continues*)

Maria: Often language…not often, always language differs from one area to another even though the official language is the same, but it changes depending on the area and the trends that come out from…What I was trying to point out was that language differs depending on the context. This (slang) language was born in the streets. I tried to draw the example with Paris.

Me: You did that elsewhere where you used another example and I guess what I was wondering is why didn't you talk to them about the point you were trying to make?

Maria: Oh, I guess by examples I'm hoping they will come up with that by themselves as a conclusion.

Me: You're hoping they'll see the pattern…

Maria: But we never come to…Can you see the pattern boys? What is the pattern? In future I could ask 'Now remember when we did that…?' and see if they have connected it.

Me: At one point you deliberately pull them up and say, 'Now remember the girls in the video'. Now, what was all that about?

Maria: Ah, yes, when I don't feel comfortable with elaborating on that…I guess if they were all girls I would feel differently but because they're all boys I feel there is that…in scientific terms… I can't think of the word, the dynamics… If I'd been a male Indonesian teacher… I don't feel comfortable so the wall comes up and I don't even realise I'm doing it. I just move on. I guess what I was trying to say is this is happening in Indonesia (i.e. liberal attitudes towards sex) but we must keep in mind there is that officialdom in Indonesia that most kids are aspiring to.

As Maria develops her understanding of an intercultural orientation, she chooses to use a text focused on contemporary colloquial language in Indonesia. As she examines the text with her students, she encounters aspects that are confronting and she avoids these in her teaching. When asked about this, she explains that her discomfort is related to her own enculturation and values, 'That's my cultural background. I didn't feel comfortable with that', together with her awareness of her teaching context of a Catholic boys school, 'I don't know how far I can go sometimes', 'if they were all girls I would feel differently', 'If I'd been a male Indonesian teacher'. She is aware of the intrapersonal dimension of teaching and of the role that identity plays in perceptions and interaction (Papademetre, 2005).

Her reluctance to address particular ideas acts as a restricting force at this point, 'I don't feel comfortable with elaborating on that', 'the wall comes up and I don't even realise I'm doing it. I just move on'. Thus, Maria operates within parameters in language teaching that are created by her identity and values, her teaching context and her orientation in language teaching, 'my issues are there'. In exploring an intercultural orientation, Maria discovers that she is in unfamiliar, more personal territory that is not required in her usual communicative orientation. She is becoming aware of her own subjectivities and how these influence her teaching and interaction (Kramsch, 2009). Her multilingual identity is a resource for her such as when she draws parallels between the linguistic diversity of cities and identifies the variability of language, '(language) changes depending on the area and the trends that come out', 'language differs depending on the context'.

An intercultural orientation, as Maria understands it, involves exploration, interpretation and reflection, hence challenging Maria's usual communication-oriented pedagogy.

Extract 50: Maria – views of intercultural language teaching (July)

Participant	Dialogue
Me:	What I noticed was that there was a lot of silence in this unit compared to the earlier one. There were long pauses and silences. Did you notice any of that?
Maria:	Mmm. Maybe…That's reflection. Do you know I've noticed that because in our culture we're not comfortable because when I've had Indonesians come to talk to my class there are those silences. Whereas here if there's silence, I think, they haven't understood, I'll have to feed them the answers. You're right.
Me:	You didn't notice it at the time? It wasn't uncomfortable?
Maria:	It wasn't too uncomfortable. I believed they were reflecting. But when it gets too long, then no. So then that's when having some tool or devices… like 'You've had time to think about that now let's go to the board'. You're right…
Me:	I noticed you trying to be really careful with the questions you were asking.
Maria:	And I was aware of that partly because of your presence… I wanted it to be… what is the right way to question? The right way is to make sure you're not giving them the answer. And

(Discussion continues)

I tend to do that because we are assuming that they are all thinking in our way.

Me: Or that they are so far off the track that we'd better tell them. Instead of allowing that space and those silences for them to say, 'What does that mean?'.

Maria: Have you noticed that I tend to say, 'There are no correct or right and wrong answers here'. Because if I'm saying, 'What verb fits in this sentence?' there can only be one or two. But if I'm asking, 'What could this sign imply?', then I'm saying, 'Look, there is no right or wrong answer here, we are getting closer to what could be the possible answer'. So, I try to make them feel comfortable about that. But especially with the young ones, there's no wrong or right here. We're just looking at pictures and coming up with some ideas of what's brought forward about the culture.

Me: So, you're trying to get across that idea that it's open to interpretation.

Maria: The whole lot is open to interpretation isn't it? …And there's nothing wrong with that silence. But as teachers, we often feel that's a sign of inability to answer. What's reflection? Reflection is time to…but I've noticed that it brings calmness on to the class whereas I'm fireworks. I'm really high energy. I'm high maintenance in the classroom.

Maria notices an increase, compared to usual, in silences in the class, relating this to the reflective aspect of an intercultural approach. She explains that silence is equated, both culturally and in teaching, with a lack of comprehension or knowledge, hence it is not comfortable for teachers. She contrasts her usual teaching style of 'fireworks' and 'high maintenance' with the 'calmness' that her effort to adopt an intercultural orientation has created. For Maria, communicative language teaching involves performance, whereas intercultural language teaching involves noticing, reflection and interpretation. She notes a difference between her previous approach, 'if I'm saying, "What verb fits in this sentence?" there can only be one or two' and an intercultural approach, 'if I'm asking, "What could this sign imply?", then I'm saying, "Look, there is no right or wrong answer here, we are getting closer to what could be the possible answer"'. She notices a shift in her questioning and focus, offering less certainty and greater possibility for diverse and individual meaning, 'the possible answer'. There is a focus here on exploration and interpretation (Liddicoat & Scarino, 2013): 'We're just looking at pictures and coming up with some ideas of what's brought forward about the culture', 'the whole lot is open to interpretation...'.

While Maria values an intercultural orientation in language teaching, she remains concerned about target language use and her overall communicative orientation.

Extract 51: Maria – views of intercultural language teaching (September)

Participant	Dialogue
Me:	So what are you understanding by interaction in this kind of way of teaching? What kinds of interaction? How important do you think it is for this way of working and for students' learning?
Maria:	Well, interactions I think are a focal point of this way of teaching, this style of teaching. However, it's not... it's not an easy one because it's a lot easier just to stand in front of a class and say 'this is the way, this, just a quick question, yeah, fine, OK, let's go on'. It really opens up a lot of, as you said too, space, time, quietness, which you're not absolutely comfortable with because you're thinking, 'Have they really understood this question?' or 'No, that answer wasn't what I was expecting'. I was hoping that uh....
Me:	So what do you see as interaction or mediation?
Maria:	OK, what do I see as interaction? Interaction is, you may be reading a sentence and you might say, you know, 'Is that clear?'. And someone like Jaxson might respond, 'So why is that word used there?' or 'What do they actually mean by that?'. You hope they would ask something like that, you would hope. Or when you see when there isn't much response, then you are feeding a little bit of... Not feeding, that's not the correct word. But you're trying. You're prompting them to give you some sort of response. And, that has not been easy. That has not been easy. I don't know why. Is it because I'm not accustomed to hearing or listening to their...teaching this way? Is it because we're not trained...?
Me:	Do you think you're listening more? Or are you aware of those spaces and those interactions?
Maria:	I think I'm aware. I don't know if I'm listening more. I'll be honest. I don't know if I'm listening more.

(Discussion continues)

Me: I don't know if teachers are good listeners. I know myself…

Maria: I know, I know. I'm constantly thinking, 'OK, let's not spend too much time on this. Let's move on', which is a little bit, I think sad, because you want them to develop oral skills whether it'll be in their own language or in the target language and you're not giving them an opportunity to discuss. I also think it's because we're meant to be doing it in the target language, so I'm very conscious of that. As a language teacher I'm very conscious of that um… interaction. I think that's why I don't always feel comfortable and I think other teachers in this situation would feel very similar. Because interaction involves spontaneity, it involves spontaneous language. Sometimes we're not always equipped with the spontaneous language in the target language. So we try to avoid those loop holes. We try to avoid them. And it's sad because it's nothing wrong to say, 'Well I actually don't know that word. Let's have a read in the dictionary'. And have it… And we can look it up together and maybe expand on it.

Maria views social interaction as central to intercultural language teaching, 'interactions…are a focal point' as it allows for exploring meaning together, 'What do they actually mean by that?'. Maria regards the process of interpretation and reflection as demanding and different to her usual approach, 'just to stand in front of a class and say, "this is the way, this, just a quick question, yeah, fine, OK, let's go on"'. In this view, content is unproblematic and interaction is minimal. This contrasts with her understanding of interaction as more complex within an intercultural perspective: 'it's not an easy one', 'you're prompting them to give you some sort of response. And, that has not been easy. That has not been easy. I don't know why'. She acknowledges her own reaction to this, 'it really opens up a lot of…space, time, quietness, which you're not absolutely comfortable with', 'that answer wasn't what I was expecting', and reflects on her capacity to manage students' interpretations, 'I'm not accustomed to hearing or listening to their…Is it because we're not trained…?'. Maria also feels concerned that an intercultural orientation requires more spontaneous language use that may confront some teachers with limited proficiency, 'sometimes we're not always equipped with the spontaneous language in the target language'. The combination, therefore, of uncertain content, interpretation and range of spontaneous language use creates a tension for her, '…we try to avoid those loop holes. We try to avoid them'. While Maria values some aspects of an intercultural orientation, she also feels concerned that these may be a distraction to her focus on communication, 'we're meant to be doing it in the target language', 'you want them to develop oral skills'. Thus, Maria, as reported in other studies (Sercu, 2005, 2007), experiences a tension between her existing frame for language teaching and her emergent understanding of intercultural language teaching.

In her final reflection, Maria considers how an intercultural orientation in language teaching relates to her overall goals and perspective as a language teacher.

Extract 52: Maria – views of intercultural language teaching (September)

Participant	Dialogue
Me:	So there's a linking to the previous lesson, so what kinds of connections are you trying to get them to make? So obviously the ones to prior learning.
Maria:	To prior learning and also with the strand of understanding culture (in the curriculum framework). I talked about the understanding of language. But the understanding culture, the links aren't... trying to... to bring out of... from them, what was the outcome of yesterday's lesson? Not just from the linguistic point of view but what were the main points you went home with? Did you think... Did anything come to mind? Was there anything, maybe on the news that perhaps, brought, refreshed, rekindled that? So I try to make connections also with, not just in the classroom, but in a topic that may have come up in another classroom because I think it's all interconnected. You can't be... I hate the idea of language learning just, this is one lesson and then that's a lesson. It's all connected.
Me:	Because it all sits within their one head. In some way, shape or form.
Maria:	And so I guess the aim of that is just to paste it. Imagine your mind as this collage. This collage. And I tend to use that, that idea of the concept of your brain and all these other topics coming out of it. To not just put it in under one umbrella.
Me:	And so how do you think you go about making those connections?
Maria:	Questioning, questioning. Whether it has been in the target language or in the dominant language. I think the questioning,

(Discussion continues)

rather than you saying, which I have a tendency to do, but I'm trying to stop that, is giving them the answers saying 'OK, yesterday we looked at this, this, this and this. Wait a minute. Hey guys, what were we looking at yesterday?' And making out a little bit. Pretending that, so the questioning is an important role model for them. It's also guidance for them. And also the connecting aspect there is just insurmountable... So I think I really do, I use the board a lot, that idea of the concept map as I said before.

I think it's more important to leave a mark in other ways. To make a difference in your teaching, whether it'll be English or Indonesian or whatever it is. And I always think these are ambassadors. These kids are ambassadors. One day I'm hoping that this will whet their palette and if they continue with Indonesian that's fine and if they don't that's fine too. But I know these things will remain. Because I remember my teachers. Those who did go beyond the boundaries were those who left a mark in my life and I wanted to be one of them. Yeah, those role models for me. Because you can, you can go off on tangents, but I think you've got to remember that well, I hope that to keep in mind that these kids you want them to be well rounded. You just don't want them to be, 'Right, I can use the passive. I can use the active. I can use...'. That's fine and I'm really impressed by that. But can you discuss, can you give a little bit of insight into this? (Language is) not the only tool and why am I teaching Indonesian? Well I often ask myself. I enjoy it, but I probably equally enjoy teaching religious education or English with that same approach. It's just that my focal point is languages, but it's so important to bring in experiences and value systems and perspectives of other cultures and other parts of the world.

I think that's what we want kids to become or to..., when they do leave school, they'll say, 'Well, that really did play an important role in shaping something in me'. Now these are all not tangible. It's not like a test...It's interesting, I think through this too, I don't want to just be the language teacher. It's interesting, you know, I don't want to be put... because I think there's a stereotype there and I hate that stereotype. I can't stand it.

(Discussion continues)

Me: Exactly. And there's more to you.

Maria: I like to be eloquent in… or erudite or not erudite, it's too big
                 a word. What I mean is to be able to teach perhaps in other…
                 or to bring into the language lesson different flavours. I know
                 it's going beyond the boundaries. But you've got to use the
                 classroom as a tool for learning about other… not just about
                 your subject area.
                 And you've got to use all the types of resources, not just
                 necessarily the conventional ones and I'm not saying teachers
                 use the conventional ones because I always think I enjoy that
                 too. But with some kids you can't do that. You've got to break
                 away a little bit from those conventions. But that's the style
                 of teacher I am. I can't, I can't be um, and I think I was like
                 that as a student. I think we tap into many things to bring
                 in, hone in on the message. The world is varied. The world
                 is diverse and we're just the crumbs. And I think this sort
                 of understanding culture can draw on that a lot. OK, we do
                 things differently. We say things differently, but there are also
                 standards here. We're just camouflaged…

Maria understands language teaching and learning within a broader
educational perspective. She views learning as multidimensional,
referring to it as a collage, 'that idea of the concept of your brain and
all these other topics coming out of it. To not just put it in under one
umbrella'. Maria sees learning as a process of making connections, a
principle advocated by Liddicoat *et al.* (2003), and perceives language
teaching as contributing to students' overall development, 'I try to make
connections also with, not just in the classroom, but in a topic that may
have come up in another classroom because I think it's all interconnected'.
For her, language learning is cumulative and interconnected, 'What was
the outcome of yesterday's lesson? Not just from the linguistic point of
view but what were the main points you went home with?', 'I hate the
idea of language learning just, this is one lesson and then that's a lesson.
It's all connected'. She perceives the importance of probing students'
understanding and encouraging connections, 'the questioning is an
important role model for them. It's also guidance for them. And also
the connecting aspect there is just insurmountable'. Maria sees her role
as a language teacher to prepare her students to act as 'ambassadors'; a
notion similar to that of an intercultural citizen (Byram, 2008). She feels

obliged to 'go beyond the boundaries' in her teaching, including going beyond grammatical knowledge and target language use, 'I can use the passive. I can use the active', to make students 'well rounded'. Maria values the impact made by her former teachers who '(went) beyond the boundaries', 'that really did play an important role in shaping something in me'. She regards herself as having a duty to transgress the conventions associated with teaching, and sees it necessary to truly transform young people. She views teaching and learning as sociocultural acts in which people are shaped and shape others, through knowledge and interaction (Vygotsky, 1978). Maria sees intercultural language teaching and learning as offering her the potential to transgress, 'I don't want to just be the language teacher', 'you've got to use all the types of resources, not just necessarily the conventional ones', 'You've got to break away a little bit from those conventions. But that's the style of teacher I am'. There is a sense here of criticality (Byram, 2008; Phipps & Gonzalez, 2004) as Maria encourages a culture of questioning and non-conformity, 'we do things differently. We say things differently, but there are also standards here. We're just camouflaged'.

Concluding comments on Maria

Maria's conceptualisation of language and culture and their relationship in general closely aligns with her view of them in language teaching. She views language in structural terms as well as semiotic terms, recognising it as dynamic, context dependent and open to interpretation. She views culture also as facts and information at one level, as well as diverse social practices and norms (Liddicoat, 2011) that operate at both national and individual levels. Maria regards language and culture as interrelated at a generic level primarily with culture providing meaning in language, and as somewhat separate at a differential level (Risager, 2007) with individuals developing their own language and culture resources. Maria's understanding of language teaching and the expectation towards communicative language use as the goal are reflected in her attention to the use of Indonesian in instruction and interaction. She understands an intercultural orientation as involving a focus on the relationship between language and culture, interaction, questioning and interpretation of meaning. It also involves learners in decentring from their own language and culture, making comparisons and reflecting on their own enculturation and identity. For Maria, teaching should be a transformative process that shapes young people for the future and she feels it is essential to transgress convention in order to do so. Maria views an intercultural orientation in language teaching as having potential to go beyond the norm. She experiments with some aspects of it, expanding her repertoire, while remaining committed overall to a communicative orientation.

Conclusion

The case studies presented in this chapter reveal how the three teachers conceptualise language, culture and their relationship as a basis for language teaching. The discussion of their conceptual framings reflects ideas outlined in Chapter 1 in relation to how language and culture and their relationship are understood in the field of language teaching.

In relation to the concept of 'language', the teachers view it largely in structural terms; vocabulary, sentences, grammar and text. The target language is seen primarily as an object of study that is somewhat unproblematic and static, with Maria also viewing it as dynamic and variable. Acquisition of the target language is regarded as difficult and effortful, but use of it is seen as the goal of language teaching. The other main language in the classroom, English, represents a source of tension for the teachers, including Maria who values it as a comparative resource, as it is perceived as conflicting with target language instruction and use. There is discomfort, therefore, with an intercultural orientation as it is seen as requiring the use of English that is not consistent with what is considered by them to be legitimate language teaching.

Similarly, although not as consistent as the perspectives on language, there are shared views among the teachers of the concept of culture, particularly its nature and place in language teaching. Kelly views culture as largely monolithic or national, Indonesian or Australian. Collette sees culture as both national and individual, as does Maria who also emphasises its multifaceted and dynamic nature. For all three teachers, culture, particularly Indonesian culture, is synonymous with difference; it is largely a cultural studies and national paradigm view. While cultural awareness, sensitivity and tolerance feature prominently in the teachers' goals of language teaching, it is problematic for them as they view it as acquired through experience. Their views reflect their own experiences, with Collette viewing culture as lived, therefore developed *in situ*; with Kelly viewing culture as belonging to others, and therefore facts and information to be taught; and Maria viewing culture as multidimensional, national and individual world views and values. Culture represents problematic content due to the potential for stereotyping and the risk of distraction from communicative language use. This tension results in pressure on the teachers to separate language and culture in practice, focusing on language and leaving culture to incidental content. Such findings reflect similar studies showing language teachers' struggle to represent their understandings of culture in their teaching.

The teachers perceive language and culture as integrated at a generic level, but this integration varies in how they see it in language teaching. The target language is central for the teachers and culture tends to be regarded as secondary or additional. The relationship between language and culture in teaching is seen in three main ways: as parallel, with culture acting as contextual information to enhance language use; as linked, with language reflecting cultural ideas and issues; and as interconnected, with culture seen as the life in language, as giving meaning to the form. These views are not necessarily discrete, however, as each teacher grapples with how to represent their understanding of language and culture as integrated in some way. It is also apparent that over the course of the study, these views evolved, and there was a stronger sense towards the end of the study, particularly for Collette and Kelly, of how culture may be integrated with language, such as through text analysis. It is arguably Maria who holds a conceptualisation of language and culture that most closely relates to the literature on intercultural language teaching, with language and culture seen as interrelated semiotic systems that are individually and collectively constructed over time. The cases overall highlight the challenge, evident in the literature, of acknowledging the distinctive nature of language and culture, while also finding ways to represent a relationship between them for the purpose of language teaching.

Furthermore, the case studies reveal how teachers' understandings of the concepts of language and culture and their relationship are influenced by their personal experiences, knowledge and identities. The relationship between teachers' personal and professional worlds, their roles as language teachers and their individual linguistic and cultural identities acts as both a resource and a source of tension for each teacher as she develops an intercultural orientation in her teaching. The teachers are all non-native speakers of Indonesian and have developed various relationships with Indonesian language and culture, and language and culture more generally. Collette tries to avoid subjectivity and values, and uses her experience of culture as supplementary content for teaching language.

Kelly keeps her personal and professional worlds discrete, wanting to use culture to provide relevance but avoiding it due to its unmanageability. Maria has multiple languages and cultures that she actively draws into her teaching, regarding these as an asset. It is a combination of the teachers' conceptual, experiential and professional frames that underpin their teaching and create both affordances (Van Lier, 2000) and tensions for them as they attempt to mediate an intercultural orientation in practice. It is the nature of mediation that is the subject of discussion in the next chapter.

3 Understandings of Mediation

In order to understand mediation in language teaching and learning, it is necessary to consider the concept of mediation itself. The term 'mediation' is commonly associated with the process of negotiation such as conflict resolution in order to resolve disputes or disagreement. It does, however, have particular meaning in relation to the field of language teaching and to teaching and learning in general. This chapter will examine how mediation is typically understood in language teaching and learning, and what might be gained from connecting with understandings of mediation from a sociocultural learning theory perspective. The discussion will then consider how an expanded view of mediation may be valuable for intercultural language teaching and learning.

Mediation From a Language Teaching and Learning Perspective

The concept of mediation in language teaching emerged during the 1990s as models of communicative competence recognised the ability needed to solve problems encountered during interaction between speakers of different languages (Byram, 2013). The intercultural mediator was viewed as someone with the skills necessary to 'handle cross-cultural problems' (Meyer, 1991: 137) and to accurately convey meanings without interfering with them. The intercultural mediator was someone who could:

> ... operate their linguistic competence and their sociolinguistic awareness of the relationship between language and culture and the context in which it is used, in order to manage interaction across cultural boundaries, to anticipate misunderstandings caused by difference in values, meanings and beliefs, and thirdly, to cope with the affective as well as cognitive demands of engagement with otherness. (Byram, 1995: 25)

Mediation, according to this view, is a process of 'managing' misunderstandings caused by difference. In order to navigate these differences, the mediator needs to become an 'insider' within a linguistic and cultural system different from that into which he/she has already been socialised (Byram, 1995). A mediator, therefore, requires knowledge and understanding of 'the other' and the ability to compare cultural frameworks in order to handle miscommunication with flexibility and tolerance (Dasli, 2011: 22). Mediation of this kind is associated with skills required in transferring meaning such as translating, interpreting, summarising and paraphrasing. The sense of translation as a mediation skill or 'highly codified quest for equivalences' (Phipps & Gonzalez, 2004) has been critiqued and more contemporary understandings of translation view it as a form of intercultural mediation:

> Translators do not just enable border crossing and mediation. They bring new worlds into being. By working along the seams of languages and different human experiences they are able to show what the world may look like from different vantage points. (Phipps & Gonzalez, 2004: 164)

As part of intercultural competence, one thus requires the skills to manage communication across languages and cultures, and also the ability to negotiate and shape intercultural communication. Byram and Alred (2002) found that during long-term study abroad programmes, students needed to develop the 'potential for social action' and both the cognitive and affective capabilities to become an 'intercultural mediator'. They claim that during sustained intercultural experience, or 'tertiary socialisation', in which one is inducted into a society beyond one's immediate or primary society of socialisation, an individual's linguistic and cultural framework is transformed. As one acquires an expanded framework for engaging in the world, one activates it according to contextual and communicative needs. An intercultural mediator, therefore, requires the ability to detach from his/her primary cultural framework and adapt behaviour, values and beliefs according to the new cultural framework, thereby 'bringing into a relationship two cultures' (Byram & Alred, 2002: 341). He/she needs to develop skills in comparative analysis of the perspectives of both parties and be able to explain the complexities and tensions that may not be apparent to either party (Byram, 2013).

Another framing of mediation in language teaching, adopted by Zarate *et al.* (2004), is that of 'cultural mediation'. This perspective views mediation as a process of navigating diverse cultures, with language learners potentially contributing to social harmony. In their study, Zarate *et al.* investigated cultural mediation through five different projects carried out across diverse contexts in Europe. One aspect of the study focused on how language teaching may develop students' empathy towards others. The researchers examined situations of miscomprehension and identified discursive functions, such as encouragement and disapproval, used by students and teachers that promoted empathy towards otherness. While some of the work focused on classroom interactions, the researchers acknowledge that theirs is 'early work in a research field still far too under exploited' and that more attention needs to be paid to aspects such as an interactional analysis of learners' discourse (Zarate et al., 2004: 218). Their study does show, however, a broadening of the concept of mediation as it has been traditionally understood in language teaching.

Others suggest that previous understandings of intercultural mediation have incorrectly assumed a starting point of distinctive difference between the 'other' culture and one's primary language and culture. Risager (2007), for example, contends that Byram and Alred's (2002) view overstates the separateness of the stages of socialisation and is based on a view of 'other' cultures as existing beyond one's primary culture. She argues that given the nature of multicultural societies, multiple cultural systems can be present in one's primary socialisation and that the phases of socialisation are constantly developing. In this way, an intercultural mediator is:

an interpreter, an intermediary, a catalyst. This role is more oriented towards social, cultural and linguistic complexity; involving the person relating to the identities of different people or groups and their concepts of each other. (Risager, 2007: 234)

In this view, the intercultural mediator responds to the intercultural status of those around him/her and, in doing so, contributes to a collective resource for making meaning. She argues that teachers are such mediators and the classroom represents such a collective resource where collective forms of learning are beneficial. From this perspective, mediation involves not just one's own linguistic and cultural framework in relation to the target language and culture, but all the possible linguistic and cultural frameworks that are brought to the interaction. Mediation, therefore, is a process of navigating multiple linguistic and cultural frameworks, the collective meaning resource that is available, at any given moment in interaction.

A further criticism of previous understandings of intercultural mediation is that it has tended to limit the view of language to that of a skill or a 'tool' for mediating. Liddicoat (2014) argues that because work has focused on perceptions and representations of others and their cultures, understandings of intercultural mediation have emphasised 'things that lie outside language'. He proposes that notions of intercultural mediation need to adopt as a starting point a view that language is the primary *site* of intercultural encounters, and that language is not just a means through which mediation occurs but it is itself part of what gets mediated. Liddicoat suggests that pragmatics provides a valuable lens through which to consider intercultural mediation, as it involves learners in analysing and interpreting language and culture for themselves and for others. In this way, an intercultural mediator adopts multiple positions, as insider and outsider, with an ability to reflect on pragmatic differences and create a position 'in-between' cultures in order to understand and create meanings that may be understood by both.

Thus, in the field of language teaching, mediation has typically been regarded as a repair or communication strategy, a skill in conveying messages between two parties who do not share the same language and culture. It is associated with translating and interpreting, in which language acts as a resource for performing these skills. These views are increasingly under challenge with recent work acknowledging translating and interpreting as acts of intercultural mediation involving, for example, identity, subjectivity, interpretation and contestation (Katan, 2008). Furthermore, the notion that mediation occurs between two distinct linguistic and cultural worlds is also contested, with recognition of 'multilingual subjects' (Kramsch, 2009), 'cross-national migrations and global communications' (Kramsch, 2012), 'global flows' of languages and cultures (Risager, 2006) and 'cosmopolitan speakers' (i Sole, 2013) prompting a rethinking of monolingual and national culture views. Byram (2013) also suggests that language teaching could benefit from 'richer' notions of mediation drawing on 'real-world' conflicts of interest and understanding such as those found in industry. These 'real-world' conflicts could be used to shape language teaching and learning. It is apparent, therefore, that the concept of mediation within language teaching is shifting and there is value in considering how it may be expanded further for the purposes of intercultural language teaching.

Mediation From a Sociocultural Learning Theory Perspective

In the field of education, the term 'mediation' has received much attention through the work of Russian psychologist Lev Vygotsky (1978) who theorised that human consciousness is a 'fundamentally mediated mental activity'. He proposed that the process of thinking itself relies on people making sense of the world around them through tools that act between the mind and the external world. According to Vygotsky, language is the most powerful tool by which humans engage with and make sense of their world. As such, language mediates human thought and action in ways that both shape and are shaped by the individuals and groups who share the same language. It is through this process of using language to represent and understand the world that people come to acquire and create new knowledge; learning, therefore, is fundamentally a social process that is dependent on human interaction in and through language.

The idea that human thought is carried out through a semiotic device means that learning necessarily requires mediation. That is, cognition is not solely carried out in the mind of the individual but it is a process of meaning creation which is realised through language in interaction (Lantolf, 1994: 7). Indeed, interpsychological interaction is considered to be a necessary precursor to cognition (Vygotsky, 1978; Wertsch, 1985). The development of new thoughts within the mind of the individual (the intrapsychological) is contingent on a meeting of minds that occurs during interaction (the interpsychological). This understanding of the socially dependent nature of mental activity places mediation at the core of the teaching and learning process:

> Mediation is the process through which humans deploy culturally constructed artifacts, concepts, and activities to regulate (i.e. gain voluntary control over and transform) the material world or their own and each other's social and mental activity. With respect to symbolic artifacts, language activity, speaking and writing, is the primary, though not exclusive, meditational means humans deploy for thinking. Human mental activity develops as a consequence of the interweaving of biological and cultural formations. (Lantolf & Thorne, 2006: 79)

Mediation, according to this view, is an active process through which people come to understand and interact in their social and physical environment through a range of artefacts. These artefacts, including language, are not naturally occurring but are instead culturally constructed. Mediation is thus a process of sense making or the transformation of an individual's thinking through shared 'tools', the most powerful of which is language.

The zone of proximal development

According to Vygotsky (1978), learning takes place within a state of cognition, the zone of proximal development (ZPD) or mental space in which the learners' existing knowledge is receptive to new knowledge. The ZPD is not a fixed state of knowledge but rather represents a 'zone', a developmental space where learning may occur. It is this 'developmental' nature of the ZPD which gives importance to the concept of mediation as it acts as a catalyst for the 'zone' to be activated, and for the difference between an individual's existing knowledge to be progressed to a more developed state. For this to occur, two conditions need to be met: a recognition (not necessarily conscious) of what is unknown to the learner, and an effort by him/her to make sense of the unknown. It is in this 'space' that mediation can occur, enabling the learner to move from his/her existing position to a more cognitively sophisticated one. Learning is therefore dependent on both social interaction, the interpsychological encounter, and individual cognition, the intrapsychological process, whereby the individual makes sense of what is 'new'. Language represents the most significant semiotic tool for mediation and learning. It is both a vehicle for conveying new ideas to the learner and a means of stimulating knowledge construction, through interaction. In this way, language is a 'master tool' (Cole, 1994), as it is the tool that mediates all other learning (Wells, 1999). As such, classroom dialogue, and in particular the language use of the more 'matured' other (Lantolf & Thorne, 2006) (the teacher), represents the primary tool through which mediation takes place.

Novice and expert

Transformation of an individual's ZPD does not occur in a vacuum and is stimulated by others with more mature developmental states. When applied to an education setting, the more knowledgeable other is typically (although not exclusively) the teacher. In classrooms, teachers and learners are constantly mediating their thoughts and actions, creating the conditions necessary for constructing new knowledge:

> For Vygotsky (1978) social interaction is a mechanism for individual development, since, in the presence of a more capable participant, the novice is drawn into, and operates within, the space of the expert's strategic processes for problem solving. More specifically, the dialogically constituted interpsychological event between individuals of unequal abilities is a way for the novice to extend current competence. (Donato, 2000: 37)

It is the teacher who understands what is known and unknown and who brings the learner across this zone with the use of appropriate tools, including language. Learners are 'novices' who are guided by an 'expert' to the requisite knowledge, including linguistic knowledge, and ways of knowing within a particular social group. Novice members gradually acquire the necessary practices to be accepted as effective members of a social group; that is, they move from novice to expert status.

Wells (1999) views the relationship between novice and expert as a 'semiotic apprenticeship' in which students are inducted into the ways of living in a given community using the tools available and, in doing so, transform both themselves and the culture of the group in the process. During the 'semiotic apprenticeship', learners acquire the cognitive frames for interpreting new ideas and information, which enable them to construct new knowledge within a shared meaning system. The expert makes use of the resources of the culture both to determine what is necessary to assist learners into the next stage of learning, and as a resource from which to draw to supply the necessary stimulus for learning. The teacher needs to know, and know how best to use, these resources or 'tools' in order to provide the most effective forms of assistance. It is through joint activity that learners come to discover the significance of these 'tools' and to apply them to making sense of, and participating in, the world. In the case of second language classrooms, it is the teacher who oversees this 'apprenticeship'. The language teacher inducts learners into the semiotic space comprising a particular discipline, school culture, class culture and the cultures of the individuals. The teacher is best placed to determine learners' needs and to provide the appropriate tools or scaffolds to assist the transformation of their knowledge.

Scaffolding through discourse: A micro perspective

Due to the significance of language as the most powerful mediation 'tool', much of the literature concerned with teaching and learning emphasises the discourse practices of teachers and learners. From a Bakhtinian (Bakhtin, 1981: 276) perspective, discourse can be understood as occurring at the level of utterance and that any utterance simultaneously holds its specific meaning at a given point in time and place, as well as the 'thousands of living dialogic threads woven by socio-ideological consciousness around the given object of an utterance'. In this way, language is understood not as a 'system of abstract grammatical categories' but rather as 'ideologically saturated' (Bakhtin, 1981: 271). According to this view, discourse can be locally and individually enacted, while simultaneously and necessarily drawing on its embedded 'semantic layers' (Bakhtin, 1981: 276). It is discourse in this sense that is prevalent in the literature related to mediation from a sociocultural learning theory perspective. Discourse is understood as a primary stimulus and support for learning in that it represents both the forms through which learners participate in joint activity and the symbolic system through which meaning is shared and ultimately personalised. During interaction between teachers and learners, both draw on a range of discourse practices in the construction of meaning. Wells (1999) refers to these practices as 'genres of discourses' which operate as mediating tools in classroom interaction in two ways. Firstly, these genres of discourse are a means of organising joint activities and represent the means for constructing new knowledge. Secondly, through participating in these discourse practices, learners are able to appropriate or make relevant for themselves, the ways and products for making meaning independently. Wells (1999) emphasises the importance of learners participating in diverse shared discourses through group work and peer assistance as a means of moving learning from the interpersonal to the intrapersonal plane.

Understandings of mediation are often concerned with teachers' talk in particular as the principal stimulus and scaffold for learning. There is an emphasis on strategies such as instruction, explanation, questioning and feedback. In the area of language teacher education, Tsui (1995) focuses on teachers' question types such as 'comprehension' or 'response' oriented, and their impact on student responses. She examines how the nature of teachers' talk can be modified to create comprehensible input and create an 'interactional structure' or opportunity for language learning. She regards teachers' questioning as important for increasing cognitive demands in learning and correlates question types with types of knowledge. She describes types of questions as open (requiring reasoning) and closed (requiring factual information), and relates these to types of knowledge (e.g. display questions are for knowledge checking and referential questions lead to new or unknown ideas). She also outlines teachers' talk in terms of purpose, i.e. explanations, error correction and feedback, highlighting the relationship between teachers' talk and cognitive processing (e.g. effective explanation is sufficient in amount and clearly sequenced). Tsui's work highlights the importance of considering teachers' discourse practices, particularly their questioning techniques, in any view of mediation in language teaching.

Similarly, in a study of the discourse practices of a particular science teacher, Verplaetse (2000) found that 'participant structures' and teacher discourse strategies impacted significantly on interaction and learners' language development. He identified three interaction phases: (1) 'inquiry' or prompted discussion; (2) 'rapid-fire review' using brief question, response and feedback turns; and (3) 'small group labwork'. He argued that the teacher's strategies and discourse patterns created the necessary opportunities for learners to practise language and to develop their social roles in the group. He highlighted two of the teacher's strategies as particularly important in promoting interaction, those of 'wondering out loud' and 'non-judgement' of students' responses. He suggests that the use of these strategies not only allows for practice but also creates a discourse that learners of the particular discipline can appropriate for themselves. This study demonstrates the importance of teachers' discourse strategies for scaffolding different kinds of learning, and simultaneously learners' language development, and in modelling ways to learn in a particular academic discipline.

Teachers' discourse practices may also scaffold learning by creating opportunities for learners to talk. For example, Anton (1999) emphasises how negotiation of meaning which leads to learning is supported through the promotion of learner talk. In her study of French and Italian tertiary language classes, Anton found a number of 'communicative moves' used by the teachers that acted as scaffolds for learning. These 'moves' included direct instruction aimed at encouraging students to notice patterns and providing open-ended questions to encourage discussions and opinions. Other 'moves' included providing feedback in simplified or manageable forms, allocating turns according to shared norms of participation and encouraging reflection on learning. She argues that these strategies enable learners to negotiate meanings and contribute to shaping the learning culture.

In the area of second language acquisition, Swain (1985) argues that a focus on learners' language 'output' as a result of interaction not only enhances language learning but also is necessary for it to occur. In her study of French immersion classes in Canada, Swain (2000) found that collaborative work among learners created the conditions for noticing differences in what students wanted to say and what they were able to say. That is, through social interaction, the students recognised the limits of their existing knowledge and sought new knowledge to address their needs. She refers to this process as 'language use mediating language learning' (Swain, 2000: 97). Indeed, the collaborative nature of the task enabled learners to engage in problem solving and to focus on the construction of meaning, leading to reflection on their learning and the use of meta-talk. The study shows the importance of learners' talk in developing metalanguage and meta-awareness that are themselves tools for mediating new learning.

The interchanges between teachers and learners in the classroom represent opportunities for different kinds of talk that can mediate learning in different ways. For example, in a study of students in a tertiary Spanish language class, Gutierrez (2008) found that there are a number of stages of mediation which are facilitated through collaborative activity on tasks. The social plane associated with collaborative tasks enables learners to experience a 'moment of awareness' in which they identify their needs. Once identified, learners move to a 'transitional' stage, moving towards self-regulation, in which they prepare to accommodate new learning according to what is offered by a 'more accomplished other'. Gutierrez (2008) identified two types of support for learning during collaborative tasks: 'requested assistance' and 'unrequested assistance'. The former included strategies such as use of learners' first language to paraphrase or exemplify a point. The latter included corrective feedback such as repetition and use of grammatical rules, as well as referencing one's knowledge to that of the collaborator. The importance of this study for understanding mediation is that collaborative dialogue offers opportunities for learners to recognise their learning needs and generate talk that facilitates their internalisation of learning.

Collaboration of any kind, however, is not sufficient and it is necessary to distinguish between forms of collaboration in order to maximise their effectiveness for mediation of learning. Guk and Kellogg (2007) for example, in their research on the micro exchanges between teachers and students, and students and students, in English classes in Korean primary schools, highlight the value of different interaction modes for providing different types of mediation. They argue that student–student interaction differs in nature and impact on language use and development from teacher–student interaction. They describe teacher–student mediation as involving processes such as demonstration, initiation of solutions, leading questioning and using metalanguage. Student–student mediation was less likely to include metalanguage and involved more imitation and demonstration, and a higher presence of learners' first language. Student–student interactions were also more likely to have more extended learner talk that, while not necessarily as accurate, more closely resembled an internalised version of the language. The authors suggest that both teacher–student and student–student interactions are different 'ends' of a whole class ZPD. Teacher–student interactions focus on explication, analysis of parts of language and using metalanguage. Student–student interactions focus on whole utterances and the use of students' first language to make sense of the target language. The study showed the importance of recognising the impact that different modes of interaction can have on mediation.

Mediating discourses of being: A macro perspective

Within learning theory, mediation can also be understood as a process of learning the ways of 'being' part of a particular group. Discourse plays a crucial role in representing, reproducing and recreating these ways of being among a group. In relation to teaching and learning, the classroom is conceived of as a community of practice (Lave & Wenger, 1991; Wenger, 1998) or an ecological system (Van Lier, 2002) into which learners are inducted into the disciplinary ways of being. Discourse both creates and reflects the shared practices that construct the roles, conditions and expectations, that is the culture of learning, in the classroom. Learning involves participating in shared activities that present opportunities for knowledge creation through new demands on a learner's existing knowledge. This means that learners need to undertake these activities and acquire the discourses associated with them. In the case of language learning, for example, undertaking language tasks is an activity that presents particular language demands. Donato and McCormick (1994) found in their study of a college French class, that changing the learning task impacted substantially on both the linguistic demands of students and their learning outcomes. They changed the design of a portfolio task to make it the basis for a class dialogue rather than as an end product in itself. That is, the portfolio was the catalyst for dialogue and further language learning strategies, which in fact became the major learning for the students. The study showed the importance of the nature of activities or tasks in shaping what is learned, not just in terms of content but also in terms of ways of learning and knowing, within a particular group.

Learning the ways of knowing is established in the daily interactions between teachers and learners that create the learning culture in a particular discipline over time. Takahashi *et al.* (2000), in a study of 'instructional conversations' in a Japanese foreign language classroom, found that teachers and students construct the shared practices of the classroom. Both groups were involved in establishing expectations of learning, connecting new learning to prior learning and attributing value to learning practices. Teachers act as guides during interactions and, in doing so, model the knowledge, skills and values that are important to learning. Through repetition and echoing others, in particular the teacher, students showed evidence of learning discipline-specific knowledge, such as linguistic forms, as well as implicit knowledge, such as relating to the teacher and expectations of being language learners. This example highlights the social and participatory nature of mediation, as well as the importance of recognising how mediation occurs both at a specific, perhaps explicit, content level, as well as at a broader, perhaps more implicit, disciplinary level.

Hall (2002) perceives language classrooms as sites where learners acquire the discourses necessary to construct new knowledge and to regulate their own learning. She examined the nature of patterns of speech in language classrooms, focusing on instructional conversations, modelling, feedback, contingency managing, directing, questioning, explaining and task structuring. She describes a relationship between strategy development and students' capacity to mediate their own learning. That is, through interaction the teacher can model the strategies necessary for learners to operate independently with their new knowledge. Hall (2002) describes three types of strategies: metacognitive (planning and reflecting on new concepts and learning), cognitive (processing, manipulating and representing new knowledge) and socio-affective strategies (engaging in shared and private speech). In her view, these strategies can be explicitly taught but tend to be acquired through interaction as teachers model ways to manage and support learning. Thus, teacher modelling of different strategies for learning is part of the process of mediation and also of what is mediated.

Van Lier (2000) proposes an ecological view of language classrooms, arguing that learning is inextricably related to the shared meanings created among members of a particular community. He suggests that communities have a 'semiotic budget' comprised of everything in the immediate environment, for example the classroom, from which learners select an 'affordance' or an opportunity for making meaning. The ways in which individuals relate to each other and to their environment (through shared activities) create opportunities for learning. He explains that the process of stimulating and supporting changes to a learner's ZPD can be achieved through formal instruction and informal interaction. It is in the joint activities of classroom life and the interactive spaces between teachers and learners that mediation takes place and in which meanings are made.

Understanding classrooms as ecologies in which teachers and learners are engaged in joint semiotic activities, both participating in and contributing to knowledge, moves away from a unidirectional view of mediation as 'help' or scaffolding to a reciprocal view of mediation as a process of mutual transformation. In studying interaction in French high school classrooms in Switzerland, for example, Doehler (2002) found that mediation is based on an interdependency of interactants and is 'simultaneously socio-historically situated and socially and locally accomplished'. In addition, she argues that mediation processes viewed at a micro level contribute to a macro level function. She gives the example of how the ways in which repairs are handled during interaction help to construct relationships between people as 'experts' or 'novices'. Mediation practices, therefore, are determined by the task and situation, and are also changed by these in the process. These changes are brought about through the constant evolution of a 'communicative culture' (Doehler, 2002: 39). Mediation is dependent on the activities which are associated, and endorsed or not, within a particular discipline and schooling context. Doehler argues that the communicative culture is itself a mediation tool that supports particular kinds of interactions and social roles. Hence, learners develop knowledge of the discipline and 'ways of dealing with a specific object of learning as well as of dealing with the situation itself as social practice' (Doehler, 2002: 24).

In her study of teacher interaction with English as a second language (ESL) students in a science classroom, Gibbons (2003) found that teachers have ways of judging learners' needs and then providing appropriate supports for them. She observed how teachers were moving between students' existing language knowledge (of ESL) and their general knowledge of science. From a micro perspective, the teachers shifted modes through recasting, signalling to learners how to reformulate their responses, indicating the need for reformulation and recontextualising personal knowledge. The teachers often signalled a gap in students' responses either directly or through seeking clarification from them, thereby indicating the need to reframe or revisit their thinking. From a macro perspective, the teachers mediated the educational and disciplinary discourse of science as a school subject particularly through the joint construction of a metalanguage that enabled students to talk about language and about science. She refers to the importance of 'contingency' or the way a teacher judges what is needed to assist a learner to advance his/her understanding. Contingency arises from the shared experiences of teachers and learners and requires the teacher to fully engage with, and interpret, learners' attempts to make meaning. This study highlights the role of teachers as mediators of discourses, their own knowledge and linguistic resources, and the specialised discourse of the educational and discipline-based context. The teacher must navigate between discourses, interpreting both and bringing to bear the appropriate resources from each in order to make sense of, and operate within, the other. Mediation can be understood, therefore, as an assisted transition into new ways of being, of acquiring new knowledge and a new discourse of the discipline.

Language choice

In relation to language teaching, language represents both the medium of instruction and the object of study. In a foreign language classroom, there are at least two languages present (the target language and the students' first language), which raises the question as to which language is used and for what purpose. The role of first language and second or additional languages and the movement between them for both teachers and learners have been studied in bilingual (Cummins & Swain, 1986; Turnbull, 2001) as well as second language contexts (Canagarajah, 1995; Ellis, 1985; Swain & Lapkin, 2000). There is increasing acknowledgement of the value and necessity of using learners' entire linguistic repertoire, including their first language, in the learning of additional languages. A learner's first language can act as a scaffold for learning, such as in assisting comparison of and reflection on linguistic forms and functions. One's first language also acts as a medium for expressing ideas beyond the current linguistic range of the second or foreign languages such as more abstracted concepts and nuanced personal opinions or perspectives. Unstunel and Seedhouse (2005) found that learners' language use typically aligns with that of the teacher and varies according to the pedagogical focus. Learners can also influence which language is used depending on their level of understanding and participation, and their expectations of language learning. Lantolf and Thorne (2006) suggest that there is insufficient understanding of the impact of first language on the internalisation processes associated with learning an additional language. They argue that if one's first language is used as a mediating tool to assist in regulating mental activity then the choice of language for instruction and interaction in the language classroom becomes a major consideration. Hence, language choice and the movement between languages, for both teachers and learners, need to be recognised as powerful mediating resources.

Thus, according to general learning theory, mediation is a process whereby new knowledge is constructed through shared interpsychological (between minds) and intrapsychological (in the mind of the individual) activity. The dialogic nature of mediation means that it necessarily involves language, as related to strategies such as questioning or giving feedback, as discourse practices such as ways of talking about language and as semiotic resource for participating in and creating disciplinary communities.

An Understanding of Mediation for Intercultural Language Teaching and Learning

A concept of mediation that is suitable for intercultural language teaching and learning needs to take account of more than either of these perspectives alone. Understandings of mediation in language teaching, as intercultural or cross-cultural mediation, have focused mainly on the skills of making sense of one language and culture for another. Meanwhile, mediation from a general learning theoretical perspective has focused on mediation as a process of supporting or scaffolding knowledge creation. Neither view is sufficient on its own and instead taken together they create an 'enriched' (Byram, 2013) understanding of mediation that is more appropriate for intercultural language teaching and learning.

It is important to consider the participants in the mediation process. In language teaching and learning, it is the learner who navigates between his/her own language and culture and the unfamiliar, new language and culture. The learner develops skills in moving between the two, building connections between the two linguistic and cultural systems. From a learning theory perspective, it is the 'more knowledgeable other' who mediates new learning for the 'novice'. This 'expert' is typically the teacher who ascertains a learner's needs and provides the necessary supports to enable the learner to construct new knowledge. In this view of mediation, the sense of movement is due to the teacher navigating between a learner's existing knowledge and the new knowledge. Mediation is the process of supporting the learner to build connections between his/her existing and new knowledge. Taken together, these views of mediation both focus on movement and building connections from what is unfamiliar to that which is familiar. In the language classroom, the language teacher is the most significant mediator who simultaneously 'translates' the new language and culture for learners, models being an intercultural mediator and provides ways to support learners to make sense of the 'new' in relation to their existing linguistic and cultural knowledge frames.

Following this, there is a need for an expanded understanding of what is being mediated. In an intercultural mediation sense, what is mediated is a new linguistic and cultural system and the ways of being in a new language and culture as distinct from one's own language and culture. There is an emphasis on acquiring knowledge of linguistic and cultural practices and values that enables the learner to enter into and construct meanings within a new world view. In general learning theory, it is knowledge, particularly discipline-specific knowledge, as well as knowledge of ways to be a learner in a particular discipline, which are mediated. An intercultural language teaching and learning perspective requires both of these understandings as learners acquire discipline-specific knowledge, that is knowledge of the new linguistic and cultural system, and knowledge of how to navigate it in relation to their existing linguistic and cultural system. It also requires knowledge of the discursive practices of belonging to the discipline of language learning, including learning ways of mediating languages and cultures.

In addition, while mediation in language teaching has traditionally assumed a starting point of two different languages and cultures, mediation in general learning theory has not. In considering mediation for an intercultural perspective on language teaching, it is necessary to adopt a multilingual starting point, assuming that mediation occurs *between* at least two languages and cultures, and *through* at least two languages and cultures. As mediation takes place on the social plane, therefore, it may be assumed that more than one language is being used. It will also be the case that within the intrapsychological plane, a learner has more than one linguistic and cultural frame of reference with which to transform his/her existing knowledge. That is, the learner has an expanded linguistic and cultural repertoire, with at least two languages and cultures from which he/she can draw to make sense of and express new realities. When considered in the context of the languages classroom, it may be that a learner's primary linguistic and cultural frame may be different from that used by the teacher and that which other learners bring. Thus, there may be multiple languages and cultures present in language classrooms that create a resource for mediation and learning. Mediation, therefore, can be understood as a macro transformational process in which not only is an individual's knowledge changed through learning a new linguistic and cultural frame of reference but his/her sense of self and identity in the world is also changed, as he/she learns new ways of being themselves within an expanded linguistic and cultural universe.

In attempting to understand mediation in relation to an intercultural perspective on language teaching and learning, it is necessary to expand existing understandings of intercultural mediation within language teaching and draw on views from general learning theory. In doing so, what can be understood as mediation in language teaching is enriched and the complexity and nuance of how language teachers mediate intercultural language learning in practice may be better understood. This kind of understanding is the focus of discussion in the following chapter.

4 Teachers' Ways of Mediating

In the context of the foreign language classroom, mediation is an idea that is under-researched and not well understood. In particular, little is known about how language teachers mediate an intercultural perspective on language teaching and learning. This chapter aims to provide insights into this dimension of language teaching by considering an enriched notion of mediation (as presented in Chapter 3) in relation to the practices of the three teachers in the study. The chapter is organised according to the same sequence of case studies presented in Chapter 2: Collette, Kelly and Maria. For each, the discussion focuses on a series of extracts of classroom practice that provide a sense of the nature and scope of each teacher's mediation practices. The discussion is framed in relation to the key concepts of language, culture and their relationship as a means of considering how mediation may vary depending on each teacher's conceptual understandings of these foundational concepts (as outlined in Chapter 2). The chapter will conclude by outlining connections between the teacher's own linguistic and cultural identity and her ways of mediating an intercultural perspective in language teaching, and furthermore, the extent to which each teacher is aware of such a relationship and its impact on mediation.

Collette's Ways of Mediating

Language

This first extract provides a window into Collette's ways of mediating, with a particular emphasis in this interaction on language as form.

Extract 53: Collette – mediating language (March)

Participant   *Dialogue*
Collette: Just put your (PowerPoint) slide up and I'm going to get other people to have a look at it and tell me what they think and whether they think it's correct.
Terus (go on), Laura. Remember you fix it up if you think there's something not quite right.

(Discussion continues)

Laura: I think what it's supposed to say is, 'He goes to school at 6.30'.

Collette: 'He leaves for school at 6.30'. OK. What's the Indonesian bit that perhaps needs fixing there? If you go to a place, what sort of 'to' are you using? *'Ke'*... [a preposition]

What's this *'tidur siang'* (afternoon nap) business?

Laura: He goes to sleep in the afternoon.

Collette: Is that what you were trying to bring across? OK.

Students: Yes.

Collette: So, *'di rumah saya'* (in my house) *'saya'* (I)... we don't actually need *'punya'* (to have) there. OK. We just *'tidur siang'*, we have an afternoon nap. OK.

Charlotte: This is a bit of a weird question but what time would an Indonesian student usually come home from school?

Collette: That's not a weird question. That's quite fine. Um, usually roughly about 2 o'clock...about then...depending on what school you go to. Most people would go to morning school and then go home, have something to eat and *'tidur siang'*, have a nap while it's really hot and then get up and go on with their routine.

I'll do this next one. *'Kapan saya...'* (When I...?) Oh! Come on girls you can fix this next one for me. Go on fix it... What about the *'Kapan'* (question word for 'When')? What should that be?

Sandra: Oh, *'waktu'* (when, indicator of time).

Collette: You want to say 'when I get home' so the whole thing needs to be done again: When I get home...*pada waktu* (at the time)... I get home...

Sandra: *Waktu saya pulang, saya mengerjakan p.r.* (When I get home, I do homework)

Collette: Pretty common for a student to have to *'mengerjakan p.r.'*. Would you say they've got this one right?

Collette's opening instruction to her students establishes the expectation that grammatical accuracy is a priority, 'look at it...and whether they think it's correct'. There is repeated emphasis on accuracy and repair, 'fix it up' and 'something not quite right', 'needs fixing', 'we don't actually need', 'Go on fix it'. Part way through when a student inquires about routines of the school day, the focus of interaction shifts and Collette provides a brief answer before returning to the focus on structure.

The effect is to emphasise the importance of language as form, with cultural information as a deviation. Collette treats the ideas as somewhat detached from language when her focus is on form and accuracy. Moreover, there is a contrast between how language and ideas are mediated at this point. Language is something to be done; it requires fixing and putting into a complete state. Ideas related to culture, on the other hand, are fluid and discursive. This fluidity is reflected in Collette's use of qualifying statements such as using 'roughly about' to indicate approximation, 'depending on' indicating contextual constraints and adding 'most people' indicating that she is generalising. Her mediation in relation to culture is nuanced, including possibilities and particularising, whereas her mediation of language is more fixed, including closed questions, references to rules and order, and certainty of answers.

Collette appeals to her students, 'Oh! come on girls you can fix this next one for me', thereby shifting the responsibility to them and signalling an inaccuracy to be addressed. She continues to focus on linguistic accuracy by posing questions and inviting students to identify solutions, 'What about…?', 'What should that be?', 'Would you say they've got this one right?'. Here, language is depicted as binary; either correct or incorrect with Collette being the final arbiter of accurate language use. She uses questioning to focus students' attention on particular inaccuracies, 'what about the "*Kapan*"?', and to prompt them to recall grammatical knowledge, 'what sort of "to" are you using?'. She is mediating the language system for her students, presenting it as structural, rule based and largely fixed. She is also mediating students' relationship to the target language, encouraging them to be both performers and analysers of it (Liddicoat & Scarino, 2013).

Culture

Later in the same lesson, as students have viewed a video about daily life in Indonesia, the focus shifts to a discussion of culture.

Extract 54: Collette – mediating culture (March)

Participant	Dialogue
Andrew:	What about *'tidur siang'* (afternoon nap)?
Collette:	What about getting up at different times or going to bed at different times? Would you want to know about the family's

(Discussion continues)

background and beliefs and would you want to share some of yours and then how would you do that?

Andrew: Would you have to take a nap?

Collette: Not necessarily. Society's a little bit more set up around...there are certain times when you've really...like you very often go visiting at 3 o'clock when it's very hot and sticky...you get tired...

Are you guys ready to share? What we'll do is...I actually want you to take this away and think seriously about it. Give some deep thought to it. There might be something you perhaps haven't thought about that somebody else may raise that gets you thinking a bit deeper about these points. So, we'll share what we've got so far. Now remember there isn't really a right answer...this is right and this is wrong. If you're not sure then we can explore it further given your response depending on what you raise some things will be really, really obvious and then there'll be some things that might require a little bit more thought or deeper understanding of Balinese culture or of Indonesia.

(Directs one group to start the sharing of observations)

Emily: The school was walking distance so it was local...and they didn't have much grass because it got burnt and died...by the sun...we think.

Collette: Why wouldn't you have as much grass as here...as much grass?

Suzie: Because there's not much rain.

Andrew: There's tonnes of rain. It's humidity...

Collette: OK. It's humid. Think about land mass, the size of Indonesia. Think about how many people live in Indonesia.

Charlotte: There's no room for grass.

Collette: Yes. Part of it is it's probably hard to maintain beautiful grass. It doesn't suit their climate as much as ours because you've got the dry season for six months and the wet season where you get a lot of rain. But also consider how many people live in Indonesia and the size of Indonesia in comparison with Australia and how many people live here. So, the land that is there is used in a productive kind of way either for housing or what else would you see? Indonesia is a beautiful country when you travel through it. We see fields with Salvation Jane and the yellow daffodil type things when we go for a drive.

(Discussion continues)

Andrew: Those yellow things are canola.

Collette: You guys know what our landscape is like. What's Indonesia's? What would you see in Indonesia?

Charlotte: Would like there be like people walking in the street? It would be quite tight.

Collette: Yes. If you were driving through the countryside what would you expect to see?

Emily: Is there like rice fields?

Collette: Yeah, rice fields. Lots of rice fields. Often terraced for irrigation purposes. So, you don't get as many, I'm not saying you don't get gardens, there's a lot of orchids and things like that and certain tropical trees that suit Indonesian's climate but you don't get your roses and manicured lawns.

Charlotte: Do they grow their own beans and things like that?

Collette: Um. Rice is the staple diet. So, there's a lot of rice grown, sweet corn. Think of tropical foods in certain regions. You'll get cassava or *singkong* (cassava). You'll get potatoes in certain areas too…

Collette depicts culture as behaviours (such as sleeping in the afternoon) and beliefs that are apparent in daily life. She adds caveats to her comments to convey the idea that culture cannot be readily known, 'there isn't really a right answer' and cannot be generalised, 'not necessarily'. She refers to culture as 'serious' with both 'obvious' and less obvious aspects, setting up students' expectations for this kind of learning. As the students report their observations from the film, the teacher probes their thinking, 'Why wouldn't…?', 'think about…'. She prompts students to give a rationale to support their observations and is providing clues about the understanding she wants them to develop. She moves into a comparative frame, the target language culture 'their' and students' Australian culture 'our'. The discussion becomes descriptive and comparative with culture portrayed as facts, 'you've got the dry season for six months…'. Collette is mediating Indonesian culture by inviting students to notice, compare and reflect on what resides beneath the surface manifestations of culture (Lo Bianco, 2003) by comparing knowledge of their own and the new culture. At this point, the view of culture being mediated is one of facts and information (Liddicoat, 2002) related to the physical environment. Collette uses students' own culture as a reference point for making sense of difference, 'You guys know what our landscape is like…'. While she attempts to convey a sense that culture cannot be fully known, she continues to question students until one of them provides the information she is seeking, 'Yeah, rice fields. Lots of rice fields'. Culture is therefore knowable in one sense; there are certain facts that distinguish the target language culture from the Australian culture, 'there's a lot of orchids and things like that and certain tropical trees that suit Indonesian's climate but you don't get your roses and manicured lawns'. She is mediating a sense of Indonesian culture by encouraging students to decentre from their own (Crozet & Liddicoat, 2000; Kramsch, 1999b), sometimes venturing into generalised statements about both, 'Part of it is it's probably hard to maintain beautiful grass'. Collette moves between a general, national sense of Indonesian culture with blanket statements such as 'rice is the staple diet...' and a view of culture as varied, using qualifications such as, 'part of it is...', 'often' and 'I'm not saying...'. She draws connections between aspects within the national culture such as the climate, crops and behaviours, showing an internal logic and coherence to culture. She scaffolds students' understanding by providing a list of examples as a way of conveying a sense of the internal diversity of culture. This extract reveals the challenge for Collette of mediating culture as she uses a range of tools to depict culture as factual, variable and also different to students' own culture. She is also mediating ways that students may know and relate to culture, both Indonesian and their own, primarily as observers (Liddicoat & Scarino, 2013).

Collette reveals a range of mediating devices from the micro to the macro in the following extract.

Extract 55: Collette – mediating culture (September)

Participant	Dialogue
Collette:	When I thought about this the other night... There were several things that I thought 'Ah, I haven't really covered with you'. Like, when you go into an Indonesian house you'll normally take your shoes off. OK. Think about how weather...you'll usually wear slip-on shoes for that reason...saves standing at the door and doing your laces up. There are some certain things if you go into the house of a Moslem you would say *Assalam walaikum* and the people in the house would say *Walaikum salam*.
	There are some things that depending on the region that you're in, there are some things that you'll need to know about

(Discussion continues)

Indonesians that not all Indonesians behave that way or do that and I think that the research that you did on traditional housing will help you to see some of those differences.

(Teacher introduces the small group task)

Talk about it first. The first one is to focus on what you've just seen OK. What does it tell you about housing in Indonesia? Whereabouts? It was in Bali, so specifically Bali that we're talking about in that first one. What did you observe about the housing, the school routine, about religion and the offerings and things like that? How do you think that all connects? So, what did you observe from the film that tells you something about Balinese society?

Then, the next question is 'What are the experiences you have learnt from this topic?'. That we can't simply translate something. There are words like *gayung* (small jug/bucket for washing) which can't translate. What is a *gayung*? You can't just give a one-word translation. If you translate it as one word how many people back here would understand that. So, why is it? What does that say about that whole concept? The *kamar mandi* (bathroom) is one where you need more than one word to explain it. So, that's just a hint about things that are unique to Indonesia and you need to go about explaining what you think.

The next bit is personal reflection. I don't mind if you do a bit of discussion on that. You all researched a house in a different area and that gave you a deeper understanding of an aspect of Indonesian culture. Remember, Indonesia is quite diverse and there are many regions that came together and became Indonesian when the Dutch left and Indonesia declared independence and they all have many cultures and traditions that they brought with them. So, what in the areas that you researched was unique and special? If you go to Indonesia and if you go to...on exchange...in Salatiga...what changes do you think that you're going to have to make? How do you prepare yourself for that? What are you perhaps not going to do and you're going to need to justify that and maybe make sure that you fitted in and feel comfortable and take some of your culture with you and share that? So, what would you take from here?

(Discussion continues)

(Students continue working on task)
What is it that you think you would need to prepare someone coming here? What would they need to know to fit in to Adelaide and go to school at (name of school)? Do you think there'll be any differences and if so, what? And one thing I've put in there is, you know, how would you be culturally sensitive? And I was going to give you an example of that. There was an exchange student last year who an Australian girl hosted. She was a lovely, cooperative, good person, had no problems with her as a student, very nice person, very nice family willing to host someone. And, when they actually had someone to host, they had an Indonesian male and part way through she came to me and said, 'You know, we're having a few problems'. And there were some issues that came up and one of them was she felt, and her mum felt, and her brother felt, that this exchange student was lazy because he didn't take the dishes out to the sink. He didn't offer to do a thing and you know from my point of view, when I went to Indonesia, I'd lived in a house where I did have to, you know, Mum and Dad said you have to clean up your room, do the dishes and things like that. That was a normal routine in our family and when I went to Indonesia it was not normal for people to expect me to do that in their house. I was a guest. They didn't expect that I would do those tasks because I was a guest. They thought you're here for a short time. We'd feel ashamed if we asked you to do the dishes. So, there's a difference of culture. It doesn't mean that the exchange student was lazy by no means. They didn't realise that was an expectation.

Collette begins by signalling to students a gap that she perceives in their knowledge, 'there were several things...I haven't really covered with you'. She then provides factual information about social norms or behaviours related to housing such as 'certain things...you would say'. Her statements are moderated with 'normally' and 'usually', reflecting a sense of variability of culture according to place, 'depending on the region', 'Whereabouts? It was in Bali, so specifically Bali' and people, 'not all Indonesians behave that way'. She invites students to notice behaviours that are different from their own and reflect on their own. She frequently moves between the general, framed as facts, and the particular, using examples from her own experience to mediate a sense of culture as both national and differential (Risager, 2007). Collette uses an example of a cultural artefact, a *'gayung'* (small jug/bucket for washing), to highlight a relationship between language and culture and the difficulty of equivalence across languages and cultures, which she explicitly states as, 'we can't simply translate something…', 'how many people back here would understand that'. She uses declarative statements such as 'Indonesia is quite diverse and there are many regions that came together…the Dutch…many cultures and traditions', to foreground the variability of Indonesian culture. She invites students to comment on aspects of Indonesian culture that are 'unique and special', thereby positioning it as divergent and somewhat exotic.

During this extract, a key theme emerges that becomes a recurrent mediating tool for Collette. She introduces the notion of 'fitting in', initially by problematising the process of intercultural experience, 'What changes do you think that you're going to have to make?'. She mediates Indonesian culture through positioning students in an imagined scenario of an intercultural encounter, and inviting them to reflect on their intracultural identity (Papademetre, 2005), 'What are you perhaps not going to do… to justify that', 'make sure that you fitted in and feel comfortable'. Collette mediates the concept of interculturality, encouraging students to consider the process of transformation, 'take some of your culture with you and share that'. She knows her students and their limited knowledge of intercultural experience, and therefore uses anecdotes to exemplify the adjustments that may be needed, 'When I went to Indonesia, I'd lived in a house where…'. She reassures students about the reasonable nature of the host student by characterising her as a 'lovely, cooperative, good person'. She then points out the source of discomfort due to differing cultural norms, 'they didn't realise that was an expectation'. Collette uses her theme of 'fitting in' as a mediating device, connecting her macro discourse, questions and narratives (Donato, 2000; Van Lier, 2000) to it as a framework for considering intercultural experience, and positioning students in the role of participants in diversity. She is mediating through offering her own identity and experiences as a way of inviting students to observe and make sense of the target culture in the absence of their own lived experience of it.

The relationship between language and culture

This final extract reveals how Collette mediates a relationship between language and culture, arising from a student's question about a single word.

Extract 56: Collette – mediating language and culture (June)

Participant	Dialogue
Jodie:	Miss, what's the word for 'singlet'?
Collette:	I think it's just a *baju kaus*. The reason I don't ...that I've got to really think about that is because a singlet in Indonesia is not something you'd walk around in. It would be a bit...
Jodie:	But what would you say for it then?
Collette:	Guys, that's another really good question. See this picture here OK some things when you translate...when you ask me something I have to think long and hard about. It was like the woollen jumper...*baju wol*...you can say...but you really don't very often walk around Indonesia in a big woolly jumper because it's too hot. This is another classic example...you would not walk around Indonesia like this because you wouldn't want to send...If you were in Bali in Kuta Beach and there's hundreds of tourists sitting around you may choose to be dressed a bit more what I would call ultra-informal in Indonesia OK. And if you're in the privacy of your own home and there was no one else around then possibly but you wouldn't want to send this message to an Indonesian by walking around like this and why wouldn't you?
Charlotte:	Like in Hong Kong I walked around in shorts and then everyone looked at me funny.
Collette:	And what ...then what message do you think you were sending?
Charlotte:	Um, I'm a prostitute?
Collette:	Well, possibly that you're fairly carefree with your values. And why?
Charlotte:	Um, because they don't wear shorts.
Collette:	When you go to Indonesia you've got to think about that and think about if you're getting a certain reaction because of your appearance and you're not happy with that reaction then what do you need to do?
Charlotte:	Don't go outside in shorts.

(Discussion continues)

Collette: Yeah, because you're actually sort of...and I'm not saying if I was in Indo I'd never wear something like that but I would never walk outside in Indonesia because the message I'm sending is that this really isn't...an Indonesian person, a male in Indonesia or even a female, would be quite embarrassed about where to look because you're revealing...that's like you're in Australia coming to school in a top where every time... like if I was a teacher and I leaned over and every time you saw everything, you wouldn't really know where to look. That's the kind of message you're sending. OK. So, that's why I have trouble translating this because in a way it is a *baju kaus* because I don't think they've got a special word for 'tank top' or loose top. To an Indonesian it is probably like wearing a bra.

What initially appears to be unproblematic (i.e. a word-for-word equivalence, the word for 'singlet' is *baju kaus*) becomes a trigger for explaining the relationship between language and culture. Collette declares a difficulty in a direct translation approach, 'I've got to really think about that', 'I have to think long and hard'. She draws on an example to mediate the idea of non-equivalence in language due to differences in cultural norms, 'See this picture here', 'you would not walk around Indonesia like this'. The picture becomes a mediating device to highlight cultural sensibilities embedded in language. She constructs a hypothetical situation, 'if you were in Bali', in order to approximate an intercultural encounter. Her scenarios are mediating tools designed to locate students as close as possible to an intercultural experience. She poses a question to gauge their understanding of the cultural sensibility she is trying to convey, 'why wouldn't you (walk around in a singlet)?'. Collette also invites students to decentre and notice their own cultural sensibilities, '(if) I leaned over and every time you saw everything...', 'it is probably like wearing a bra'. She is scaffolding students' understanding by using equivalent norms within their own cultural context. She draws attention to the problem she is experiencing, 'that's why I have trouble translating this...I don't think they've got a special word for tank top', but it remains at the level of description and she does not explicitly state that non-equivalence is an inherent feature of language and culture. Collette is attempting to 'translate' intercultural experience and cultural values for her students through highlighting an interdependence between language and culture at the level of a word.

These extracts reveal ways in which Collette mediates language, culture, their relationship and intercultural experience for her students. In relation to language, she mediates by attending to form and grammar such as through direct questioning and explanation. In relation to culture, Collette uses two key devices: decentring (by noticing, comparing and reflecting) and the macro theme 'fitting in'. She mediates, somewhat incidentally, a relationship between language and culture as that of 'culture-in-language', by unpacking cultural meanings in words. Identity also forms part of Collette's mediating repertoire as she draws on her life experiences as an overall frame and as content for teaching. She identifies examples from students' own cultural context to create points of connection to enable students to make sense of the unfamiliar culture, and she extends their knowledge of cultural contexts by creating imagined scenarios in which they consider their own reactions.

Kelly's Ways of Mediating

Language

In this first extract, Kelly invites her students to notice and analyse language in an authentic text, a letter to the editor of a teenage magazine.

Extract 57: Kelly – mediating language (July)

Participant	Dialogue
Kelly:	Who can have an idea of what's being asked in this letter to the editor? You don't have to have word-for-word perfect but even if there are some words in the texts that you can remember from last term or when we did the food unit. OK. Just have a quick look at the vocab words and a quick look at the text.
Sandra:	Something about fried chicken and KFC.
Kelly:	OK. So fried chicken and KFC. What else? Is there anything else you can pick up?
Rose:	Something about the skin of the chicken.
Kelly:	Yes, something about how it's cooked. What else?
Rose:	It's asking a lot of questions.
Kelly:	Yes, it is asking a lot of questions there.
Shannon:	That KFC and McDonald's are junk food.

(Discussion continues)

Kelly: Yes, it's asking whether KFC and McDonald's can be seen as junk food. You've got the main idea so that's a good thing. I'll just read to you briefly in English, in a roundabout way, what it means. Now, *tanya* (to ask) is not the name of the person. It is the person asking the question. *'Penasu yang terhormat'* now I'm not sure whether this is the correct translation but in the dictionary it had *penasu* as guardian or caretakers so I wasn't sure … but it's basically to a person who is respected within that newspaper who is writing a column.
(Teacher translates the passage into English)
So, they're just seeking clarification of what 'junk food' means.

Rose: That's a lot of words just for that.

Kelly: That's just the main ideas coming from that text. So, let's have a bit of a brainstorm. We'll do this in English for the moment and then I'll hand out the article. What are some of the main issues if you were the person reading that? How would you respond? What do you think about it? Rose?

Rose: Well, the difference is that with McDonald's and that, you don't know what chemicals they're putting into it… Like, for money, so that you go back for more. Whereas if you cook it at home you know exactly what's gone into it.

Kelly: Yeah, so you don't know whether they're putting extra preservatives and flavourings in the food to make you, not addicted, but like the food so you keep going back to try it.

Rose: Like so much salt on the chips so that you buy more drinks.

Kelly: Yep, because you get thirsty. So, they're using other ways to get you to buy other food.
I want to start linking in some of the language related to the topic. OK, and one thing I'd like you to do for homework tonight is go over this and the handouts I've given you so that some of the language you start to try and remember so that it's useful for Wednesday. So, these are the main issues, *isu-isu utama*. The main issues that emerged from the article. What I'll do just to save a bit of time is I'll get one of you just to read the sentence in Indonesian and then I'll say what it means in English and then you can write either above it or underneath in the space below what it means.

(Discussion continues)

Toby:	Why don't you just tell us what it means and we don't have to read it?
Kelly:	Well, because then you can practise your pronunciation as well. OK.

The sequence begins with the teacher inviting students to read for gist, 'Who can have an idea…?' and reassuring them that accuracy is not the main concern, '(not) word-for-word perfect'. At this early stage, Kelly is creating a culture of language learning that focuses on language for meaning. She encourages students to look for familiar words, 'vocab words', as a way of drawing on their existing knowledge as a basis for new knowledge, 'anything else you can pick up?'. She affirms students' responses and continues to question until they move from single words to broader meanings, 'main issues'. Kelly is mediating language by inviting points of connection with it, including asking for opinions about it. She models language use through reading aloud parts of the passage. Then there is a noticeable shift in Kelly's approach as she offers an English translation of the text, 'I'll just read to you briefly in English…what it means'. She uses students' first language (English) as a scaffold; however, by using it in this way, Kelly privileges it as the main vehicle for making meaning and at the same time implies that there is a singular interpretation of language, 'I'm not sure whether this is the correct translation'. The original emphasis on reading for gist has become a focus on accurate decoding and when Kelly invites personal opinions about the ideas in the text, the discussion moves away from the text. Kelly is mediating the target language by using English as an alternate code for making meaning; a code that she considers more expedient, 'to save a bit of time', and more readily available as a resource for learning, 'We'll do this in English for the moment', 'I'll just say what it means in English and then you can write… what it means'. When one student, Toby, challenges her about the need to read the Indonesian when she is providing the meaning in English, Kelly tries to justify her request in terms of the benefits of pronunciation practice. In trying to mediate the target language through analysis of an authentic text, Kelly has disconnected Indonesian from meaning and has instead reinforced the idea that Indonesian is a code whose meaning is only understood through the code of English.

In the following interaction, Kelly has asked students to use Indonesian to describe their local area, during which she attempts to mediate the new language and culture in relation to the students' existing language and culture.

Extract 58: Kelly – mediating language (April)

Participant	Dialogue
Tammy:	That's pathetic because there's nothing in my street.
Kelly:	Well, you can say that. You just said to me earlier that your neighbours get up early and feed their horses. So, you can say something like that. You can say *'jalan saya sangat sepi'* (My street is very quiet).
Toby:	How do you say 'dead'?
Kelly:	Just say *'lebih sepi'* (quieter), 'it's very quiet'.
Toby:	But there's nothing.
Kelly:	Well, then you can say *'tidak ada orang di jalan saya'*. There are no people in my street.
Toby:	Or 'dead'!
Kelly:	Toby, the thing is Indonesians wouldn't say a 'dead' street. They'd just say it's either quiet or...
Toby:	I'm not Indonesian.
Kelly:	No, but we're doing Indonesian and you've got to think in Indonesian when you're writing.

The initial emphasis in this interaction is on communicating in the target language. When one student asks, 'How do you say "dead"?', the teacher responds with an attempt at equivalence, 'just say *"lebih sepi"* (more quiet)'. The student is not satisfied, however, as he understands that it does not represent his sense of 'dead'. As someone who herself grew up in the local area, Kelly understands the sense of space and isolation that the student wishes to convey and she attempts to provide an alternative expression to move closer to his meaning. When this is unsuccessful, she moves into explanatory mode, 'Indonesians wouldn't say a "dead" street', signalling that there are differences in cultural perspectives between the target language and the student's own. He perceives her response as wanting him to 'be' Indonesian, which he rejects, 'I'm not Indonesian'. She reminds him that learning a new language involves new ways of thinking, 'you've got to think in Indonesian', signalling that language is related to thought and that using Indonesian involves navigating a new world view (Kramsch, 2004b). Kelly is attempting to use Indonesian as a vehicle through which students can communicate aspects of their identities, lives and world. When the target language does not adequately address the student's communicative needs or cultural context, Kelly gives alternative expressions in Indonesian and also uses English to try to develop the student's awareness of the culturally bound nature of language.

Kelly's primary mediation strategy in relation to language is that of forming equivalence in meaning between Indonesian and English. Initially, Kelly constructs Indonesian as a different code, thereby creating a relationship between the students and the target language as that of codebreakers. Later, she begins to position students as discoverers of meaning, albeit largely predetermined meaning, located in target language words and texts. Kelly's primary tool for mediating between the familiar and the unfamiliar is English. She uses English for discussion, description, comparison and explanation. English represents an alternative code in terms of form and the primary code in terms of meaning. Apart from explicit mediating practices, Kelly also mediates ways of being an intercultural mediator through her own use of Indonesian. She refers to knowing and memorising words, reading for meaning beyond words, and she models how to be a codebreaker and translate between languages and cultures. In these ways, she is mediating a sense of the relationship that one might have with a new language and culture.

Culture

In the following extract, Kelly uses a number of ways to mediate the concept of culture as different practices and values, particularly through positioning students as analysers of culture, including their own.

Extract 59: Kelly – mediating culture (March)

Participant	Dialogue
Kelly:	(Following a brainstorming activity about significant places in the city of Adelaide)
	Let's think about why these places are important and why an Indonesian may want to visit them. Think back to why it was important to learn about Indonesian places of interest. Do you think any of them are the same as our well-known places or why we should study about them here?
Rose:	Well, it's part of our history and part of our culture.
Kelly:	Who can remember the word for history? It started with an 's'. *Sejarah.* So, we should study about well-known places because it tells us information about our past. What other reasons do you think we should study about these places? Now, all of you

(Discussion continues)

would have done the (local winemakers) study tour in Year 9. Why do you think you were sent there to go on an excursion?

Rose: To learn about the German heritage.

Kelly: Yes, the German heritage. And learning about wine techniques. That tells us about our past and our heritage. What other reasons? What do you think Logan? Why should we study about well-known places in Indonesia?

Logan: So it can help you learn about the culture.

Kelly: It helps you learn more about the culture. Who can remember the word for culture? (pauses) *Kebudayaan.*

Shannon: It's a long word.

Kelly: So we are able to learn a different way of life. How people live differently than the way we live. Why they do certain things compared to the way we do them?

Rose: It can be like um how Adelaide is identified.

Kelly: Yeah, so it can be how Adelaide is identified as a state, as a capital city.
Identitas. Besides history, identity and culture is there anything else?

Simon: Religion.

Kelly: Religion. Who can remember about religion? Who knows the word for religion? It starts with an 'a'.

Nina: *Agama*

Kelly: *Agama*, thanks Nina. Who can think of any places related to religion?

Simon: The churches.

Kelly: Yes, the churches. We can also say there are mosques... (describes various places). Can we be a bit more specific and give examples of places and how they link to *identitas*, our culture and our religion?
Why do you think people visiting the Barossa Valley is important?

Rose: We've got a lot of famous wines.

Kelly: Australians are more likely to go to the Barossa Valley because they know there's good wine produce there and they can sample different types of foods as well. This sort of links up

(Discussion continues)

to our next question as well. If you were an Indonesian person would you be more likely to go to the Barossa Valley than not want to go?

Rose: It would depend on how much history that they know about South Australia.

Kelly: So, it depends on the Indonesian person's knowledge or interest in South Australia.

Nina: They might not know about it but they might go there and think I'll learn all about it and they might taste some wine and buy some wine.

Kelly: So, OK. Think a little bit about Indonesian culture and think more about their way of life and the majority of Indonesians. What is the main religion of Indonesia?

Several students: Moslem.

Kelly: Moslem. And what's part of the religion?

Joanne: They don't drink.

Kelly: They don't drink. The majority of Moslems wouldn't drink alcohol. So, do you think if a Moslem person were to come to South Australia, would they be more inclined to go to the Barossa Valley or to Kangaroo Island?

Several students: Kangaroo Island

Nina: The Barossa

Kelly: Why do you still say the Barossa Valley? Why do you think that?

Nina: Just because they can't drink doesn't mean they couldn't try it to see if they liked it.

Kelly: Guys, if that's their religion and they were brought up respecting the beliefs ...the pillars of Islam, why would you then go against that?

Nina: You have to do something...like you can't just stay that person all of your life. You have to take risks. You have to do stuff.

Joanne: They might still go to the Barossa for other things not just for the wineries or not even just go for the wine.

(Discussion continues)

Kelly: Indonesians who come to Australia may just come and visit the Barossa Valley just to see what it looks like and other places of interest in that area than the wineries. So, can you see now how you've got to think about culture and religion when you think about what places people are more inclined to go to? If... we've said that we have got a lot of churches. If you were a Moslem person, would you be more inclined to go and visit a church or would you go somewhere else like would you try to find a mosque or a *mesjid* and look at how it's structured and its architecture in Adelaide?

Nina: Well, we're still Catholics or Christians and when we go to Indonesia we still go to their mosques. It's pretty much the same thing.

Kelly: I just want you to be aware that you have to think a bit more about the culture and the background rather than just saying it's a well-known place and everyone would want to go there because that may not be the case.

Kelly opens the exchange with a series of broad, open-ended questions inviting students to consider the cultural significance of local places. She responds by echoing students' comments, 'Yes, the German heritage' and reinforcing their value by paraphrasing them. She also states the idea in her own terms, 'information about our past' and then continues to invite other responses. When there are no responses, Kelly turns to the shared experience of a previous excursion as a way of tapping into students' experiences. The same student responds with the notion of 'heritage' and Kelly restates the point and invites more comments, signalling that the responses thus far are not quite sufficient. When a student responds with 'learn about the culture', Kelly confirms, then labels it with the Indonesian term, *'kebudayaan'*. This sequence reflects a pattern that she uses which begins with a broad question, followed by restating and sometimes expressing the student's response in simple terms, labelling the idea with an Indonesian word and then seeking further responses, 'Any other reasons?'. She tries to focus the discussion through inviting tangible examples, 'Can we be a bit more specific and give examples?'. She is attempting to ground what is a somewhat generalised discussion in more specific cultural facts and experiences familiar to her students; she is probing for points of connection. Her labelling of key ideas using

Indonesian is an attempt to retain a focus on language within a discussion conducted in English about culture. In fact, when one student observes the form of a word, 'It's a long word', this reflects the emphasis that Kelly has created on words as labels but the comment goes unexplored as a possible mediatory moment.

As the interaction proceeds, Kelly shapes the relationship between her students and language and culture, Indonesian and their own. She encourages them to adopt an 'outsider' perspective on their own culture by considering Indonesian visitors' interests in visiting local sites. Kelly prompts students, 'think a little bit about Indonesian culture…their way of life…' and follows this with a more targeted questions, 'What is the main religion of Indonesia?'. She moves to a more generalised view, 'The majority of Moslems wouldn't drink alcohol' and then tries to position students as cultural insiders, 'If you were a Moslem…' as she attempts to show connections between religion and attitudes. When one student, Nina, gives the 'wrong' answer, Kelly appeals to them, 'Guys, if that's their religion… why would you then go against that?'. She is challenging their understanding through questioning their assumptions, but she does not connect with their cultural framework that values risk taking. Later, she acknowledges students' views, albeit labelling these unlikely, and then states her intention to make them 'think a bit more' about their own culture. She is inviting them to decentre, but is unsure how to manage their differing views and their own cultural values that emerge as they are asked to adopt a new position. Kelly is mediating on a number of levels during this exchange; moving between abstract ideas and concrete experiences, using English for discussion and Indonesian for labelling key concepts, and moving between generalised and personal views, all the while encouraging students to decentre and expand their world view.

The relationship between language and culture

Part way through the study, Kelly develops a text analysis task for her students as a way of encouraging them to become analysers of language and culture.

Extract 60: Kelly – mediating language and culture (July)

Participant	Dialogue
Kelly:	Just pick up little word or words that you can recognise and see if you can work out the purpose of the ad just from

(Discussion continues)

recognising those few words. But I'm not expecting you to understand everything.

[Teacher leaves the room]

Jim: *Kopi susu.* (White coffee) *Kapal api.* (Steamship)

Anna: *Kopi susu.* That's something to do with coffee.

Jim: A white coffee.

Anna: So, it's like an instant white coffee.

[Teacher re-enters the room]

Casey: Delicious. Is that *enak?*

Kelly: Yeah. So, *jelas lebih enak...*(clearly more delicious). What do you think that might be? Are you looking up all the words and then...?

Anna: Problem solving!

Kelly: So, I'd write that down *jelas lebih enak* and write what you think it means also. So, you guys have done really well just by guessing and seeing what you can pick up.

Jim: We picked up it was white coffee after seeing *kopi susu.*

Anna: We guessed like instant white coffee.

Kelly: Or evidently more delicious I suppose you could say.

Me: Why would they be promoting white coffee?

Kelly: Think about in Australia our diets with white coffee and other milk-related products and think about how there's a big concern especially for young women and elderly women about not having enough milk in their diet.

Jim: Would it be because they've got an aging population like us and they want to get more calcium in their diets?

Kelly: OK, you're on the right track. Why would you think they'd be advertising a product that's got milk in it? Think about the Indonesian diet.

Jim: Because they don't have a lot of milk when you look at it. They only have buffaloes. They didn't have dairy cattle ever and I don't think they do.

Kelly: They have them there for the food like for the meat. They don't really have them there for...

Jim: They don't give good meat...beef cattle are disgusting.

Kelly: They have a lot of goat milk as well.

Me: What's most of their land used to produce?

(Discussion continues)

Anna & Jim:	Rice.
Kelly:	And tea as well. And also because Indonesians don't have a high dairy...like...a lot of dairy products in their diets as well. So, putting I guess powdered milk...that's what it really is... in their coffee products it's basically encouraging Indonesians to drink it because it's...
Anna:	Because it's a source of calcium.
Jim:	Oh, OK. [The group views the next advertisement.]
Kelly:	OK. So, it's in English. So, why do you think they're using English?
Anna:	'Cause probably the younger population know a lot more English than the older people and this would be appealing to the younger people it being a cleanser ...
Kelly:	So, just moving on from that the younger people are more inclined to understand English but how do you think that...?
Jim:	Would it be more 'cool' because it's advertised in English so it's a Western product?
Kelly:	OK. So, it's a Western product. So, what do you think...?
Anna:	It would be more appealing.
Kelly:	So, what do you think that's telling us about Indonesian society? What do you think they would consider more powerful for the youth whether it's an ad done in English or an ad done in Indonesian?
Anna:	They think like they're becoming more and more westernised so it's more appealing because it's from somewhere else and it's not an Indonesian-based product.
Jim:	We've already seen that with the 'No. 1 in America'.
Anna:	Yeah. Like the Wrigley's ad it says 'No. 1 in America'.
Jim:	You wouldn't mention that now on an Australian ad or a British one or possibly even most of the European countries; that it's number one in America. You certainly wouldn't mention it in the Arab world.
Anna:	Because it's...um...it's westernised.
Kelly:	So, you're saying people are more influenced by the West to change their lifestyles.

(Discussion continues)

Anna:	Because it's from a completely different place, it's more appealing because it's foreign.
Kelly:	Exotic maybe. Something different.
Anna:	Yeah, something completely different.

Kelly's initial emphasis is on encouraging students to notice familiar language and text features, 'Just pick up little word or words that you can recognise and see if you can work out the purpose'. The students proceed to decipher the meaning using a dictionary and visual clues. Kelly confirms their translation and reminds them to note it for later discussion, 'write what you think it means also'. She uses writing as a scaffold to allow time and space for students to process their understanding. Then, Kelly prompts students to reflect on their own culture, 'Think about... our diets... having enough milk' as a way to connect to the meaning and purpose of the text. She uses feedback to reassure a student saying, 'You're on the right track', and then directs them to reflect more deeply, 'Think about...'. When the suggestion does not elicit the answer she expects, she provides her interpretation, 'it's basically encouraging Indonesians to drink it...'. The discussion shifts to the next text and the influence of English on Indonesian, with Kelly probing students' interpretations throughout, 'Why do you think...?'. She then asks directly about the connection between language and culture, 'What do you think that's telling us about Indonesian society?'. Her next question is a leading one designed to make students adopt one position or the other, which they do and then they extend the discussion to other examples. Jim takes the connection further to other cultural contexts, 'the Arab world' and Kelly acknowledges his statement and abstracts it further, checking his understanding by saying, 'So, you're saying...' and then paraphrasing his comment. She closes the interaction by confirming their line of reasoning, 'Exotic maybe. Something different', and providing terms to assist them articulate their views, which is echoed by Anna, 'Yeah, something completely different'. Kelly is using the target language as a resource for exploring the relationship between language and culture. She uses English as the medium for mediating new knowledge, with recurring questions designed to probe and extend students' interpretations and encourage them to justify their views.

There are a series of phases to Kelly's mediation in this interaction. The focus initially is on predicting meaning, 'What do you think that might be?', 'guessing and seeing what you can pick up'. After this noticing phase, Kelly prompts students with a comparison to their own culture, 'Think about in Australia our diets with white coffee...'. She is encouraging students to make connections (Liddicoat *et al.*, 2003) by reflecting on their own culture. The interaction moves to an explanatory and reasoning phase, 'Why do you think they're using English?'. Kelly is explicitly using processes of noticing, analysing, comparing and interpreting language for cultural meanings (Liddicoat & Scarino, 2013). She is creating a discourse of how to be an analyser of the target language with its embedded cultural references. She is simultaneously scaffolding students' understanding of the particular text and mediating how to be a language learner, and how to understand the relationship between language and culture.

The series of extracts show Kelly's ways of mediating and her emerging pedagogy as she develops her understanding of an intercultural perspective in language teaching. When Kelly focuses on the target language, her main mediation process is that of translation and positioning students as codebreakers. During the study, her emphasis changes somewhat and she invites students to engage with texts for meaning and she encourages interpretation. In relation to culture, Kelly initially uses English as the primary mediation tool, discussing aspects of culture with some comparison to students' own cultural realities. She extends the focus on comparison and decentring later in the study through using text analysis to unpack cultural meanings in language. Through her own modelling, Kelly also mediates ways of relating to language and culture, initially as a codebreaker and observer, and later also as an analyser and interpreter.

Maria's Ways of Mediating

Language

The following extract reveals how Maria uses the target language as a means of communicating, as she encourages her students to use Indonesian to perform a spontaneous role play of meeting a friend at the bus stop.

Extract 61: Maria – mediating language (March)

Participant	Dialogue
Mark:	*Anda tidak berubah Phung.*
Phung:	*Dan Anda juga.*
Jaxson:	*Mengapa lama sekali kita bertemu?*
Mark:	*Saya gagal kelas sebelas.*
Jaxson:	*Tentu saja.....Saya bercanda saja.*

(Discussion continues)

Maria:	OK, so now you've done the small talk.
Jaxson:	*Mau ikut ke Mount Gambier? Berjalan-jalan.*
Mark:	*Oh ya.*
Jaxson:	What's the word for 'bring'?
Maria:	*Membawa.*
Jaxson:	*Membawa air.*
Mark:	*Jam berapa bertemu besok? Jam setengah tujuh?*
Jaxson:	*Jam dua.*
Mark:	*OK. Jam dua. Sampai besok.* Oh, that was the worst unscripted dialogue I've done.
Maria:	OK, so now you go home and tell Mum and Dad 'I've seen an old friend from school'.
Mark:	*Bagaimana hari ibu?*
Jaxson:	*Oh, baik.*
Maria:	Oh, that's nice, asking about Mum's day. Now Jaxson tell him…
Jaxson:	Wait, wait. That's what I'm about to say. *Saya memasak makan malam.*
Maria:	How stereotypical is this! There are Indonesian mothers who…
Jaxson:	I'm in Australia.
Maria:	OK, she's Australian now. (The conversation continues)
Jaxson:	*Kamar tidur Mark sudah bersih.*
Mark:	*Terima kasih ibu. Oh, kami bertemu dengan teman-teman dari sekolah dasar hari ini di tempat bis.*
Jaxson:	*Oh, siapa?*
Mark:	*Teman-teman kami namanya…*
Maria:	Now Phung, get up and play Dad. Quickly.
Jaxson:	*Mengapa …sudah…Sudah lama tidak bertemu, mengapa?*
Mark:	*Karena, dia bersekolah di Saint Andrew's sekarang.*
Maria:	Now, tell Mum there's a plan at the weekend. We're in Australia aren't we?
Mark:	*Ya. Boleh saya pergi ke danau hari Minggu dengan teman-teman dari Sekolah Dasar?*
Jaxson & **Phung:**	No!

(Discussion continues)

Mark: *Mengapa?*
Maria: Now, tell him 'You haven't cleaned your room or done your homework'. This sounds like an Australian household.
Jaxson: *Kamu belum membersihkan kamar dan mengerjakan P.R.*
Mark: *Saya tidak cinta Anda!*
Maria: Oh, boys. This is supposed to be serious. Come on.
Jaxson: We're a dysfunctional family. (All laugh)
Maria: It's interesting when you have to use the language in everyday circumstances you realise you lack that spontaneity. Me too! But you were using imperatives, *'boleh'* requests. You used the formal, leaving the jokes aside. There comes into it lots of cultural issues too. Are we in Australia? Would it be different in Indonesia? Why would it be *Ibu* home or would it be *Bapak* or would there be anyone?

Translation

Mark: You haven't changed Phung.
Phung: Nor have you.
Jaxson: Why is it so long since we've met?
Mark: I failed Year 11.
Jaxson: Of course...I'm just joking.
Maria: OK, so now you've done the small talk.
Jaxson: Do you want to come to Mount Gambier? To hang out.
Mark: Oh yeah.
Jaxson: What's the word for 'bring'?
Maria: Bring.
Jaxson: Bring some water.
Mark: What time shall we meet tomorrow? Half past six?
Jaxson: Two o'clock.
Mark: OK. Two o'clock. See you tomorrow. Oh, that was the worst unscripted dialogue I've done.
Maria: OK, so now you go home and tell Mum and Dad 'I've seen an old friend from school'.
Mark: How was your day Mum?
Jaxson: Oh, good.

(Discussion continues)

Maria:	Oh, that's nice, asking about Mum's day. Now Jaxson, tell him…
Jaxson:	Wait, wait. That's what I'm about to say. I'm cooking dinner.
Maria:	How stereotypical is this! There are Indonesian mothers who…
Jaxson:	I'm in Australia.
Maria:	OK, she's Australian now. (The conversation continues)
Jaxson:	Your bedroom has been cleaned Mark.
Mark:	Thanks Mum. Oh, we met up with some friends from primary school today at the bus stop.
Jaxson:	Oh, who?
Mark:	Their names are…
Maria:	Now Phung, get up and play Dad. Quickly.
Jaxson:	Why …haven't…Why haven't you seen them for a long time?
Mark:	Because he's going to school at St Andrew's now.
Maria:	Now, tell Mum there's a plan at the weekend. We're in Australia aren't we?
Mark:	Yeah. Can I go to the lake on Sunday with them?
Jaxson & Phung:	No!
Mark:	Why?
Maria:	Now, tell him 'You haven't cleaned your room or done your homework'. This sounds like an Australian household.
Jaxson:	You haven't cleaned your room or done your homework.
Mark:	I don't love you! (All laugh)
Maria:	Oh, boys. This is supposed to be serious. Come on.
Jaxson:	We're a dysfunctional family. (All laugh)
Maria:	It's interesting when you have to use the language in everyday circumstances you realise you lack that spontaneity. Me too! But you were using imperatives, 'may I' requests. You used the formal, leaving the jokes aside. There comes into it lots of cultural issues too. Are we in Australia? Would it be different in Indonesia? Why would it be Mum home or would it be Dad or would there be anyone?

The initial part of this conversation involves students using Indonesian by drawing on the model used in the previous lesson; they are experimenting with memory and expression. The students use the language to make their own jokes, '*Saya bercanda saja*' (I'm just joking), exerting their individuality on the task and using Indonesian for self-expression. Maria interjects occasionally to remind them of the trajectory of the conversation, providing suggestions or words in Indonesian in order to keep the flow and focus of the interaction. When Jaxson plays out the role of 'mother cooking dinner', Maria derides his comment saying, 'How stereotypical is this!' assuming he is operating in an Indonesian context. The student takes issue with this, declaring that he has assumed an Australian context. Maria has assumed that the use of Indonesian is aligned with Indonesia; a national paradigm view. Realising that differing assumptions have been made, she clarifies and confirms the context by saying 'We're in Australia aren't we?'. Maria has not recognised her students' own realities and has assumed that using the target language requires students to be 'other' than themselves. This is in part due to the nature of the task that builds on a previous text and therefore Maria has assumed the same context applies. It is also related to communicative language teaching that assumes a native speaker norm and context. Her students, however, are performing their own multilingual identities, using Indonesian to be themselves within their immediate context, and not in this moment perceiving a difference between themselves and the 'other' (i Sole, 2013).

Throughout the conversation, Maria mediates students' knowledge and use of Indonesian, offering support by providing an unknown word and at various times prompting students, 'Now Phung, get up and play Dad. Quickly', enabling them to maintain the conversation. She marks the different phases of the conversation, 'now you've done the small talk', and intersperses her opinion and feedback on its progress, 'Oh, that's nice, asking about Mum's day'. She draws the interaction to a close by directing the turn, 'Now, tell him, "You haven't cleaned your room..."' and then appealing to them, while joining in their laughter and admitting that the conversation has gone astray, 'Oh boys, this is supposed to be serious'. Maria is mediating a way of being a language user, initially assuming an Indonesian context and then adjusting her assumptions and recognising learners' assumptions. She positions Indonesian as a language for communication, albeit somewhat contrived, and supports students to maintain the interaction through offering words, directions and feedback to guide them. She joins in with the students' humour, recognising that they have adapted the task to their own frame of reference, and thereby endorsing their personalising of the target language to express their own meanings.

Culture

Maria uses a range of devices to mediate a view of culture within an overall comparative perspective, drawing connections with students' own cultural frames.

Extract 62: Maria – mediating culture (August)

Participant	Dialogue
Maria:	What would we put alongside here? Freedom of press, media. What about in Indonesia? Or here? (She points to the centre of a Venn diagram)
Jaxson:	Indonesia tends to be stricter.
Maria:	Stricter laws, policies on *apa* (what)?
Jaxson:	It's too broad to narrow it down.
Maria:	*Ya*, OK. On media? What issues...? How did you come up with this? What impressions...what led you to believe ...to come up with a statement like this?
Jaxson:	The article on Inul Daratista.
Maria:	What can you tell me about Inul?
Jaxson:	She's a dangdut (pop music with Arab and Indian influence) dancer.
Maria:	She's a *penari dangdut*...she's a *dangdut* dancer, So, what's the problem?
Jaxson:	The way she dances. It's very controversial for some Islamic leaders.
Maria:	So, controversial...*kontroversi* exists in Indonesian.
Jaxson:	They're trying to ban her from doing it.
Maria:	Right. So, *melarang dia* (forbade her)...*pemerintah* (government)? Or *tokoh* (prominent figures)...
Jaxson:	*Tokoh Islam.* (Islamic leaders)
Maria:	*Tokoh Islam ingin melarang show Inul Daratista karena dia sangat ...tariannya sangat erotis menurut pendapat mereka... menurut pengalamannya*...[Islamic leaders wanted to ban Inul Daratista's show because she's very...her dancing is very erotic in their view...(according to their experience) from their perspective]. Do we have anything like that here? Have we heard of anything like that here?

(Discussion continues)

Jaxson: No.

Maria: So, we're *bebas* (free)?

Jaxson: No. I can't say not to that degree. We're less strict on stuff like that.

Maria: Is there anything that had come up in the news like that... that you know that could be put on a par or that could say something about how we feel about that sort of thing?

Jaxson: I don't know but on a par like that you'd see stuff like on Video Hits on Saturday mornings.

Maria: *Ya*, mm. Good point. *Bagus* (Good). *Bagus sekali* (Very good). What do you see on those Video Hits?

Jaxson: Women dancing half naked.

Maria: Right, OK. So, do you think it's caused any controversy? If there were controversy where would it come from? *Dari mana?* Do you think it would come from the government?

All: No.

Maria: Or from political groups?

Jaxson: *Mungkin.* (Maybe)

Maria: But what sort of political groups?

Mark: Maybe like local government.

Jaxson: I don't think they'd be too upset with it. It's not an issue I think they'd deal with. I reckon it would cause more outrage with the public than it would at a higher level.

Mark: That's like when...was it Madonna who brought out that film clip when someone got shot in a car park and they completely banned it? They made her remove the film clip. They were like a parents' committee on like a local level who took it higher and it got banned.

Maria: But isn't that interesting. That video is to do with violence...not really sex or eroticism. So, perhaps controversy can be caused by...maybe we can conclude by saying violence is more of an issue on television than it is...not an issue but not a concern on Indonesian television as much as it is on our television. But you're right then to say that a lot of the controversy from that may come out of these Video Hits comes not from a political party but from ...*orang tua* (parents)...or maybe from a political party such as Family First...maybe ...*partai Kristen* (a Christian party) that have foundations that have some religious connection. *Apakah kamu setuju?* (Do you agree?)

The discussion follows a brainstorming exercise in which students identified similarities and differences between Indonesian and Australian cultures using a Venn diagram. This device supports the process of differentiating and drawing connections between aspects across cultures. The comparative perspective recurs throughout the discussion with Maria challenging students to reflect on their own cultural values, 'Do we have anything like that here?', 'So, we're *bebas* (free)?', 'Is there anything ...that could be put on a par?'. She encourages students to reference against their understanding of their own culture and use it to explain their opinions, 'Stricter laws, policies on *apa* (what)?', 'How did you come up with this?', 'What do you see...?', 'If there were controversy where would it come from?'. She invites students to make parallels across cultures, 'Is there anything...that could say something about how we feel about that sort of thing?', 'violence...but not a concern on Indonesian television as much as it is on our television', and problematises cultural values and practices, 'freedom of press' through her open-ended and probing questioning, 'If there were controversy, where would it come from?', 'What sort of political groups?'. Maria highlights the internal diversity of culture through making references to subgroups such as religious groups and parent groups, and she uses caveats to moderate generalised statements, '...(according to their experience) from their perspective'. Her use of qualifiers is particularly marked when she offers her own perspective, such as 'perhaps', 'maybe', 'not an issue but not a concern'. In drawing the discussion to a close, Maria suggests a summary position, 'maybe we can conclude by saying...'; however, she qualifies this with 'maybe' and the follow-up question, '*Apakah kamu setuju?* (Do you agree?)', inviting contestation. By qualifying and moderating her comments and constantly questioning opinions, Maria is creating a discourse of culture learning and presenting culture as dynamic, multifaceted and open to interpretation.

A further mediation practice evident in this extract is the way in which Maria blends languages, English and Indonesian. She uses both languages within an utterance, 'stricter laws, policies on *apa?*', and by doing so demonstrates that languages are not confined to distinct uses but that language is an overall resource for making meaning. There is little sense in this exchange of 'doing' language or 'doing' culture for a language learning task; it is an open discussion about ideas and the students use both English and Indonesian without prompting or a requirement to do so. They are following the model provided by Maria who blends her languages to express ideas and opinions; they are participating in the discourse practices and learning culture established by the teacher (Doehler, 2002; Ustunel & Seedhouse, 2005). By modelling language use in this way, Maria is mediating a way of being in relation to language per se; a way of being multilingual.

In addition to comparison, Maria uses self-reflection as a process for mediating the concept of culture, particularly as it shapes linguistic and cultural identity.

Extract 63: Maria – mediating culture (August)

Participant	Dialogue
Mark:	Maybe it wouldn't be with religion though. Maybe it wouldn't be so much religion [inaudible] but it might be more just people's opinions.
Maria:	Yes. I accept that Mark but how are opinions formed? Where do they come from?
Jaxson:	Beliefs.
Maria:	Yes. That's right Jaxson. Where do beliefs come from? You showed me in your PowerPoints last week that your belief system and your attitudes and approach ....and... you only touched the surface...the source comes from your family. Much of your belief system comes from the way you were brought up. Am I wrong or...? Your likes in music and so on ... also can be influenced by your environment. Your aspirations in life as well could be influenced or have been influenced (even though you might or we might not want to admit it) by the environment you were brought up in. That's your family, *keluarga*, your school, *sekolah*, and why your parents chose a Christian school and not a public school, that says something about your background already and also your aspirations for the future have they been patterned or shaped also by this upbringing and the school has played a very important part in the way you approach life and perhaps will approach it in future. So, all of these factors have played a big part in who you are and who you will become. So, that's how we started. In fact, we have done almost a full circle. We've talked about in the beginning the symbols and icons in our personal life that reflect our beliefs system. We also looked at, on a wider scale, what symbols represented by each religion and you last week almost did a collage of the symbols in your life that are intertwined in some way or another with *agama*, even though we might not see a direct link there is some kind of influence.

(Discussion continues)

Mark: What about culture?

Maria: Also, culture plays a very important part. Where you were born plays a very important part. We weren't born in Sydney or Perth or Darwin or East Timor or Indonesia. We were born in Adelaide, South Australia. *Tetapi* (however), we've all had cultural influences on the way we have become and will become. Phung, you've had a background that's quite different from Jaxson, even though we were all born here. Mark, you informed us your great grandmother...was it your great grandmother...? Something that belonged to your ancestor and how your family had developed from that. Yours Jaxson...you've got *nenek dan kakek* (grandmother and grandfather) in *Inggeris* (England) and your connection to that country and that background and do you have some connection to India too? And you Phung. You have Vietnamese straddling over your background and will have in your future too. So, that's played a part in who you are and will become. So, that's really how we actually started this unit and finished this unit and how these factors all played a big role. So, what about all the stuff in the middle of the unit? That we've had to enhance the unit, to make it more alive. What's that all got to do...?

Mark: [inaudible]

Maria: I think my aim with those particular pieces was to show you how religion can also affect or influence the justice system or lack of justice system in a country. And because we were looking at Indonesia, those issues are (1) related to religion, (2) they are contemporary, (3) they are controversial, (4) they are political and (5) they do reflect the changing world, the changing times. They are all intertwined with *kebudayaan* (culture), and *kebudayaan* cannot be severed or separated from *agama* (religion), particularly in Indonesia, where you do have these extreme groups who do want to change what they see as moderate laws. And where does that perspective come from? Understandably from their beliefs, from religion. They believe that women should be covered. They believe that Indonesian society is being affected negatively be these laws. So, where had the liberal influence come from? Is it from *pengaruh Barat* (Western influence)? Is it from the West? Is it since the Suharto

(Discussion continues)

regime ended that there had been more liberalism? Where is it coming from? It's certainly coming from the trade winds. The trade winds are bringing…the trade winds once brought the traders from China and Saudi Arabia to Indonesian shores. These trade winds are bringing changes. Changes that are more and more evident. So, for these groups it is difficult for them to accept that *Generasi Muda* (The young generation) are going to be affected by these liberal laws.

The extract begins with Maria affirming a student's statement and then probing further, 'but how are opinions formed?'. From the start, the teacher is problematising and inviting critical awareness of students' own perspectives. The teacher makes statements which explicitly connect culture with aspects of students' lives, 'Your aspirations…have been influenced…by the environment you were brought up in', '…symbols in your life that are intertwined in some way or another with *agama*'. She is indicating that culture is personal and social. This is highlighted further by her movement between particular and abstracted points, 'you have Vietnamese straddling over your background', and later, 'traders from China and Saudi Arabia'. Maria draws attention to the individual identities of her students, making observations and drawing connections between aspects of their identities such as their schooling, birthplace, family and religion. She holds up a mirror to each of the student's historicities (Kramsch, 2009) and foreshadows the extension into the future, 'who you are', 'who you will become', 'shaped also by this upbringing', 'your aspirations for the future', 'the way you approach life'. She is conveying a macro idea about one's enculturation being a lifelong experience through the examples provided by students' individual lives. In fact, the idea that language and culture are a 'journey' is an overarching theme for her that she weaves through the teaching sequence. She uses signposts to reference back and forth to aspects of the discussion, and then recaps on the content covered and provides a summary statement to draw the sequence to a close. She summarises the characteristics of culture that were evident to her in the teaching sequence as 'related to religion', 'contemporary', 'controversial', 'political' and 'changing'. She has moved away from the particular and personal to the more abstract position of the nature of culture in general. Maria shares her teaching intentions with the students, '…those particular pieces was to show you how religion can also affect or influence the justice system or lack of justice system in a country. And because we were looking at Indonesia…'. She is inviting them into a language learning community

(Lave & Wenger, 1991) that she is trying to create, reflecting her sense of critical intercultural awareness.

Throughout the discussion, Maria constructs a view of Indonesian culture as internally diverse, particularly in relation to religion, characterising different religious groups using the terms 'extreme' and 'moderate'. She presents culture as dynamic, referencing aspects in the past, 'the Suharto regime', 'traders from China and Saudi Arabia', and linking to contemporary times, *'Generasi muda'*. Maria uses an analogy of 'the trade winds', with literal and metaphorical significance, to emphasise the idea that cultural change is unstoppable, akin to the forces of nature. Her choice of language here positions students as observers of diversity at this point, focusing on the internal variability of a national culture. She frequently moderates her statements with terms such as 'could be', 'perhaps', and invites contestation by asking, 'Am I wrong or…?'. At times, she slows the pace of interaction and pauses to give students' time to consider their own perspectives. She invites students to make connections, 'What's that all got to do…?', 'Where is it coming from?', at times adding her own views, 'It's certainly coming from the trade winds'. By allowing silences and time for thinking, Maria is not only scaffolding students' processing of ideas and constructing their own perspectives but she is also creating the sense that these ideas are open to interpretation and personalisation.

The relationship between language and culture

For Maria, language and culture are intertwined, and she explores this relationship through the use of authentic texts, analysing language for culturally embedded meanings.

Extract 64: Maria – mediating language and culture (June)

Participant	Dialogue
Maria:	What about the use of the language? How can you determine today if you were to explain to a tourist or a student going over there…just from the short experience we've had yesterday and a little bit today what would he or she need to know to recognise the severity of a sign?
Jaxson:	I would say just to get a rough image like a nice sign or something that would be the least severe would have words like *Selamat datang* (Welcome) or *terima kasih* (thank you)

(Discussion continues)

	which are nicer words but something more severe would have words like *jangan* (don't) or *dilarang* (It's forbidden). Yeah, harsher words.
Maria:	What about the use of the subject pronoun like *kamu* (you), *Anda* (formal you), *kami* (exclusive we), *kita* (inclusive we)? Um, anyone…now this is broad…but just from what you've seen…
Jaxson:	Maybe signs that use *Anda*, *kamu* are more detailed, might be addressing you personally and would probably mean that they might be nice signs of course this is very general…Something might be the most severe probably would just say, 'Don't do this' and address you specifically yes but there's exceptions…
Maria:	Perhaps government type messages. Messages that promote certain behaviour that perhaps are not as seen here in public. What about signs like *Apakah bapak sudah pakai kondom hari ini*? (Have you [men] worn a condom today?) Now have you ever seen a sign like that out in the open, say going down King William Street? Have you ever seen a sign like that? No, I haven't either because I'm sure a lot of brakes would go on! Um. *Apakah bapak sudah pakai kondom hari ini* or *Apakah ibu sudah pakai obat hari ini*? (Have you [women] taken your pill today?) Have you taken the pill? Because it could go both ways couldn't it? But that leads us to another discussion, doesn't it? That's a different sign isn't it? Generally what could it fit under?
Jaxson:	I reckon it could be *diumumkan* (announced) but it's also saying it's not telling you…it's recommended. It's implying it.
Maria:	Yeah. Excellent. That's true. It's a bit like that *Mari kita* (let us)…Going back to that *Apakah bapak*…it doesn't say *Pakailah kondom* (Wear a condom)… maybe there are signs like that around but I haven't found them as yet but if I'm ever back in Indonesia I'll certainly be doing research on this.
Jaxson:	It would be a very aggressive sign! I wouldn't like a sign shouting at me, telling me to wear a condom. Like the whole Uncle Sam thing…

(Discussion continues)

Maria:	Actually that's a very good analogy. That's a very good analogy. It gives you an idea of what people think; what they prioritise. So, let's come up with some ideas, some observations of the signs we've looked at.
	So, what does the language tell us about the culture and I use this very, very carefully because when you talk about a culture it's never one and I don't think so anyway because as you know Indonesia is an archipelago and it's made up of many, many...and relatively recently it's become a united country so it's made up of many cultures.
	(Students choose a text and discuss their observations)
Jaxson:	It really reminds me of...you're doing something everybody pitches in...you're doing it for the good of the nation. Fresh, beautiful. Start today...
Mark:	It looks like a primary school poster.
Jaxson:	Yeah. It does. I can't really describe it but...
Phung:	I suppose he's putting rubbish in the bin.
Maria:	Yeah. All...I find that all the posters regarding the city talk about this clean *bersih. Jagalah kebersihan* (Take care of cleanliness). Those ways of communicating and who's in control. Who has an influence on society? Who do you think...?
Jaxson:	Maybe the local council. It's put up by the local council or government.

The extract begins with Maria drawing students' attention to language use, 'What about the use of the language?'. She refers back to a prior discussion in which the class has discussed the impact of examples of public signs and creates an imagined scenario of advising a traveller about how to interpret such signs. The students echo her characterisation of the emotional load of the language, offering examples of their own, 'a rough image', 'a nice sign', 'the least severe', 'harsher words'. She poses an open-ended question to probe their awareness of the function of particular language features in the text, 'What about the use of the subject pronoun...?'. Maria is deconstructing the text with her students, inviting them to critically analyse language for possible meanings. She is building a shared discourse with her students about the power of language to position, frame and represent relationships between people, thereby highlighting language-in-culture (Crozet & Liddicoat, 2000). Maria declares a connection between language and culture with statements such as, 'Messages that promote certain behaviour', and directs students to notice how language is being used, 'What about signs like...?'. She uses comparison with students' own language and culture to mediate differing cultural norms, 'Now have you ever seen a sign like that...?'. When a student observes that modifying the structure (from a question to an imperative form) impacts on the emotional content of a sign and makes an analogy to military recruitment posters, the teacher endorses and praises his interpretation and uses his comment to open a new area of exploration, 'So, let's come up with some ideas...'. The emphasis is on individual and collective observation and analysis. There is little sense that meaning is singular or known by Maria *a priori* but rather that she is making her own sense of language and culture as she guides students to do the same. She builds on students' comments and encourages critical cultural awareness or *savoir s'engager* (Byram & Zarate, 1994), 'Who's in control?', 'Who has an influence on society?'.

Maria explicitly invites students' opinions about the relationship between language and culture, 'What does the language tell us about the culture...?' and opens the discussion for their interpretations of the text and connections they make with their own experiences and cultural frames. She qualifies her use of the term 'culture' and draws attention to her own sense of caution about overgeneralising, 'I use this very, very carefully'. She moves between the particular (the signs) and the general (the power of language), modelling how to be an analyser of language and culture. She draws the discussion to a close by offering a reflection on and question about the power of communication that then prompts a further view from a student. Maria mediates an integrated view of language and culture through the use of text analysis, open-ended questioning, inviting interpretations, caveating generalised statements and encouraging students to compare and connect with their own language and culture. She is constructing a path through learning for her students, scaffolding social interaction and individual meaning making, and normalising interpretation and reflection as part of the culture of language learning (Liddicoat & Scarino, 2013).

One further mediation practice that Maria employs is that of using the target language as a medium for self-expression.

Extract 65: Maria – mediating language and culture (August)

Participant	Dialogue
Maria:	*Mengapa Jaxson tertarik pada menjadi ahli hukum? Karena banyak tugas...*
Jaxson:	*Ya. Banyak tahun saya suka dan saya selalu pikir bahwa ahli hukum pekerjaan yang bagus untuk saya.*
Maria:	*Uang gajinya penting untuk Jaxson atau tidak?*
Jaxson:	*Tidak. Karena pada tahun awal ahli hukum, gajinya tidak bagus.*
Maria:	*Bagaimana agama tradisional mempengaruhi mungkin pilihan karir Jaxson atau mungkin tidak ada hubungan?*
Jaxson:	*Ya. Agama mempengaruhi banyak aspek dari kehidupan saya. Putusan dan perspektif...*
Maria:	*Perspektif terhadap apa?*
Jaxson:	*Perspektif terhadap ahli hukum.*
Maria:	*Dan perspektif terhadap keadilan?*
Jaxson:	*Ya. Yesus mengajar saya banyak pelajaran.*
Maria:	*Dan Edmund Rice juga?*
Jaxson:	*Ya.*
Maria:	*Apakah Anda bisa menjelaskan siapa Edmund Rice karena* Michelle *tidak mengajar di sini...*
Jaxson:	*Edmund Rice pendiri sekolah-sekolah* Christian Brothers...

Translation

Participant	Dialogue
Maria:	Why do you want to become a lawyer? Because they have lots to do...
Jaxson:	Yes. For a long time I have liked it and have always thought that being a lawyer would be a good job for me.
Maria:	Was the money an important thing for you or not?
Jaxson:	No. Because at first lawyers' salaries are not that good.
Maria:	How has religion affected your choice of career or maybe there isn't a connection?

(*Discussion continues*)

Jaxson:	Yes. Religion affects lots of aspects of my life. My decisions and my perspective…
Maria:	Your perspective towards what?
Jaxson:	Towards being a lawyer.
Maria:	And towards justice?
Jaxson:	Yes. Jesus has taught me many lessons.
Maria:	And Edmund Rice too?
Jaxson:	Yes.
Maria:	Could you explain a little about who Edmund Rice is because Michelle hasn't taught here?
Jaxson:	Edmund Rice was the founder of Christian Brothers' Schools… (Student gives further description.)

This interaction follows a formal oral presentation in which students used Indonesian to describe significant symbols or influences in their lives. In this case, the student, Jaxson, presented his family, education and interest in music as the major influences in his life. It is a spontaneous discussion, albeit led by the teacher, intended to gain insights into the student's aspirations and identity. The conversation is structured through the teacher's interest in the student; there is no predefined grammatical point or structure being practised. There is a seamless transition from the formal presentation to the informal discussion following the teacher's question, *'Mengapa Jaxson tertarik pada menjadi ahli hukum?'* (Why do you want to become a lawyer?). Maria is encouraging self-reflection through prompting Jaxson to reveal more of his personal perspective. She reveals her own assumption by asking, 'Was the money an important thing for you or not?' and then tries to make connections with Jaxson's religious values, exploring his intraculturality (Liddicoat *et al.*, 2003). At each turn, Maria responds to the comment and offers a further question that encourages deeper reflection on the student's part. She is extending the use of Indonesian beyond the parameters of a language learning task, challenging expectations about which language is used for what purpose. While Indonesian is often meshed in Maria's talk, it is usually reserved for 'doing' language learning, whereas English is the language for discussing ideas. In this interaction, however, Maria extends the role that Indonesian can have, showing that it can be a vehicle for expressing oneself. She is mediating the student's way of being in relation to the target language. Her questions are exploratory, inviting Jaxson's perspectives, 'How has religion affected your choice…?', 'Your perspective towards what?'. The focus is on the student's identity and not on his language use, and there is no correction or instruction per se.

At this moment, the student is more than a student learning Indonesian; he is using the target language as a vehicle for articulating his own identity, in his own context and for a personal purpose. The target language is used as a legitimate medium for self-expression, a personal meaning-making resource that is part of who the student is (i Sole, 2013). Moreover, the individual student is the subject of interest here and not the target language and/or culture. That is, the target language is decoupled from any construction of Indonesia and Indonesians only, as the interaction is not focused on the 'other', but on the self. The target language is a means of mediating one's own identity and relationship to the target language and culture. By using Indonesian to explore Jaxson's identity and values, Maria has mediated his relationship to it, showing him that it is not just something that he performs but that the language is a legitimate part of who he is.

Connections Between Teachers' Conceptions and Ways of Mediating

The cases in this chapter reveal an interplay between language teachers' conceptual frameworks and their ways of mediating an intercultural orientation in their teaching. Specifically, the teachers' understandings of language, culture and their relationship, both in general and for language teaching, are fundamental to both what is being mediated and how it is being mediated in the language classroom. While some aspects are similar across the three cases, there are also ways of mediating that are particular to each teacher. The discussion that follows, therefore, focuses on each case to explore this sameness and distinctiveness, leading to the chapter conclusion that reflects on the relationship overall between the teachers' conceptions and their mediation practices.

Collette's conceptions and her ways of mediating

For Collette, language (that is, Indonesian) is the primary focus for teaching and learning. She uses both Indonesian and English as mediating tools in relation to the concept of language. She focuses on Indonesian as an object of study and presents, explains, orders, rehearses and gives corrective feedback on it in order to render it comprehensible to students. She uses scaffolding talk in English such as questioning, giving examples, inviting observations and reinforcing grammatical knowledge in order to support students' noticing and understanding of the language system (Tsui, 1995; Wells, 1999). Collette also uses Indonesian as a mediating device to model accurate language use and uses it in routine tasks and exchanges to create a culture of communicative language use. Her modelling of how to use the target language in a functional way is a form of scaffolding which supports students to mimic and attempt their own communication using the target language (Guk & Kellogg, 2007). Her identity as a language user is an implicit form of mediation as she interweaves target language use in her teaching, showing possible ways of being in relation to it. Collette's use of Indonesian also reinforces her identity as the language teacher. Both Collette and her students perform their schooling identities through using Indonesian and, in addition, Collette performs her personal identity (Menard-Warwick, 2008). For learners, the target language represents disciplinary content (Doehler, 2002) through which they can perform their identities as language learners.

In relation to culture, Collette holds two main views: culture as facts and information, and culture as lived experience, both of which are mediated in particular ways. Collette gives factual descriptions and explanations in English about Indonesian culture, and occasionally invites students to question cultural phenomena. Her primary mediation process in relation to culture as facts is that of comparison. She uses comparative statements to encourage students to notice similarities and differences between Indonesian and their own culture. She creates a discourse about culture as difference and recounts personal experiences that frame culture as personal and comprehensible for students. Collette's view of culture as personal experience is mediated through her meta-theme of 'fitting in'. She presents examples from her life experience to render intercultural encounters as real and to enable students to contemplate their own reactions. Collette creates a role for students as 'potential' intercultural mediators, locating interculturality within a national paradigm, and therefore positioning students as observers until they reach Indonesia where they can participate for real.

Collette's goal in language teaching is to enable her students to interact with native speakers of Indonesian, and to become intercultural mediators, as she herself has done. Her focus is primarily on the former, and while she attempts to present culture as diverse and integrated with language, she also regards it as a distraction from language. Collette's view of language and culture for teaching and learning are distinct from language and culture in life. She sees language and culture as integrally connected in life through experience as she herself lives an intercultural life, using Indonesian at home and having family connections in Indonesia. Collette moves between two representations of language and culture: the one for teaching and learning, and the one that exists in her own life. She actively encourages students to experience the former and provides glimpses into the latter. Collette uses her own life experiences, through stories and examples, to mediate Indonesian language and culture to her students, yet she seems unaware of how her identity as an intercultural person is represented through her discourse, modelling and interaction with students, that is, how her own stance is mediatory.

Kelly's conceptions and her ways of mediating

Kelly primarily views language as content: a code comprising words, sentences and texts. Her predominantly structural view of language is mediated through the ways she draws attention to form, and engages in translating and decoding Indonesian for her students. Language not only comprises Kelly's primary pedagogic content knowledge (Shulman, 1987) but it is also the pedagogic knowledge used by her in managing teaching and learning. Language also represents unproblematic content for Kelly, as it is fixed and incontestable, and useful in structuring teaching and interaction. As she engages with an intercultural perspective through the research, Kelly's view of language expands somewhat and she begins to focus on language and meaning. She uses text analysis, encouraging students to read for gist and explore meaning in text. Text analysis is a mediating device for her that enables her to focus on the 'link' that she sees between language and culture, while retaining a degree of structure and focus on language.

If language is aligned with structure and control, then culture is just the opposite in Kelly's view. Her conception of culture as both exciting and challenging is evident in her ways of mediating it in practice. Culture represents a risk in that Kelly perceives she lacks adequate cultural knowledge and pedagogical skills in managing cultural content. For Kelly, culture is both extensive in its scope and loaded with content that is potentially confronting, uncomfortable and disruptive in the classroom. She uses structured tasks to render culture manageable in her teaching, particularly directing students to notice behaviours and assimilate facts. Her view of culture as 'sided', the familiar Australian side, and the unfamiliar 'other' Indonesian side, is reflected in her use of comparison as a mediating device. This encourages students to decentre somewhat, but it largely remains at the level of observable features of culture. There is a recurring pattern in

Kelly's teaching of encouraging observation, discussion and opinion, only to close it down (through a return to language) when it becomes personal and interpretative. Her view of language teaching and learning as oriented towards communicative competence does not readily accommodate affective and subjective dimensions of language learning.

The ways in which Kelly models her own relationship with language and culture are a further mediating practice. There is little inclusion of Kelly's personal connection with Indonesian language and culture in her teaching. The few instances where it is evident, it is presented as factual content, typically examples and anecdotes, which appear incidentally in discussions. She offers her own examples to add legitimacy, authenticity and also to counter what she regards as students' inaccurate or limited views. In this way, Kelly demonstrates her own relationship with Indonesian culture as being the same as that which she constructs for her students, as an observer of difference. Kelly's own sense of having limited knowledge and experience of Indonesian culture, and her communicative competence orientation towards language teaching (which positions culture as secondary to language use) create a relationship of distance between Kelly and the target language and culture, and this influences the relationship that she constructs for her students.

Kelly's case reveals how her views of language, culture and their relationship are integrally related to her ways of mediating, and actually create a number of tensions as she develops an intercultural language learning perspective. As the person standing between the target language and culture and students' own, Kelly filters the target language and culture, allowing it through as observable facts and information that render it teachable and manageable. She uses comparison to make connections to students' existing knowledge, but the comparison is rather generalised and homogeneous within a national perspective. Her ways of mediating reflect Kelly's lack of comfort and limited awareness of her own linguistic and cultural identity as it relates to her teaching. Kelly perceives herself largely as an observer of Indonesian language and culture, and this is the relationship that she ultimately mediates for her students.

Maria's conceptions and her ways of mediating

Maria conceives language as inclusive of the target language, English and, for her and her students, other languages. She sees language as comprised of linguistic structures and features that operate as a resource for making meaning. Indonesian represents the main content of her teaching within a communicative language use orientation. Her conception of language as diverse and variable in both form and meaning is mediated through her use of multiple examples, and her explicit statements about language as diverse, contextually bound and associated with subcultures. Maria draws attention to aspects of language, noticing features, exploring their function and comparing examples with students' knowledge of English. She also uses metalanguage to comment on the function, form and rules of language and its power to impact on people. She compares and contrasts the distinctive and common nature of languages as part of developing students' language awareness overall. She also scaffolds students' learning by varying the pace of instruction and building connections to previous lessons, topics and other subjects.

Maria's other main way of mediating language is by modelling multilinguality. She is conscious of being multilingual in her life and in her teaching, and she actively draws on her various languages in her teaching. She mediates a semiotic view of language through blending languages, weaving Indonesian into informal conversations, explanations, examples and discussions in class. She creates the expectations of what is permissible, and shows that uncertainty and risk-taking are acceptable and necessary in language learning and use (Byram & Zarate, 1994; Zarate et al., 2004). She encourages students to interpret unfamiliar language and models the act of interpreting herself. Maria positions herself as having multiple roles in relation to the target language including that of teacher, user and learner.

There is a strong association between Maria's view that culture is a 'kaleidoscope' and her ways of mediating culture. She views culture as dynamic and diverse, and therefore selects texts with differing, even conflicting, perspectives. She makes both general and caveated statements, often playing devil's advocate and proposing an alternative position or view. Maria builds connections over time, referencing back to historical events and linking these to contemporary aspects of language and culture. She promotes students' observations, interpretations and opinions, and uses increasingly sophisticated questions to probe students' thinking and encourage reasoning. When she deems the conceptual load to be greater than students' proficiency in the target language, she uses English as a scaffold and often blends both languages.

For Maria, language and culture are integrally connected, with culture providing the 'life in language'. This view carries into her teaching, particularly through her discourse related to the relationship between language and culture. She invites students to analyse language closely, drawing connections between language forms, use and meanings, and cultural context, relationships and world view. She depicts the target language and culture as accessible, contemporary and relevant to students' lives. She compares the target language and culture and students' own, highlighting the commonality and distinctiveness of each and thereby rendering the target language and culture as more familiar and knowable. Maria mediates an integrated relationship between language and culture through her attention to her own and her students' enculturation and situatedness. She positions students as intercultural mediators by asking them to decentre and notice their own cultural values and identities in their interpretations of a new linguistic and cultural system. Maria blurs the boundaries between formal learning and social interaction, between performing the roles of a teacher and students, and of being themselves (Tsai & Houghton, 2010).

Maria's case also shows how her conceptual frames influence her ways of mediating language and culture for her students. Her own linguistic and cultural identity, and awareness of this, is a primary mediating resource for her; she draws on her cultural identity to give examples, make comparisons and connections, and to model ways of being in more than one linguistic and cultural reality (Liddicoat & Kohler, 2012). She acknowledges and describes the tensions of differing values, the benefits of new ideas and the reconciliation required when one person holds multiple linguistic and cultural frames.

Conclusion

The cases of Collette, Kelly and Maria provide a window into understanding how language teachers' ways of mediating are intimately related to their understandings of language, culture and their relationship in language teaching. There are both commonalities and differences between the teachers, which provide a useful starting point for considering why this might be the case.

All of the teachers adopted a structural view of language at some point. When they did this, their ways of mediating were characterised by closed questioning, explanation, correction and translation, with the target language (particularly vocabulary and grammatical structures) being an object for study and learning being mediated through English. While it was not explicitly investigated in the study, there may be underlying reasons as to why there is a commonly held structural view of language. It may be, as found in previous studies (Klein, 2004), related to the teachers' own experiences in learning the target language such as through their university language courses which have also adopted this view. Furthermore, despite communicative language teaching, materials (particularly textbooks) are typically based on grammatical structures and communicative tasks are often designed to practice these (Eisenchlas, 2010). Hence, the prevailing view among language teachers is that communicative language use relies primarily on grammatical competence. Maria is somewhat different, in that, as a native speaker of Italian, she has acquired English through both formal schooling and an immersion experience. As such, this may have heightened her awareness of the nature of language and she shows an understanding of language as both structure and semiotic system.

All of the teachers also used the target language as a medium for classroom interaction and performing language learning tasks. Typically, these were routine classroom exchanges or teacher-directed interactions using display questions. Maria was the only one, and this may be in part due to having more senior students, who used the target language for genuine communication and self-expression by the student. All of the teachers, possibly in response to my suggestions, also experimented with using target language texts for analysis and interpretation, and thereby focused more on language and meaning. The teachers' ways of mediating then included open-ended questioning, invitations to notice and interpret meaning and comparisons with students' own language and culture, using English for discussion and comparison. The teachers found this kind of mediation challenging, noting as Maria did, 'That has not been easy. I don't know why. Is it because I'm not accustomed to hearing or listening to their...teaching this way? Is it because we're not trained...?' (Extract 51). This is a valid question and it is quite likely that the teachers' training, even for Kelly as a more recent graduate, did not address interaction and mediation of this nature.

A further area of similarity among the teachers is the relationship between their conceptions of, and ways of mediating, culture. When the teachers viewed culture as facts and information, their mediation largely comprised discussion in English with examples and anecdotes to provide authenticity and relevance. As the teachers engaged with a social practice view of culture, their discourse more explicitly included qualified statements and caveats, multiple and varied examples and a movement between generalised statements and particular, often personal, examples. The teachers' ways of mediating culture focused on building connections between macro and micro perspectives of culture, between national and individual identities, and between students' own and the new culture. The expansion of Kelly's understanding of culture was particularly noticeable (including by herself), even within the limited scope of the study, moving from culture as facts and information, to culture as social organisation, values and world view embedded in language. While the study did not probe where teachers' conceptions came from, it is likely that they were influenced by their language study at university where culture is commonly taught separately from language. This is particularly the case in Australian universities where the teaching of Indonesian often resides within social sciences, and is strongly associated with cultural studies and anthropology. The kinds of more integrated understandings shown by Collette and Maria may be attributable to their additional life experiences of residing in other countries.

Finally, in relation to the teachers' ways of mediating the relationship between language and culture, their practices varied depending on whether the teaching was incidental or planned. When the teaching was incidental, for example responding to a student's impromptu question, the teachers provided explicit instruction or explanation that was typically focused on a particular word or sentence. When the teaching was planned, for example text analysis, there was greater focus on interpreting text and deliberate attention to meaning in language including open-ended questioning and building connections between the new language and culture by referencing to students' known language and culture (English). The teachers constructed a relationship between language and culture, and the kind of relationship that students could have to it: positioning them variously as observers, analysts and, occasionally, participants. The teachers all experimented with how to show the integration of language and culture in their teaching, and they expressed their desire but also uncertainty about how to do so. This may not be surprising in that language teachers have to date received little training in conceptualising the relationship between language and culture, let alone how to address this in planning and programming, teaching and assessment.

This chapter has outlined the teachers' range of ways of mediating an intercultural perspective in their language teaching. It has revealed the interconnection between teachers' conceptions and their mediating practices, at times showing firmly held views and practices, and other times, showing struggles and emergent understandings and practices. The cases also highlight commonalities and differences between the teachers, providing a basis to consider possible reasons for these, and leading to implications for further work and research that are outlined in the following chapter.

5 Understanding Language Teachers as Mediators and the Implications for Intercultural Language Teaching and Learning

From the outset, this book was intended to shed light on the mediation dimension of intercultural language teaching and learning. In doing so, it has also examined the nature of language teachers' understandings of the foundational concepts of language teaching – language, culture and their relationship. Through the cases presented, a number of insights have emerged about the nature of mediation, language teachers' conceptual frameworks and case study research. This concluding chapter outlines these insights and explores some of the implications for language teacher education and for future research on intercultural language teaching and learning and mediation.

Revisiting the Concept of Mediation

The complexities and challenges revealed in the case studies indicate a need to revisit the concept of mediation and how it is understood in language teaching, and more specifically, intercultural language teaching. Mediation is not a matter of translation skills, teaching strategies or scaffolding alone; it is also an embodied process that draws upon a teacher's orientation towards his/her own language and culture, understanding of language and culture (and their relationship) and overall stance towards language teaching and learning.

Mediation involves a constellation of teachers' conceptual frames, practices and ways of being that are at play in any given moment and which are interwoven over time in the act of language teaching. Language teachers hold knowledge that is discipline specific, pedagogic, experiential and contextual, which may enhance or inhibit their ways of mediating intercultural language learning. Teachers of languages must simultaneously mediate learners' knowledge of the target language and culture, the relationship between language and culture and their knowledge of ways to act as intercultural mediators. They are constantly building connections between a familiar and a new language and culture, and through this, a familiar and new way of being.

In order to understand and do justice to this complexity, it is necessary to conceive mediation in the richest possible terms, drawing on both sociocultural learning theory and intercultural language teaching, and understanding mediation as both an intercultural and an educative process. It means recognising that mediation occurs at both micro and macro levels: from a single utterance, question or example, to a classroom and disciplinary discourse and learning culture. Teachers use processes such as questioning, explaining, elaborating, exemplifying and cross-referencing to actively build connections between the known language and culture and the new. They explicitly draw attention to linguistic and cultural content, inviting observation, analysis, interpretation and reflection. They move between the particular and the generalised, and weave connections between learning experiences in the language classroom and beyond (Tsai & Houghton, 2010). Language teachers construct representations of the target language and culture, such as through choices of texts and examples, and they construct students' relationships to the target language and culture through comparing with, and critically reflecting on, their own language and culture.

The case studies show that language teachers' mediation practices are integrally bound with their conceptions of language, culture and their relationship. The more that they viewed language as structure and culture as information, the more they focused on giving factual, often generalised information, asking display questions and providing explanations. The more that the teachers understood language and culture as social semiotic, the more they used exploratory discussion, open-ended questioning, interpretation, personalisation, comparison and reflection. They were also more likely to challenge students' assumptions about the target language and culture, encourage them to see their own language and culture more critically, and to normalise linguistic and cultural diversity and variability. It is this latter kind of mediation that most closely relates to theories of intercultural language teaching and learning.

As reported in other studies (Diaz, 2013; Sercu, 2007), the teachers conceptualised language and culture as integrated, but struggled with how to represent this view in their teaching. Through the action research process, the teachers became more conscious of their understandings of language and culture and were more likely to actively draw on them in their teaching. For example, using text analysis to explore both language and culture in a way that retained a focus on language use, reading, and analysis and reflection on language and culture. The teachers' separation of language and culture was partly due to their communicative competence orientation which positions culture as secondary to language use. It was also related to their conceptualisation of language and culture, which was integrated at a generic level, as adopted in their teaching, but was at a differential level (Risager, 2006) in their lived experience. It is one of the challenges of teaching of any kind that teachers must transform their conceptual understandings into 'teachable' content. This study highlights this process, revealing that these language teachers hold one kind of conception of language and culture in general, and another for language teaching, with little awareness of the process of moving between the two.

Finally, the cases foreground the role of the language teacher as the primary mediator or 'quintessential go-between' in the foreign language classroom (Kramsch, 2004a). They offer representations, both explicit and implicit, of linguistic and cultural ways of viewing the world and of ways to act interculturally. They mediate subject content, including transforming their own intercultural identities and experiences to enrich such content. On occasions, aspects of their knowledge are in tension, presenting a conflict between a teacher's personal and professional worlds. Other times, aspects of their knowledge are complementary, presenting a valuable resource for language teaching. The teachers construct relationships between students and the new language and culture, positioning them as observers, analysts, interpreters and participants, and creating the possibilities of how learners can relate to 'otherness' and in the process become intercultural mediators.

Arguably, the greatest resource for mediating an intercultural perspective in language teaching and learning is the language teacher's own linguistic and cultural identity (Kramsch, 2004a; Menard-Warwick, 2008; Papademetre, 2005). While this may be the case, having a resource alone is not sufficient and the cases highlight that a language teacher's degree of self-awareness impacts significantly on the nature and extent to which such a resource is explicitly used for mediation. The teachers varied in their awareness of themselves as embodiments of a new language and culture, and as models of ways to be intercultural mediators. In general, the greater the teacher's awareness of her own linguistic and cultural identity, the more she attended to the linguistic and cultural construction of the identity of her students, and therefore the more an intercultural perspective was evident in her teaching. A language teacher's capability to decentre from his/her own linguistic and cultural identity and employ it as a resource for mediating an intercultural perspective is, however, not a given and self-awareness and reflection need to be actively fostered. Therein lies one of a number of challenges for the profession and those involved in language teacher education.

Implications for Language Teacher Education

The insights gained through the case studies have a number of implications for those interested in furthering intercultural language teaching and learning, both in theory and practice. Since language teachers are the primary mediators in the foreign language classroom, the discussion here will focus on them in the first instance.

Language teachers' conceptual frameworks are a crucial starting point in advancing intercultural language teaching and learning in practice. Teachers develop their conceptual frameworks primarily through their initial training and ongoing professional learning. It would be a useful starting point to investigate what, if any, attention is given in language teacher education to the concept of mediation and to the mediatory role of the language teacher. Furthermore, language teachers need support to recognise their own linguistic and cultural identities, historicities and subjectivities (Kramsch, 2009, 2011) and consider how these may enhance and inhibit mediation. Language teachers could also be encouraged to systematically, and over time, investigate the ways in which they act as intercultural mediators in their own teaching. An 'investigative stance' (Crichton, 2008) and critical perspective (Byram, 2008; Diaz, 2013; Phipps & Gonzalez, 2004) could foster the kinds of learning within the language teaching profession that intercultural language teaching aims to engender in students.

Reflections on the Experience and Directions for Further Research

This book originated from a desire to better understand the nature of intercultural language teaching and the role of language teachers in mediating this in practice. It started with a number of assumptions that influenced the design of the study and the choice of research methodology. The fact that intercultural language teaching was, and continues to be, an emergent orientation for many language teachers was a primary concern. From the outset, it could not be assumed that the teachers were fully versed in and already teaching with an intercultural approach and instead the research needed to assume that some change was necessary. The study was therefore designed to be iterative, with each episode building on the previous one, and through professional discussions and critical reflection, enabling the teachers to act as 'transformative intellectuals' (Giroux, 1988), developing their understandings and enacting these in practice. As evident in her final reflections, each teacher gained new insights into intercultural language teaching, her ways of mediating and her own linguistic and cultural identity. While these changes should not be overstated given the constraints of the study, they also show that, with support, language teachers develop conceptual frames and ways of mediating that align with theories of intercultural language teaching.

Apart from the participants and their teaching contexts, there are aspects of the broader context in which the study was conducted that are distinctive. The fact that the language being taught and learned was Indonesian, particularly during a difficult period in the relations between Australia and Indonesia, meant that the teachers were in part responding to negative community perceptions of Indonesia and this possibly amplified their desires to counter public perceptions and raise students' critical cultural awareness. Furthermore, the teachers' identities as non-native speakers of Indonesian meant that they tended to perceive themselves as 'outsiders', viewing culture from within a national paradigm (Risager, 2007), at times constructing a similar position for their students. The proximity of Indonesia, and the assumption of teaching the language in order for students to communicate with native speakers in Indonesia, may have also strengthened the communicative orientation of the programme.

While some aspects were distinctive, the research methods and findings may have wider relevance to those interested in further investigation of intercultural language teaching and mediation. Participatory action research, for example, assumes principles such as negotiation of meaning, interpretation and valuing of multiple perspectives that are complementary to intercultural language teaching and learning. A case study proved to be an invaluable means of capturing teachers' experiences and understandings in a rich and context-sensitive way, recognising the situatedness of individuals, their knowledge and actions. The study presented in this book was small scale and aimed at gaining in-depth insights more so than generalisable ones. A case study approach, however, could be expanded to a wider range of teachers with varied relationships to the target language and culture, a wider range of languages and cultures, and a wider range of teaching contexts, examining how these factors may influence mediation. Further research could incorporate additional means of capturing a longitudinal perspective on teachers' learning and changed practices such as through a self-reflection journal or blog. This could also encourage teacher reflexivity as they would have a direct basis for noticing, decentring and reinterpreting their own views and practices. Indeed, Diaz (2013) argues that a longitudinal study using participatory action research would be valuable to illuminate the kinds of professional learning processes that facilitate changes in teachers' practices. Similarly, in the spirit of reflexivity, researcher–participants could also record their own reflections as their understandings change over time during the research experience.

Finally, the insights contained in this book highlight the need for greater investigation and theorising of mediation in relation to intercultural language teaching and learning. Attention is warranted, for example, to the discourse of the language teaching profession itself and how mediation and the concepts underpinning intercultural language teaching and learning are understood. In this way, views that may have become entrenched, such as a structural view of language and a cultural studies view of culture, may be contested and more contemporary understandings may be developed. While it was not possible within the scope of this study to consider mediation from the perspective of students, there is also merit in exploring their experience in future research. For example, investigating the relationship between teachers' ways of mediating and the nature of language and culture learning that students develop. Such research would need to be sensitive to the highly personal and developmental nature of intercultural language teaching and learning, and could also yield valuable insights into the undertheorised area of assessment.

Continuing the Dialogue

This book has presented a research study focused on language teachers as mediators in the foreign language classroom. It has illustrated the complexities and challenges of language teachers' work: how their conceptions, practices and own linguistic and cultural identities are integral to the ways that they mediate intercultural language learning, at times being an asset and other times creating tensions for them. I hope that this account has provided insights into mediation that may bring language teaching closer to realising an intercultural orientation. It is offered in the spirit of furthering our understandings and enriching our practices, contributing to the 'journey' (to adopt Maria's metaphor) of language and culture learning. It is an invitation to researchers, language teachers and students to continue the dialogue.

Appendix 1: Materials Used in Establishing and Guiding the Study Overall

1.1   Schedule of Collaborative Planning, Observation and Debriefing Sessions

Notes: The following table outlines the schedule of planning, observation and debriefing discussions held with the group and individual teachers during the course of one school year.

Term	Activity and purpose
Prior to school year	Initial planning meeting with group to establish the project
	Initial meeting with each teacher to identify first episode
1	*For each teacher:*
	Video recording of lesson (1)
	Audio recording of out-of-class discussion
	Video recording of lesson (2)
	Debrief with teacher
2	Video recording of lesson (3)
	Audio recording of out-of-class discussion
	Video recording of lesson (4)
	Debrief with teacher
	Debrief with all teachers (end of semester)
3	Video recording of lesson (5)
	Audio recording of out-of-class discussion
	Video recording of lesson (6)
	Debrief with teacher
4	Video recording of lesson (7)
	Debrief with teacher
	Debrief with each teacher (end of year)

1.2   Considerations in Observing Lessons

Notes: The following is a series of broad questions used to guide observation of mediation and intercultural language teaching during the lessons.

(1) What messages are conveyed, explicitly or implicitly, about language, culture and their relationship?
(2) What kinds of interactions constitute mediation of intercultural language learning in the classroom?
(3) What kinds of mediation occur between teacher and students?
(4) What kind of discourse was used by the teachers in mediating intercultural language learning?
(5) How are teachers' identities invested in their teaching – explicitly or implicitly?
(6) To what extent are teachers aware of their identities and mediation practices?

1.3   Notes From the Initial Group Discussion

Notes: The following is my record of the initial group discussion in order to establish understanding of the study and the focus on mediation in relation to intercultural language teaching and learning.

We discussed the meaning of 'mediation' as it is a central concept in the study and we need to give it more thought in future episodes. We do have some data already (from other research studies) which focus on the concept of intercultural language teaching from the teacher's perspective, and this study is designed to take that further and see how such concepts are conveyed in teaching and learning.

Mediation is a concept from psychology (and learning theory) that is based on understandings of how the brain operates and interacts with the world around it. It is essentially the process by which our brains make sense, interpret and learn using 'tools' – most importantly language. So, mediation is central to the teaching and learning process. Mediation (from language teaching) is the process of learning how to make sense of and communicate in a new language and culture system.

We discussed the concept of 'intercultural language teaching and learning' and explored our understanding of each of the major ideas involved, particularly language and culture and their interrelationship.

We discussed that while it is artificial to separate these out (i.e. in the real world we know they are inseparable) it is important for our thinking and teaching to do this and then bring them back together (it was felt that in a sense we already separate out language!).

We discussed that we currently have a strong sense of a 'framework' for thinking about language, due to years of theorising, researching and teaching languages. Our framework includes, for example:

- Grammar.
- Sentence structure.
- Nouns, verbs, adverbs, etc.
- Vocabulary.
- Metalinguistic awareness/language awareness e.g. non-equivalence.
- Idiomatic language.
- Skills for language learning.

I suggested that we might also ask the following about language: How does

- Language shape people's lives?
- Language shape and reveal world views?
- Language reveal beliefs, values, relationships, social order, etc.?
- Language affect people's life chances/pathways?

On the other hand, we felt that we don't have a similar framework for thinking about culture. We began brainstorming and formed the following ideas about culture:

- The nature of culture itself (e.g. changing, dynamic, flexible, influenced/shaped by others, layered, …. It's a system).
- Culture provides the why in language learning, it is the conceptual basis for learning and therefore needs to go beyond the 'descriptive' e.g. houses in Indonesia are …., houses in Australia are….
- Culture includes values, e.g. diversity.
- Culture includes phenomena, e.g. similarities and differences, i.e. comparing, facts about…, e.g. geography, climate, religion.
- Culture teaching should include cultural awareness, e.g. there are no specific rules for culture.
- Learners need to understand culture as a process, e.g. the abstract nature of culture, it is present/all around us every day, not something that belongs to 'others' but alive and well in ourselves also.

– We need to include meta-cultural awareness, i.e. students' language/ ways of talking about culture.

Overall, our aims in teaching culture are to enable students to develop awareness, evaluate, adopt aspects of cultures – their own and others. The group discussed the idea that the ultimate aim of our curriculum is to develop students' tolerance and respect for difference.

We noticed that these are of a different nature to the language list and the culture list includes more 'process' and 'understanding' type goals. Need to challenge the idea that culture is an imposition/distraction from language learning, e.g. What else do students need to know besides Indonesian?

We also discussed the meaning of 'inter-' and established that we can think of it as 'between'. We explored possible implications for language and culture teaching and learning, such as 'inter-' could mean, between:

- One or more cultures.
- One's own culture and the target language culture and other cultures.
- Language and culture.
- Individuals, groups, subgroups and whole cultures.

In the classroom, between:

- Students and teacher, student and student, text and student, text and teacher, language and all.
- Your teaching and students' thinking/connections they are making.

Also, in the school context, between:

- Teacher and school culture, students and school culture, culture of schooling, your class culture, culture of the school including parents/ community.

We closed with a brief discussion of possible programme ideas for the coming term.

1.4   Notes to Guide the Mid-Year Group Discussion

Notes: The following notes were developed by me and used to guide the mid-year group discussion.

This study is concerned with the *pedagogy* of *intercultural* language learning. There are two key concepts:

- Language and culture (and their interrelationship).
- Mediation (or at this point, kinds of interaction).

Language and culture

We have had some discussion of language and culture and regard them as inseparable in the 'real world'. It is an ongoing process to see them as inseparable in teaching practice.

Mediation

Diverse interactions leading to sense making, e.g. at the micro level of moment to moment, and at the macro level of how students respond to teachers' feedback and the overall 'picture' being presented to them. There are some 'types' of interaction that could support mediation, e.g.

Mode of interaction	Pedagogy/teacher explanation	Thinking processes	Tasks (and texts)
For example, student–student teacher–student	For example, construct concepts through diagnostic questions, giving explanations, instructions	For example, problem solving, reflection, prioritising	For example, text analysis, text composition, comparison

We need to consider different types of interaction that go on in the classroom to understand how this relates to mediation of intercultural language learning, e.g. do particular tasks better mediate different kinds of language learning? We need explicit documentation of the mediation so it can be reviewed and analysed.

For the next 'episode', we need to plan a series of lessons, e.g. over a week with various interactions. May need to consider working closely with a small group of students (4–5) to really focus on the interaction.

The debriefing discussions will invite reflection on your teaching, in particular:

- The relationship of language and culture.
- The mediation taking place, e.g. how do you help students develop new concepts and understandings? What do you do to help them do this? What strategies or talk/scaffolds do you use?

1.5   Questions to Guide End-of-Year Debriefing with Each Teacher

Notes: The following notes were used to guide the final debriefing discussion with each teacher.

- Tell me about how you see language and culture and the relationship between them.
- When we talk about mediation, what do you understand by this?
- What does that mean for you/the teacher and students (e.g. what roles, processes)?
- What kinds of mediation do you feel have been effective in developing students' intercultural language learning?
- What do you think about your own teaching from an intercultural language learning perspective, e.g. the way you teach, what you teach, how you go about teaching, how you move around, questioning, use of language, examples, etc.?
- Would you go about doing things differently at all? If so, what and why?
- What, if anything, has 'clicked' for you in this process overall? What have you learned?
- What do you now see as important/valuable for your teaching in future?

Appendix 2: Examples of Materials Developed by Participating Teachers

2.1 Collette

2.1.1 A short-term teaching and learning programme

Notes: The following is an example of a teaching programme with an intercultural language learning orientation that was developed collaboratively by Collette and me. The proforma was one that I developed prior to this study and was based on the local curriculum framework that Collette was not required to use but chose to do so for this unit of work. Normally, Collette followed a textbook.

Idola Saya

Band: Middle years (9/10)   **Learner pathway:** Typically 1B (Year 8 entry)
Programme duration and link to long-term programme: 3–4 weeks, Year 9 Term 3

Programme purpose: *(keep in mind how this unit links to your long-term plan)*
To explore how students' sense of identity is influenced and constructed by their group memberships and choices in relationships. Students will examine significant relationships and the different roles that different people have in our lives and how this reflects our values and contributes to our sense of selves.

Curriculum scope: *Key ideas – identify the key ideas that specifically relate to this unit*

### Understanding Language	### Understanding Culture
Consider: Target language structures and conventions	*Consider: Concepts about culture in general*
Making comparisons across languages	*Concepts about the target culture specifically*
	Comparisons across cultures
Language structures and features:	
Ber- verbs e.g. berpakaian, bermotif, bersifat	How does language i.e. adjectives reflect values in
Simple me- verbs e.g. memakai, mengenakan	the society e.g. murah hati, berdisiplin
Adjectives e.g. related to appearance (rupanya), character (sifat) and	Exploring how personal qualities reflect students'
behaviour (kelakuan)	own values
Conjunctions i.e. karena	How identity is influenced by the context,
Ordinal numbers i.e. pertama, kedua etc.	particularly relationships with those around us, and
Comparatives and superlatives i.e. lebih... daripada..., ter-/paling	how we choose to identify with particular people
Skills in language analysis and language awareness:	
Exploring authentic texts for patterns in language, particularly use of	
adjectives and descriptions of people and their actions	

Communication

Consider: Macro skills (L, S, R, W – in the target language)

Texts (as stimulus and to be produced), general knowledge

Listening/viewing: Class interaction, group reading of texts; view film (subtitles – relates to reading also)

Speaking: mini-oral presentations (×2)

Reading: Sample description of an admired person/idol; film review; agony aunt advice column

Writing: Language exercises; descriptions of people, ranking and reasons for preferences; article about best friend/ideal partner

Essential learnings: *Consider how this contributes to students' essential learnings (i.e. those that are dominant)*

Identity: Students explore how their identity is individually and socially constructed/shaped. They reflect on values that are important to them and how these values have been developed. They understand that personal values differ according to factors including language and culture.

Sequence of teaching and learning: Tasks and exercises, forms of interaction e.g. nature of tasks, mode e.g. group/pairs/class etc., teacher instruction and key focus/explanations....

Students...	Teacher talk/key questions etc.
Undertake language exercises for describing physical appearances of people e.g. *Dia tinggi dan berpakaian modern. Dia memakai rok ungu dan baju cokelat.* Students find a picture to describe the physical appearance of a person orally to the class – pictures on board – students guess which person is being described – spontaneous with no supporting cue cards etc.	*Rupanya, sifatnya, lakunya* contributes to who we are and how we are seen by others.
Read the text related to a famous person (i.e. teacher model) and discuss the language and reflection questions.	Teacher questioning of individuals and class e.g. *Bagaimana sifat orang ini? Mengapa dia terkenal? Bagaimana pendapat Anda tentang sifat dan lakunya?*

(Continued)

Students collect a number of (e.g. 5–10) pictures of famous people and describe in Indonesian their appearance and qualities. Give a priority order/rank them in terms of your favourites and give reasons for your ranking e.g. *Nicole Kidman sangat tinggi dan cantik. Dia orang pertama karena dia pandai bermain peranan sulit dan sangat baik hati memberikan uang kepada rumah sakit di Sydney.*

Students reflect on their choices of people and consider how an Indonesian person may agree/disagree with their choices and why.

Students ask parents/siblings about their ranked list of famous/admired people and seek their views about their top five. Students report orally to the class one of their family member's views and explain why they think their list is different from their own. (English and/or Indonesian)

(Extension) Create a class ranking/list and discuss who has been chosen and why. Explore how it may differ among different groups in society e.g. would teachers agree with their choices – why/why not? What factors influence our preferences e.g. age, position/role, culture/upbringing etc.

Previewing task: Read a film review of the film *Ada apa dengan Cinta?* and discuss what students expect to see: main characters, plot, issues.

View film: *Ada apa dengan Cinta?*

Kenalkan pelaku utama:

– Describe the main characters.

– Choose one character from the film and write a description of him/her in Indonesian. Describe his/her physical appearance and character and how he/she relates to the others in the film. What similarities and differences do I share with the main characters? What values do we share? (e.g. *Cinta sangat cantik dan baik hati. Dia berani dan suka membantu temannya*)

Class discussion/individuals reflect on choices made e.g.

Menurut pendapat Anda siapa yang pertama, kedua, ketiga... Mengapa?

Explore/discuss if and why choices are different and how factors influence our preferences e.g.

Apakah ada perbedaan? Ceritakanlah yang sama dan yang berbeda. Mengapa ada perbedaan?karena bapak saya tidak begitu suka musik rap....

Comparing, ranking, expressing preferences and reaching compromises to create a common set e.g. *Saya lebih suka... karena... ; Ok...bisa tetapi saya pikir bahwa... lebih ...daripada...; Saya setuju dengan...*

– What do I value in my friendships? What do I consider to be a 'good' friend? What ways am I a good friend? How do friends work through issues? Who do I confide in and why?

– What are your key relationships e.g. at home, school, wider community? Develop a concept map outlining your main relationships e.g. brainstorm categories in Indonesian.

Consider the relationships we have and why we have them e.g. family, choice, need etc. e.g.

Gambar itu termasuk siapa? Mengapa?

Describe who is part of your map and why e.g. Teman saya di sekolah *adalah* orang yang penting. Dia *selalu* mendengarkan saya dan *karena* dia lucu, saya *selalu* tertawa kalau dia ada. Saya sangat *menghormati* kakek saya. Dia tua tetapi coba mengerti remaja. Dia *sering* bercerita tentang *kehidupannya* yang sangat menarik, seperti waktu dia di Vietnam.

Apa perhubungan Anda dengan orang itu?

Bagaimana perhubungan antara orang itu dan Anda?

Pikirlah tentang mengapa orang itu penting untuk Anda.

Select a text/agony aunt column about a relationship of concern. Students work in pairs to analyse the article for language features and examine how the ideas are expressed, including the attitudes and values that come through e.g. promiscuity, loyalty, embarrassment etc. Teacher explores how attitudes towards sexual relationships at certain ages. What sort of person are you? Describe yourself – physical appearance and what you value in others.

(Additional exercise could be to collect your horoscope/shio and explore the qualities expected of you and how these actually relate/compare to how you see yourself.)

Final task: Create a 'sahabat setia' or 'pacar ideal' poster. Give a physical description of the person and explain what makes them a good friend or perfect match. Describe how they make you feel and who you are when you are around them.

What does the language show about what is important?

Identify aspects of the language that show values or concerns of the author.

How do you react to these values?

'What kinds of views do you and your culture have of such ideas? (How does this get shown in language?)

Exploring who we hold dear in our lives and why, including their role/impact they have on us

e.g. *teman akrab, terbaik, yang paling... perasaan...; karena...*

(Continued)

Resources: *Indicate the texts, materials, artefacts, stimuli which will be used*

Links with Bersama-sama 1: Mau beli apa?

Film: *Ada apa dengan Cinta?*

Magazine advice column extract

Film review (modified authentic text)

Evaluation/teacher reflection

What key language did students develop as a result of the unit?

What did students take away with them from this unit?

How does this connect with their ongoing learning?

What kinds of interactions were students engaged in during the unit?

What best supported them to make their own connections in their learning?

How did the unit enable students to reflect on themselves?

2.1.2   Questions to guide a debriefing discussion

Notes: The following is an example of semi-structured questions used to guide a debriefing discussion with Collette.

- What were you trying to achieve in this lesson i.e. what were you teaching them from an intercultural perspective? And why?
- You do lots of 'describing' features of houses in the lesson. What is the conceptual content/focus? e.g. 'fitting in'? Where does this come from? Are you planning to touch on social dynamics and interactions related to housing?
- 'We've got a week's work to do before the chapter test…'. This reveals the emphasis (the school's?) on a testing culture. How does this affect your programme goals and interaction?
- You did most of the lesson in English with only a few words in Indonesian. Why?
- Is there another way to do it? What is the message that students will take away? What are you seeing as the relationship between language and culture?

2.2   Kelly

2.2.1   Notes from initial planning meeting

Notes: The following are notes from the initial planning meeting with Kelly in which she considers what an intercultural orientation might mean in her teaching.

Kelly raised the issue of working through a 'culture' topic/lesson based on the textbook 'culture note'. Her dilemma was how to match the language difficulty with the conceptual demands of the topic. The topic chosen was the Indonesian national identity card (KTP). She had chosen this to fit with the textbook chapter and was then planning to give some more information in Indonesian from authentic sources to support the note.

Kelly was concerned that the language level she had found in seeking authentic texts was too advanced for students and would take a long time and lots of patience to work through. She wanted to discuss how to modify or adapt it. I asked Kelly some questions along the lines of:

- What is it important for students to learn about the KTP?
- Why are identity cards important in cultures? How does it relate to the world of Year 10 students?

We discussed that it may be more relevant to Year 11/12s who have licences and Medicare cards etc. ID cards are very politically loaded and although you can simplify the language, the conceptual load may be too much/too remote from this group.

I asked her to explain what her current programme focus was and what students would be learning. I then suggested pulling back even further and asking 'What is important for students to learn about their neighbourhood? What makes places important to people? What places are important in Australia and why? What places are important to you/ students and why?' (trying to connect with who they are and what is important and relevant to them).

We then discussed how this could look in practice and planned that students could:

- have a class discussion about what places are most significant in Australia, they could even rank the top 10 and debate what should be there or not and why;
- then, individually they choose two or three places of interest to them and describe them in Indonesian (language task) and then in English, explain why they chose these places, what is important about them and how an Indonesian would react to them or what places would be of most interest to an Indonesian visiting Australia.

Kelly commented 'I didn't think culture would be that' i.e. she thought culture had to be informational/data about lifestyle. I explained that it can be about getting more from existing texts and using students' thinking and identity as a resource for interaction in the classroom i.e. seeing what is inside their heads and what connections they are making (undoubtedly). I also explained that much of the reflection and discussion might be in English and that that was ok/to be expected and actually might be necessary to get the deeper connections of culture *and* language. We are using the language as the 'way in'. It is a different kind of teaching – more open-ended questioning and there are unknown answers and multiple interpretations that students will make as you ask for their input/ideas/interpretations and reasoning. I explained that I see an intercultural orientation as not about 'adding' to the curriculum or even swapping 'non-authentic' texts for authentic ones but as a way of getting more meaning out of what we already use.

Questions that I asked about culture – How does this relate to who students are? Why is it important learning?

There is a need to focus on the *understanding* part of 'understanding culture' using the South Australian Curriculum, Standards and

Accountability (SACSA) framework e.g. values, how cultures are organised, comparing similarities and differences, common humanity and 'mining' the language for meaning.

We also discussed the limitations of textbooks and the 'sprinkled facts' approach to culture. This approach leaves you and the students asking 'What was that all about? How did it connect to my language development?'. These 'notes' are not sufficiently rich or cognitively relevant or connected with the language development in the topic itself to be of use and be meaningful for students.

As a result of the discussion, Kelly shifted from the original idea of an isolated topic and isolated one-off 'culture' lesson to an integrated lesson both in terms of content and sequence. She is now focusing on 'pulling the culture out' of her existing 'language-oriented' topic i.e. the neighbourhood. Her focus is extended to the notion of 'significant sites' and why they are significant – what makes somewhere significant in different cultures. She expressed several times that she felt relieved that we had discussed this and changed her approach – not just from the perspective of teaching something that she wasn't comfortable with– but also that she had a better understanding of what might be possible in teaching culture in language teaching.

2.2.2 A short-term teaching and learning programme

Notes: The following is an example of a teaching programme with an intercultural language learning orientation that was developed by Kelly and includes a unit on advertising that we had discussed in detail. The proforma was developed by Kelly and includes references to the local curriculum framework that Kelly was required to use. It shows an expansion of her usual planning for a 'cultural lesson' based on the textbook cultural information and the unit based around text analysis using authentic online texts.

TERM 3 UNIT PLAN

Topics: City vs village life, the influence of advertising, (unit designed for research study) sickness and health.

Rationale: Students will gain an understanding of the 'gotong-royong' concept of mutual cooperation, the differences between city and country life, the influence of food advertising in Indonesia and how does food advertising contribute to lifestyle concerns. Students will gain an understanding of the health system in Indonesia and herbal remedies. Students will also be able to describe illnesses and conditions to a doctor.

Essential learnings: Futures, identity, thinking, communication

Key competencies: KC1, KC2, KC3, KC4, KC6, KC7

Week/term	Content	Assessment and homework
9/T2	**Lesson 1:** Introduction to new topic city vs village life. Brainstorm useful vocab words/phrases. Cultural lesson: gotong-royong, what is the significance of gotong-royong, what are the examples of this in Australia? Read cultural notes in textbook page 152. **Lesson 2:** Look at PowerPoint presentation and answer questions on the differences between the city and village. **Lesson 3:** Language lesson: pe- table. Copy notes and read notes from textbook. Watch video on city vs country life in Indonesia. What are the similarities and differences? How is it in Australia?	Vocab words taken from brainstorm activity Revision exercises on gotong-royong and pe- function
10/T2	**Lesson 1:** Language lesson: conjunctions supaya and sehingga. Copy board notes and practice exercises. **Lesson 2:** Reading comprehension: Kehidupan di desa dan di kota. Pages 148–149 textbook. Listening comprehension. **Lesson 3:** Grammar lesson the suffix –kan pages 158/159. Copy o/h notes on the causative and beneficial –kan. Worksheet exercises.	Vocab words Exercise sheets: Reading comprehension Listening comprehension
1/3	**Lesson 1:** Brainstorm words associated with food advertising. Use KFC and other ads. Highlight the language used. How is it different to food ads in Australia. Outline the format for Lesson 2. **Lesson 2:** Introduction to topic on food advertising in Indonesia. Students will work in groups – analysing advertisements using KFC Indonesia website, DANCOW website, print advertisements, video of advertisements from Indonesian TV. Students will need to watch the ads several times to identify main parts of the ad. Each group will have questions to answer and discuss. Each group will then report their findings to others in the class.	Vocab words Reflection task **If students are doing the KFC ads they need to bring in headphones. Groups will be allocated.**

	Lesson 3: Debrief from previous lesson. Each group will inform other students of their research findings. Discussion: What is the purpose of the ads? How are these ads different to ads in Australia? What does food advertising tell us about our society and Indonesian society? What influences our lifestyle choices? How are food ads responsible for obesity and health issues? (this will link to newspaper article)	
2/3	**Lesson 1/2:** Read article taken from *Kompas* on the link of food advertisements and obesity. Translate the text as a class. This will take two lessons. Discuss the article. Who is the intended audience? What is the purpose of the article? **Lesson 3:** Reflection quiz re lifestyle choices.	
3/3	**Lesson 1:** Use the questions from an exam paper on nutrients and health, obesity as a practice for assessment task. Read one text analysis as a class, provide a vocab list. **Lesson 2:** Assessment task: text analysis task. **Lesson 3:** Assessment task: text analysis task. **Evaluation sheet: If students learnt anything, did they prefer these teaching pedagogies etc?**	Assessment task: Text analysis task (S)
4/3	**Lesson 1:** Introduction to topic on sickness and health. Body parts and describing symptoms to a doctor. Pages 92/93 textbook. Worksheets on Anda sakit apa? Fill in the blank sentences.	Provide a vocab list
	Lesson 2: The role of the Puskesmas compared to health facilities in Australia. Reading taken from textbook. Copy o/h notes on the uses of the Puskesmas. Brief lesson on acronyms in Indonesia. **Lesson 3:** Grammar lesson ber verbs. Copy notes and complete worksheets from textbook.	

(Continued)

Date	Content	Notes
5/3	**CULTURAL LESSON** **Lesson 1:** Traditional vs modern medicine. What is jamu? Who uses jamu? Why do some Indonesians prefer to use herbal remedies instead of modern medicine? Do Australians use herbal remedies? Why are our perceptions changing towards herbal alternatives? Read article from textbook. Use jamu advertisements and packaging to reinforce language content. **Lesson 2:** Find an article/report re jamu. **Lesson 3:** Reading comprehension: Kominex, apa itu? Read together as a class, answer questions in English/Indonesian.	Homework: Read pages 105–107 Keren 2 on Jamu before cultural lesson
6/3	**Lesson 1:** Listening comprehension: True or false 'Kenapa Dedi tidak bersekolah hari ini?'. Revision sheet on language functions and a short reading task. **Lesson 2:** School closure day – no lesson. **Lesson 3:** Begin assessment task: outline role play. Students follow model, change illness and body parts.	
7/3	**Lesson 1:** Assessment task: drafts to be checked. **Lesson 2:** Assessment task: practice role play. **Lesson 3:** Present role plays to class.	Assessment task: Oral – going to the doctors (S)
8/3	**Lesson 1:** Revision for test: City vs country life and the role of advertising. **Lesson 2:** Health/sickness/puskesmas/jamu. **Lesson 3:** End of unit test.	Assessment task: End of unit test (S)

2.2.3   Questions to guide a debriefing discussion

Notes: The following are questions used to guide one of the debriefing discussions.

- What kinds of interactions did you include in this unit and why?
- What did you notice about the kinds of interactions and students' learning? e.g. How did you feel about their participation?
- How did you feel about the kind of discussion and reactions students had to the content of the article? (e.g. handling the discussion, leaving some things unresolved?)
- What did you notice about your contribution? Not just the teaching but your questioning, movement, the ways you get them to engage with the texts/ideas? Was it your usual interaction? What were you trying to mediate?
- How did you feel about the 'intercultural-ness' of the unit? What about the use of English and Indonesian? What were you using these for and why?

2.3 Maria

2.3.1   A short-term teaching and learning programme

Notes: The following is an example of a teaching programme with an intercultural language learning orientation that was developed collaboratively by Maria and me. The proforma was one that I developed prior to this study and was based on the local curriculum framework that Maria used in some of her junior school planning. Her programmes for senior students were normally developed in accordance with the senior secondary syllabus for Indonesian but Maria felt that this proforma enabled her to better plan with an intercultural language learning perspective.

Learners: Stage 1 or 2 continuers

Programme/aims and objectives: *The language of signs*

- Expose students to the 'text type' of Indonesian signs
- Draw comparisons with use of language of signs in English
- Identify possible contexts for particular signs
- Form categories by analysing particular linguistic constructions in these signs
- Reflect and discuss how linguistic structures tell us something about Indonesian culture

Understanding Language	Understanding Culture
Consider: Target language structures and conventions	*Consider: Concepts about culture in general*
Making comparisons across languages	*Concepts about the target culture specifically*
	Comparisons across cultures
Imperative forms of transitive/intransitive verbs	The use of 'you' in Indonesian signs is more evident whereas in English it is implied but not used in public signs, 'you' is substituted by words such as 'customers/trespassers/pedestrians/drivers, prosecutors'
Polite imperatives: -lah, silahkan, tolong, coba. Harap	
Passive imperative: diharapkan	No standing/dilarang parkir di sini/'Don't' not commonly used on public signs but in Indonesian 'jangan' is frequently used. Passive form very common in Indonesian signs
Negative imperative: jangan	
Subject pronouns: Mari kita.........Anda	Discuss ways language [and culture] are used to influence people and affect their thoughts or actions [e.g. creating culture]
Sebaiknya	
Seharusnya	Discuss degrees of 'force' within language and how this relates to culture
Abstract nouns: ke + adjective+ an	
Consider limitations of translating ideas across languages	Consider how signs are part of own culture [school, local community, country/Australia]

Sequence of teaching and learning:

Tasks and supporting exercises

Teaching activity

Brainstorm by asking students what signs do, i.e. their function. List on board reasons both in English and Indonesian: to encourage, to inform, to welcome, to announce, to advertise, to serve, to apologise, to advise, to recommend, to warn, to prohibit

List on board:

- **Recommend, hope ,inform, apologise**
- **Danger, attention, prohibited, warning, No...... Stop**
- **Give way, turn left/right, keep clean, Don't....please don't...**
- **Penalty, fine, trespassers prosecuted...**

Give students examples of three categories

(1) Pengumuman [announcement] e.g. hati-hati ada banyak anak kecil.
(2) Di puji/dianjurkan [Recommended]e.g. jagalah kebersihan di kota anda.
(3) Dilarang [prohibited]e.g. Dilarang masuk, kecuali petugas.

Teacher talk+forms of interaction e.g. open-ended questions such as 'what do you think .... Tell me about.....'

Discuss where we find signs and how they are a part of our daily lives.
Why do we have them?
Discuss common English structures that appear in signs.
Ask students to identify categories and to explain what cues they found in the sign to come to that conclusion.
Give student a set of signs in Indonesian and in small group discussion ask them to put them under the three categories giving reasons for their choice.
Tell me about the use of language in the sign.
Where would you find the sign?

(Continued)

Is the aim of the message clear?

Students categorise these signs giving reasons for their choice and keeping in mind possible context. Students also order the signs according to degree of command or force. Discuss linguistic structures and common patterns across the set of signs.

Review the imperative forms, polite, passive and negative. Complete exercises.

Design five signs in Indonesian you could find on a fun beach walk. The signs should include various language forms.

Discuss with students the type of signs we find on Australian beaches.

Give examples of signs that would fit the three categories discussed in the unit.

Is it encouraging certain behaviour?

Is it prohibiting certain behaviour?

Is it warning?

Is it informing?

Is it promoting certain behaviour?

ASSESSMENT

(1) Gather evidence of five signs in the community and explain, compare and translate into Indonesian.

(2) Compare three Indonesian signs explaining use of language i.e. imperative structures. Discuss what the sign is trying to do or point out. Is it encouraging, punitive, authoritarian, apologetic, polite, harsh? Give examples/evidence from the texts.

(3) Write an informative piece in English for a school exchange group, outlining language structures students may encounter in signs in Indonesia. Give examples of these language structures and where and why they are possibly used.

(4) **Reflection question:** What have you learned about the use of language in signs and its impact on people and their behaviour?

2.3.2   An assessment task

Notes: The following is an example of an assessment task (based on text analysis and reflection) drawn from the short-term programme and designed to capture students' intercultural language learning. The task was developed by Maria with feedback from me.

Stage 2 Bahasa Indonesia

Assessment Task

Topic: Bahasa Tanda-Tanda (The language of signs)

Part A

Gather evidence of five signs in our community and explain/compare/ see if they are translatable into Indonesian. Explain its location, language used, put into category, translate if possible or explain why not.

Part B

Compare three Indonesian signs explaining use of language e.g. imperative structures (-lah, coba, harap) and use of personal pronouns (Kita, Anda) and the passive form (di-) and the impact or effect of such language e.g. What is each sign trying to do or point out? Is it encouraging, punitive, authoritarian, apologetic, helpful such as offering a service, warning, polite/ harsh etc.?

Part C

Write an informative piece in English for a school exchange group, outlining language structures students may encounter in signs they find during their trip. Give examples of these structures and where and why they are used.

Reflection question: What have you learnt about the use of language in signs and its impact on people in society?

2.3.3   Questions to guide a debriefing discussion

Notes: The following are questions that were used to guide the debriefing discussion at the end of the unit on 'signs'.

Teacher and student reactions/perceptions
* What are your reactions to this teaching sequence?
* How is it different from your usual approach?
* What messages had you hoped students would go away with?
* What messages do you think they went away with?

Language and culture
- How did this sequence add to students' language development?
- How do you feel about the integration of language and culture in the sequence?
- Do you see the intercultural focus as compatible with their language development? If so, how? If not, why not?

Mediation
- Do you have any comments about the interaction and how the learning was mediated?
- What, if anything, was different about the interactions and your mediation processes?
- What did you notice about the metalanguage in these lessons? (e.g. the language used about language and culture?)

2.3.4   Questions to guide the final debriefing discussion

Notes: The following are questions that were used to guide the final debriefing discussion with Maria. They are based on the general questions in Appendix 1.5 but were slightly modified for Maria (e.g. the third and final questions).

- Tell me about your idea of what intercultural language teaching is e.g. what key points would you say to others?
- What do you understand by the term 'mediation' (particularly as a key idea for intercultural language teaching)?
- What kinds of 'mediation' have been critical to developing your students' intercultural language learning? (For example, you are always trying to get 'connections' happening – what kinds and how do you think you do this? Why?)
- What has been your own learning in the process? (e.g. about the nature of language and culture, about pedagogy, about students' learning, ways of talking, planning for intercultural language learning etc.)
- What do you see as valuable that you have/will adopt in your teaching in future?
- What has been particularly fruitful/useful/significant/influential in our interactions e.g. key moments, style of interaction, frequency, examples, metalanguage etc.?

Appendix 3: Data Analysis

3.1 Description of the Data Analysis Process

The raw data in this study consisted of 50 discs of video and audio recordings. In the first instance, these discs were coded according to the teacher's initials, date of school visit and number of discs. The coding system provided a way of accessing the data by teacher, by type and by date order. A first impressionistic analysis was done by viewing or listening to each set of discs according to teacher and in chronological order. This provided the strongest initial impressions of each teacher's particular 'case'.

From the initial analysis, the data were further analysed in order to select a series of extracts that would be transcribed for detailed analysis. From the video data, extracts were chosen due to the focus on mediation, while from the audio data, extracts were chosen based on evidence of teachers' conceptual frameworks and biographies that reflected their views on language teaching and learning.

During lessons, I did not regularly take field notes but focused on noting key points for further planning and debriefing discussions (see Appendix 1 for an example). The next layer of analysis could be described as the deductive process. It involved a number of stages beginning with transcription of the relevant extracts. The transcription was intended as a record of what had been said in interactions both in the classroom and in the teacher–researcher discussions, with a view to a thematic analysis of the discourse. The thematic analysis was conducted with reference to key concepts drawn from the literature, in particular language, culture and their relationship.

The transcriptions of classroom interaction focused on evidence of teachers' ways of mediating language, culture and their relationship. Any data which related to teachers' explicit or implicit mediation of language, culture and their relationship were noted and characterised using a 'commentary' column next to the dialogue in the transcription table.

Following the separate analysis of each set of data, audio and video, the final stage of analysis was to consider the two sets of data in relation to each other. The assumption underlying this process was to examine the connection, if any, between teachers' conceptions and their ways of mediating. A matrix was developed to consider points of connection between teachers' conceptions and their ways of mediating (see Appendix 3.2).

3.2   Matrix for Analysing the Two Data Sets

Relationship between data sets 1 and 2

Case study	Ways of mediating (learning theory)	Ways of mediating (language teaching)	Further comments
Views of key concepts			
Language			
Culture			
Relationship of language and culture			
Overall relationship			

References

Agar, M. (1994) *Language Shock. Understanding the Culture of Conversation.* New York: William Morrow.

Anton, M. (1999) The discourse of a learner-centred classroom: Sociocultural perspectives on teacher–learner interaction in the second-language classroom. *The Modern Language Journal* 83 (3), 303–318.

Bachman, L.F. (1990) *Fundamental Considerations in Language Testing.* Oxford: Oxford University Press.

Bachman, L.F. and Palmer, A.S. (1996) *Language Testing in Practice: Designing and Developing Useful Language Tests.* Oxford: Oxford University Press.

Bakhtin, M. (ed.) (1981) *The Dialogic Imagination: Four Essays by M. M. Bakhtin* (Vol. No. 1). Austin, TX: University of Texas Press.

Bennett, J.M., Bennett, M.J. and Allen, W. (2003) Developing intercultural competence in the language classroom. In D.L. Lange and M. Paige (eds) *Culture as the Core: Perspectives on Culture in Second Language Learning* (pp. 237–270). Greenwich, CT: Information Age Publishing.

Bhabha, H.K. (1994) *The Location of Culture.* New York: Routledge.

Bloomaert, J., Leppänen, S., Pahta, P. and Räisänen, T. (eds) (2012) *Dangerous Multilingualism: Northern Perspectives on Order, Purity and Normality.* Basingstoke: Palgrave Macmillan.

Buttjes, D. (1991) Mediating languages and cultures: The social and intercultural dimension restored. In D. Buttjes and M. Byram (eds) *Mediating Languages and Cultures: Towards an Intercultural Theory of Foreign Language Education* (pp. 3–16). Clevedon: Multilingual Matters.

Byram, M. (1988) Foreign language education and cultural studies. *Language, Culture and Curriculum* 1 (1), 15–31.

Byram, M. (1989) *Cultural Studies in Foreign Language Education.* Clevedon: Multilingual Matters.

Byram, M. (1991) Teaching culture and language: Towards an integrated model. In D. Buttjes and M. Byram (eds) *Mediating Languages and Cultures: Towards an Intercultural Theory of Foreign Language Education* (pp. 17–30). Clevedon: Multilingual Matters.

Byram, M. (1995) Intercultural competence and mobility in multinational contexts: A European view. In M.L. Tickoo (ed.) *Language and Culture in Multilingual Societies: Viewpoints and Visions* (pp. 21–36). Singapore: SEAMO Regional Language Centre.

Byram, M. (1997) *Teaching and Assessing Intercultural Communicative Competence.* Clevedon: Multilingual Matters.

Byram, M. (2003) On being 'bicultural' and 'intercultural'. In G. Alred, M. Byram and G. Fleming (eds) *Intercultural Experience and Education* (pp. 50–66). Clevedon: Multilingual Matters.

Byram, M. (2008) *From Foreign Language Education to Education for Intercultural Citizenship: Essays and Reflections.* Clevedon: Multilingual Matters.

Byram, M. (2012) Conceptualizing intercultural (communicative) competence and intercultural citizenship. In J. Jackson (ed.) *The Routledge Handbook of Language and Intercultural Communication* (pp. 85–97). Hoboken, NJ: Taylor & Francis.

Byram, M. (2013) Mediation. In M. Byram and A. Hu (eds) *Routledge Encyclopedia of Language Teaching and Learning* (2 edn, pp. 456–457). New York: Routledge.

Byram, M. and Zarate, G. (1994) Definitions, objectives and assessment of sociocultural competence. In M. Byram, G. Zarate and G. Neuner (eds) *Sociocultural Competence in Language Learning and Teaching* (pp. 7–43). Strasbourg: Council of Europe.

Byram, M. and Risager, K. (1999) *Language Teachers, Politics and Cultures*. Clevedon: Multilingual Matters.

Byram, M., Nichols, A. and Stephens, D. (2001) *Developing Intercultural Competence in Practice*. Clevedon: Multilingual Matters.

Byram, M. and Alred, G. (2002) Becoming an intercultural mediator: A longitudinal study of residence abroad. *Journal of Multilingual and Multicultural Development* 23 (5), 339–352.

Byram, M., Gribkova, B. and Starkey, H. (2002) *Developing the Intercultural Dimension in Language Teaching. A Practical Introduction for Teachers*. Strasbourg: Council of Europe.

Byram, M. and Feng, A. (2004) Culture and language learning: Teaching, research and scholarship. *Language Teaching* 37 (3), 149–168.

Byrnes, H. (2006) Perspectives: Interrogating communicative competence as a framework for collegiate foreign language study. *The Modern Language Journal* 90 (2), 244–246.

Canagarajah, S. (1995) Functions of code-switching in ESL classrooms: Socialising bilingualism in Jaffna. *Journal of Multilingual and Multicultural Development* 6 (3), 173–195.

Canale, G. and Swain, M. (1981) Theoretical bases of communicative approaches to second language teaching and learning. *Applied Linguistics* 1 (1), 1–47.

Carr, J. (1999) From 'sympathetic' to 'dialogic' imagination: Cultural study in the foreign language classroom. In J. Lo Bianco, A.J. Liddicoat and C. Crozet (eds) *Striving for the Third Place: Intercultural Competence Through Language Education* (pp. 103–112). Canberra: Language Australia.

Chomsky, N. (1965) *Aspects of a Theory of Syntax*. Cambridge, MA: MIT Press.

Cole, M. (1994) A conception of culture for a communication theory of mind. In D.R. Vocate (ed.) *Intrapersonal Communication: Different Views, Different Minds* (pp. 77–98). Hillsdale, NJ: Erlbaum.

Creswell, J.W. (2007) Five qualitative approaches to inquiry. In J.W. Cresswell (ed.) *Qualitative Inquiry and Research Design: Choosing Among Five Approaches* (pp. 53–84). Thousand Oaks, CA: Sage Publications.

Crichton, J. (2008) Why an investigative stance matters in intercultural language teaching and learning: An orientation to classroom-based investigation. *Babel* 43 (1), 31–33, 39.

Crozet, C. (2003) A conceptual framework to help teachers identify where culture is located in language use. In J. Lo Bianco and C. Crozet (eds) *Teaching Invisible Culture: Classroom Practice and Theory* (pp. 39–49). Melbourne: Language Australia.

Crozet, C. and Liddicoat, A.J. (1999a) The challenge of intercultural language teaching: Engaging with culture in the classroom. In J. Lo Bianco, A.J. Liddicoat and C. Crozet (eds) *Striving for the Third Place: Intercultural Competence Through Language Education* (pp. 113–126). Canberra: Language Australia.

Crozet, C. and Liddicoat, A.J. (1999b) Turning promises into practices: The challenge of intercultural language teaching. *Australian Language Matters* 1 (Jan–Mar), 12.

Crozet, C. and Liddicoat, A.J. (2000) Teaching culture as an integrated part of language: Implications for the aims, approaches and pedagogies of language teaching. In A.J. Liddicoat and C. Crozet (eds) *Teaching Languages, Teaching Cultures* (pp. 1–18). Melbourne: Language Australia.

Cummins, J. and Swain, M. (1986) *Bilingualism in Education: Aspects of Theory, Research, and Practice*. London: Longman.

Damen, L. (1987) *Culture Learning: The Fifth Dimension in the Language Classroom*. Reading: Addison-Wesley.

Damen, L. (2003) Closing the language and culture gap: An intercultural communication perspective. In D.L. Lange and M.R. Paige (eds) *Culture as the Core: Perspectives on Culture Teaching and Learning* (pp. 71–88). Greenwich, CT: Information Age Publishing.

Dasli, M. (2011) Reviving the 'moments': From cultural awareness and cross-cultural mediation to critical intercultural language pedagogy. *Pedagogy, Culture and Society* 19 (1), 21–39.

Demorgon, J. (1989) *L'exploration interculturelle. Pour une pédagogic internationale*. Paris: Armand Colin.

Denzin, N.K. and Lincoln, Y.S. (2000) Introduction: The discipline and practice of qualitative research. In N.K. Denzin and Y.S. Lincoln (eds) *The Handbook of Qualitative Research* (pp. 1–20). Thousand Oaks, CA: Sage Publications.

Diaz, A.R. (2013) *Developing Critical Languaculture Pedagogies in Higher Education: Theory and Practice*. Bristol: Multilingual Matters.

Doehler, S. (2002) Mediation revisited: The interactive organization of mediation in learning environments. *Mind, Culture and Activity* 9 (1), 22–42.

Donato, R. (2000) Sociocultural contributions to understanding the foreign and second language classroom. In J.P. Lantolf (ed.) *Sociocultural Theory and Second Language Learning* (pp. 28–50). Oxford: Oxford University Press.

Donato, R. and McCormick, D. (1994) A sociocultural perspective on language learning strategies: The role of mediation. *The Modern Language Journal* 78 (iv), 453–464.

Eisenchlas, S. (2010) Conceptualising 'communication' in foreign language instruction. *Babel* 44 (2), 13–21.

Ellis, R. (1985) *Understanding Second Language Acquisition*. Oxford: Oxford University Press.

Fantini, A.E. (1991) Bilingualism: Exploring language and culture. In L.M. Malave-Lopez and G. Duquette (eds) *Language, Culture, and Cognition: A Collection of Studies in First and Second Language Acquisition* (pp. 110–119). Clevedon: Multilingual Matters.

Friedrich, P. (1986) *The Language Parallax: Linguistic Relativism and Poetic Indeterminacy*. Austin, TX: University of Texas Press.

Geertz, C. (1973) *The Interpretation of Cultures*. New York: Basic Books.

Gibbons, P. (2003) Mediating language learning: Teacher interactions with ESL students in a content-based classroom. *TESOL Quarterly* 37 (2), 247–273.

Giroux, H.A. (1988) *Teachers as Intellectuals: Towards a Critical Pedagogy of Learning*. New York: Bergin and Garvey.

Gouldner, A.W. (1970) *The Coming Crisis of Western Sociology*. London: Heinemann.

Guk, I. and Kellogg, D. (2007) The ZPD and whole class teaching: Teacher-led and student-led interactional mediation of tasks. *Language Teaching Research* 11 (2), 281–299.

Gumperz, J.J. (1982) *Discourse Strategies*. Cambridge: Cambridge University Press.

Gutierrez, A.G. (2008) Microgenesis, method and object: A study of collaborative activity in a Spanish as a foreign language classroom. *Applied Linguistics* 29 (1), 120–148.

Hall, J.K. (2002) *Methods for Teaching Foreign Languages: Creating a Community of Learners in the Classroom*. Upper Saddle River, NJ: Merrill Prentice Hall.

Hall, J.K. and Ramirez, A. (1993) How a group of high school learners of Spanish perceives the cultural identities of speakers, English speakers, and themselves. *Hispania* 76, 613–620.

Halliday, M.A.K. (1975) *Learning How to Mean: Explorations in the Development of Language*. London: Edward Arnold.

Halliday, M.A.K. (1978) *Language as Social Semiotic: The Social Interpretation of Language and Meaning*. London: Edward Arnold.

Houghton, S.A. (2013) Making intercultural communicative competence and identity-development visible for assessment purposes in foreign language education. *The Language Learning Journal* 41 (3), 311–325.

Hymes, D.H. (1972) On communicative competence. In J.B. Pride and J. Holmes (eds) *Sociolinguistics: Selected Readings* (pp. 269–293). Harmondsworth: Penguin.

Hymes, D.H. (1974) *Foundations in Sociolinguistics: An Ethnographic Approach*. Philadelphia, PA: University of Pennsylvania Press.

Hymes, D.H. (1986) Models of the interaction of language and social life. In J.J. Gumperz and D.H. Hymes (eds) *Directions in Sociolinguistics* (pp. 35–71). Oxford: Basil Blackwell.

i Sole, C.R. (2013) Cosmopolitan speakers and their cultural cartographies. *The Language Learning Journal* 41 (3), 326–339.

Katan, D. (2008) Translation as intercultural communication. In J. Munday (ed.) *The Routledge Companion to Translation Studies* (pp. 74–92). Hoboken, NJ: Taylor & Francis.

Kemmis, S. and Wilkinson, M. (1998) Participatory action research and the study of practice. In B. Atweh, S. Kemmis and P. Weeks (eds) *Action Research in Practice: Partnerships for Social Justice in Education* (pp. 21–36). London: Routledge.

Klein, F.M. (2004) *Culture in the Foreign Language Classroom: Teachers' Beliefs, Opportunities and Practice*. Minneapolis, MN: Minnesota Press.

Kohler, M. and Mahnken, P. (2010) *The Current State of Indonesian Language Education in Australian Schools*. Canberra: Department of Education, Employment and Workplace Relations.

Kramsch, C. (1987) Foreign language textbooks' construction of foreign reality. *Canadian Modern Language Review* 44 (1), 95–119.

Kramsch, C. (1989) New directions in the teaching of language and culture. *NFLC Occasional Papers* 1–13.

Kramsch, C. (1993) *Context and Culture in Language Teaching*. Oxford: Oxford University Press.

Kramsch, C. (1994) Foreign languages for a global age. *ADFL* 25 (1), 5–12.

Kramsch, C. (1995) The cultural component of language teaching. *Language, Culture and Curriculum* 8 (1), 83–92.

Kramsch, C. (1998) *Language and Culture*. Oxford: Oxford University Press.

Kramsch, C. (1999a) The privilege of the intercultural speaker. In M. Byram and M. Fleming (eds) *Language Learning in Intercultural Perspective: Approaches Through Drama and Ethnography* (pp. 16–31). Cambridge: Cambridge University Press.

Kramsch, C. (1999b) Thirdness: The intercultural stance. In T. Vestergaard (ed.) *Language, Culture and Identity* (pp. 41–58). Aalborg: Aalborg University Press.

Kramsch, C. (2003) Teaching along the cultural faultline. In D.L. Lange and R.M. Paige (eds) *Culture as the Core: Perspectives on Culture in Second Language Learning* (pp. 19–36). Greenwich, CT: Information Age Publishing.

Kramsch, C. (2004a) The language teacher as go-between. *Utbildning & Demokrati* 13 (3), 37–60.

Kramsch, C. (2004b) Language, thought and culture. In A. Davies and C. Elder (eds) *Handbook of Applied Linguistics* (pp. 235–261). Oxford: Blackwell.

Kramsch, C. (2006) From communicative competence to symbolic competence. *Modern Language Journal* 90 (2), 249–252.

Kramsch, C. (2008) Ecological perspectives on foreign language education. *Language Teaching* 41 (3), 389–408.

Kramsch, C. (2009) *The Multilingual Subject: What Foreign Language Learners Say about Their Experience and Why it Matters.* New York: Oxford University Press.

Kramsch, C. (2011) The symbolic dimensions of the intercultural. *Language Teaching* 44 (3), 354–367.

Kramsch, C. (2012) Theorizing translingual/transcultural competence. In G.S. Levin and A. Phipps (eds) *Critical and Intercultural Theory and Language Pedagogy* (pp. 15–31). Boston, MA: Heinle Cengage Learning.

Kramsch, C. and Nolden, T. (1994) Redefining literacy in a foreign language. *Die Unterrichtspraxis* 27 (1), 28–35.

Kramsch, C. and Whiteside, A. (2008) Language ecology in multilingual settings: Towards a theory of symbolic competence. *Applied Linguistics* 29 (4), 645–671.

Krashen, S. (1982) *Principles and Practice in Second Language Acquisition.* New York: Prentice-Hall.

Lantolf, J.P. (1994) *Vygotskian Approaches to Second Language Learning.* Oxford: Oxford University Press.

Lantolf, J.P. and Thorne, S.L. (2006) *Sociocultural Theory and the Genesis of Second Language Development.* New York: Oxford University Press.

Lave, J. and Wenger, E. (1991) *Situated Learning: Legitimate Peripheral Participation.* Cambridge and New York: Cambridge University Press.

Legutke, M. and Thomas, H. (1991) *Process and Experience in the Language Classroom.* Harlow: Longman.

Leung, C. (2005) Convivial communication: Recontextualising communicative competence. *International Journal of Applied Linguistics* 15 (2), 119–144.

Liddicoat, A.J. (2002) Static and dynamic views of culture and intercultural language acquisition. *Babel* 36 (3), 4–11.

Liddicoat, A.J. (2005) Culture for language learning in Australia language-in-education policy. *Australian Review of Applied Linguistics* 28 (2), 28–43.

Liddicoat, A.J. (2011) Language teaching and learning from an intercultural perspective. In E. Hinkel (ed.) *Handbook of Research in Second Language Teaching and Learning* (Vol. 2, pp. 837–855). New York: Taylor & Francis.

Liddicoat, A.J. (2014) Pragmatics and intercultural mediation in intercultural language learning. *Intercultural Pragmatics* 11 (2), 259–277.

Liddicoat, A.J., Scarino, A., Papademetre, L. and Kohler, M. (2003) *Report on Intercultural Language Learning.* Canberra: Department of Education, Science and Training.

Liddicoat, A.J. and Scarino, A. (2010) Eliciting the intercultural in foreign language education at school. In L. Sercu and A. Paran (eds) *Testing the Untestable in Language and Education* (pp. 52–76). New York: Routledge.

Liddicoat, A.J. and Kohler, M. (2012) Teaching Asian languages from an intercultural perspective: Building bridges for and with students of Indonesian. In S.X. and K. Cadman (eds) *Bridging Transcultural Divides: Asian Languages and Cultures in Global Higher Education* (pp. 73–100). Adelaide: University of Adelaide Press.

Liddicoat, A.J. and Scarino, A. (2013) *Intercultural Language Teaching and Learning.* Chichester: Wiley-Blackwell.

Lo Bianco, J. (2003) Culture: Visible, invisible and multiple. In J. Lo Bianco and C. Crozet (eds) *Teaching Invisible Culture: Classroom Practice and Theory* (pp. 11–38). Melbourne: Language Australia.

MCEETYA (1994) National Asian Languages and Studies in Schools Program. See http://www1.curriculum.edu.au/nalsas/about.htm (accessed 15 May 2012).

MCEETYA (2005) *National Statement for Languages Education in Australian Schools: National Plan for Languages Education in Australian Schools 2005–2008.* Hindmarsh: DECS Publishing.

Menard-Warwick, J. (2008) The cultural and intercultural identities of transnational English teachers: Two case studies from the Americas. *TESOL Quarterly* 42 (4), 617–640.

Meyer, M. (1991) Developing transcultural competence: Case studies of advanced language learners. In D. Buttjes and M. Byram (eds) *Mediating Languages and Cultures: Towards an Intercultural Theory of Foreign Language Education* (pp. 136–158). Clevedon: Multilingual Matters.

Moran, P.R. (2001) *Teaching Culture: Perspectives in Practice.* Scarborough, Ontario: Heinle & Heinle.

Nostrand, H. (1991) Basic intercultural education needs breadth and depth: The role of second culture. In E. Silber (ed.) *Critical Issues in Foreign Language Instruction* (pp. 131–159). New York: Garland.

Paige, R.M. (1993) On the nature of intercultural experience and intercultural education. In R.M. Paige (ed.) *Education for the Intercultural Experience* (pp. 1–20). Boston, MA: Intercultural Press Inc.

Paige, R.M., Jorstad, H., Siaya, L., Klein, F. and Colby, J. (1999) Culture learning in language education: A review of the literature. In R.M. Paige, D.L. Lange and Y.A. Yeshova (eds) *Culture as the Core: Integrating Culture into the Language Curriculum* (pp. 47–113). Minneapolis, MN: University of Minnesota.

Paige, R.M., Jorstad, H., Siaya, L., Klein, F. and Colby, J. (eds) (2003) *Culture Learning in Language Education: A Review of the Literature.* Greenwich, CT: Information Age Publishing.

Papademetre, L. (2000) Developing pathways for conceptualising the integration of culture-and-language. In A.J. Liddicoat and C. Crozet (eds) *Teaching Languages, Teaching Cultures* (pp. 141–149). Melbourne: Language Australia.

Papademetre, L. (2005) Intra-cultural considerations for intercultural teacher education. *Australian Language and Literacy Matters* 2 (1), 5–10.

Papademetre, L. and Scarino, A. (2000) *Integrating Culture Learning in the Languages Classroom: A Multi-Perspective Conceptual Journey for Teachers.* Melbourne: Language Australia.

Phipps, A. and Gonzalez, M. (2004) *Modern Languages: Learning and Teaching in an Intercultural Field.* Thousand Oaks, CA: Sage Publications.

Reason, P. and Bradbury, H. (eds) (2008) *The Sage Handbook of Action Research: Participative Inquiry and Practice.* Thousand Oaks, CA: Sage Publications.

Risager, K. (2006) *Language and Culture: Global Flows and Local Complexity.* Clevedon: Multilingual Matters.

Risager, K. (2007) *Language and Culture Pedagogy: From a National to a Transnational Paradigm.* Clevedon: Multilingual Matters.

Risager, K. (2011) Research timeline: The cultural dimensions of language teaching and learning. *Language Teaching* 44 (4), 485–499.

Roberts, C., Byram, M., Barro, A., Jordan, S. and Street, B. (2001) *Language Learners as Ethnographers.* Clevedon: Multilingual Matters.

Robertson, J. (2006) The three Rs of action research methodology: Reciprocity, reflexivity and reflection-on-reality. *Educational Action Research* 8 (2), 307–326.

Scarino, A. (2001) *Teachers as Mediators of Language and Culture.* Adelaide: University of South Australia.

Scarino, A. (2009) Assessing intercultural capability in language learning: Some issues. *Language Teaching* 42 (1), 67–80.

Scarino, A., Liddicoat, A.J., Dellit, J., Crozet, C., Carr, J., Crichton, J., Papademetre, L., Kohler, M., Scrimgeour, A., Morgan, A-M., Mercurio, N. and Loechel, K. (2007) *Intercultural Language Teaching and Learning in Practice.* Adelaide: Document Services, University of South Australia.

Scarino, A., Liddicoat, A.J., Crichton, J., Curnow, T., Kohler, M., Loechel, K., Mercurio, N., Morgan, A-M, Papademetre, L. and Scrimgeour, A. (2008) *Professional Standards for Teaching Languages.* Adelaide: Document Services, University of South Australia.

Scarino, A. and Liddicoat, A.J. (2009) *Teaching Languages and Cultures: A Guide.* Melbourne: Curriculum Corporation.

Sercu, L. (2000) *Acquiring Intercultural Communicative Competence from Textbooks: The Case of Flemish Adolescents Learning German.* Leuven: Leuven University Press.

Sercu, L. (2004) Assessing intercultural competence: A framework for systematic test development in foreign language education and beyond. *Intercultural Education* 15 (1), 73–89.

Sercu, L. (2005) Foreign language teachers and the implementation of intercultural education: A comparative investigation of the professional self-concepts and teaching practices of Belgian teachers of English, French and German. *European Journal of Teacher Education* 28 (1), 87–105.

Sercu, L. (2006) The foreign language and intercultural competence teacher: The acquisition of a new professional identity. *Intercultural Education* 17 (1), 55–72.

Sercu, L. (2007) Foreign language teachers and intercultural competence: What keeps teachers from doing what they believe in? In M. Jimenez-Raya and L. Sercu (eds) *Challenges in Teacher Development: Learner Autonomy and Intercultural Competence* (pp. 65–80). Frankfurt: Peter Lang.

Sfard, A. (1998) On two metaphors for learning and the dangers of choosing just one. *Educational Researcher* 27 (2), 4–13.

Shohamy, E. (2001) *The Power of Tests: A Critical Perspective on the Uses of Language Tests.* Harlow: Pearson Education Limited.

Shohamy, E. (2006) Expanding language. In E. Shohamy (ed.) *Language Policy. Hidden Agendas and New Approaches* (pp. 5–21). London and New York: Routledge.

Shulman, L.S. (1987) Knowledge and teaching: Foundations of the new reform. *Harvard Educational Review* 57 (1), 1–22.

Slaughter, Y. (2007) The study of Asian languages in two Australian states: Considerations for language-in-education policy and planning. PhD thesis, University of Melbourne.

Slaughter, Y. (2009) Money and policy make languages go round: Language programs in Australia after NALSAS. *Babel* 42 (3), 4–11.

Sobolewski, P. (2009) Use of ethnographic interviews as a resource for developing intercultural understanding. *Babel* 43 (2), 28–34.

Stake, R.E. (2005) Case studies. In N.K. Denzin and Y.S. Lincoln (eds) *Qualitative Research Methods* (pp. 435–454). Thousand Oaks, CA: Sage Publications.

Swain, M. (1985) Communicative competence: Some roles of comprehensible input and comprehensible output in its development. In S. Gass and C.G. Madden (eds) *Input in Second Language Acquisition* (pp. 235–253). Rowley, MA: Newbury House.

Swain, M. (2000) French immersion research in Canada: Recent contributions to SLA and applied linguistics. *Annual Review of Applied Linguistics* 20, 199–212.

Swain, M. and Lapkin, S. (2000) Task-based second language learning: The uses of the first language. *Language Teaching Research* 4 (3), 251–274.

Takahashi, E., Austin, T. and Morimoto, Y. (2000) Social interaction and language development in a FLES classroom. In J.K. Hall and L.S. Verplaetse (eds) *Second and Foreign Language Learning Through Classroom Interaction* (pp. 139–161). Mahwah, NJ: Erlbaum.

Tsai, Y. and Houghton, S.A. (eds). (2010) *Becoming Intercultural Inside and Outside the Classroom*. Newcastle upon Tyne: Cambridge Scholars.

Tsui, A.B.M. (1995) *Introducing Classroom Interaction*. London: Penguin.

Turnbull, M. (2001) There is a role for the L1 in second and foreign language teaching, but ... *Canadian Modern Language Review* 57 (4), 531–540.

Ustunel, E. and Seedhouse, P. (2005) Why that, in that language, right now? Code-switching and pedagogical focus. *International Journal of Applied Linguistics* 15 (3), 302–325.

Van Ek, J.A. (1986) *Objectives for Modern Language Learning*. Strasbourg: Council of Europe.

Van Lier, L. (2000) From input to affordance: Social-interactive learning from an ecological perspective. In J.P. Lantolf (ed.) *Sociocultural Theory and Second Language Learning* (pp. 155–177). Oxford: Oxford University Press.

Van Lier, L. (2002) An ecological-semiotic perspective on language and linguistics. In C. Kramsch (ed.) *Language Acquisition and Language Socialization: Ecological Perspectives* (pp. 140–164). London: Continuum.

Verplaetse, L.S. (2000) Mr Wonder-ful: Portrait of a dialogic teacher. In J.K. Hall and L.S. Verplaetse (eds) *Second and Foreign Language Learning Through Classroom Interaction* (pp. 221–242). Mahwah, NJ: Erlbaum.

Vertovec, S. (2010) Towards post-multiculturalism? Changing communities, conditions and contexts of diversity. *International Social Sciences Journal* 61 (199), 83–95.

Vygotsky, L.S. (1978) *Mind in Society. The Development of Higher Psychological Processes*. Cambridge, MA: Harvard University Press.

Wells, G. (1999) *Dialogic Inquiry*. Cambridge: Cambridge University Press.

Wenger, E. (1998) *Communities of Practice: Learning, Meaning and Identity*. Cambridge and New York: Cambridge University Press.

Wertsch, J.V. (1985) *Culture, Communication and Cognition: Vygotskian Perspectives*. Cambridge: Cambridge University Press.

Worsley, P. (1994) *Unlocking Australia's Language Potential, Profiles of 9 Key Languages in Australia: Vol. 5 Indonesian/Malay*. Canberra: The National Languages and Literacy Institute of Australia.

Zarate, G. (1986) *Enseigner une culture estrangere*. Paris: Hachette.

Zarate, G., Gohard-Radenkovic, A., Lussier, D. and Penz, H. (2004) *Cultural Mediation in Language Learning and Teaching*. Kapfenberg: Council of Europe Publishing.

Index